"I know of no other book like this. Expanc
'who is a proph
necting their messages with issues of our
ets stands out as a novel contemporary approach to drawing us closer
to the Bible."

—RABBI STEVEN BOB, author of *Jonah and the Meaning of Our Lives*

"With a lifetime of learning, fresh insights, and deeply felt personal commitment, Barry Schwartz has assembled a distinctive, life-sustaining crew of eighteen biblical figures—prophets, visionaries, dreamers, seers—whom he has grouped, half a dozen each, around one of the three principles proclaimed by Micah: justice, compassion, faith. With each example we gain fresh courage and companionship to confront the urgent demands of our times, sustained by a sense of eternity."

—RABBI EVERETT GENDLER, author, *Judaism for Universalists*

"Adding to biblical scholarship, *Path of the Prophets* presents unusual and important prophetic voices—Shiphrah's path of civil disobedience, Judah's path of repentance, Tirzah's path of equality, Hannah's path of prayer, and Ezra's path of wisdom—that vividly demonstrate moral courage. Its study guide asks poignant moral questions, such as 'What injustices call for resistance today?'

I truly enjoyed this magnificent book and highly recommend it for all interested in serious biblical study that engages the mind, touches the soul, and imbues one with a sense of justice."

—RABBI WARREN STONE, Temple Emanuel, Kensington, Maryland, and a leader in Jewish environmental activism

"*Path of the Prophets* is the most significant new contribution to our understanding of the prophets so far in the twenty-first century—filled with new insights, important for Jewish scholarship, and a joy to read for anyone who has ever grappled with the meaning and contemporary relevance of the Bible."

—RABBI MICHAEL LERNER, editor of *Tikkun* magazine

"Schwartz brings new life to the men and women of the Bible, ordinary people who did extraordinary things—and challenges us to do the same, to make the most of life's journey."

—RABBI SALLY J. PRIESAND, author of *Judaism and the New Woman*

"The prophets call us passionately to justice—but alas, the prophetic books are not easy to understand. Schwartz has done the seemingly impossible—delving clearly into the prophets' ethical dilemmas and urging readers to face those injustices of yesterday and today. As we yearn for religious voices that will challenge entrenched ideologies, this is a desperately needed volume."

—RABBI ERIC YOFFIE, president emeritus of Union for Reform Judaism

Path of the Prophets

University of Nebraska Press
Lincoln

Path of the Prophets

The Ethics-Driven Life

RABBI BARRY L. SCHWARTZ

The Jewish Publication Society
Philadelphia

 Published by the University of Nebraska Press as a Jewish Publication Society book. Manufactured in the United States of America.

∞

Library of Congress Cataloging-in-Publication Data

Names: Schwartz, Barry L., author.
Title: Path of the prophets: the ethics-driven life / Rabbi Barry L. Schwartz.
Description: Philadelphia: University of Nebraska Press, [2018]
Identifiers: LCCN 2017030386 (print)
LCCN 2017031514 (ebook)
ISBN 9780827613096 (pbk.: alk. paper)
ISBN 9780827613843 (epub)
ISBN 9780827613850 (mobi)
ISBN 9780827613867 (pdf)
Subjects: LCSH: Prophets—Biography. | Justice—Biblical teaching. | Jewish ethics—Biblical teaching. | Bible. Prophets—Criticism, interpretation, etc.
Classification: LCC BS1505.55 (ebook) | LCC BS1505.55 .S39 2018 (print) | DDC 221.9/22—dc23
LC record available at https://lccn.loc.gov/2017030386

Set in Merope Basic by E. Cuddy.

"Justice, justice shall you pursue."
(Deuteronomy 16:20)

In gratitude to Harold Cramer, Esq. (z"l)
for his devotion to justice and his
unfailing support of The Jewish
Publication Society, from the Board
of Trustees of JPS.

"But leave it to Israel: if they
are not prophets, yet they are
the children of prophets."

— HILLEL

Contents

PART 3. TO WALK HUMBLY

Acknowledgments

"And the Lord put it in his heart to teach" (Exod. 35:34). In my own small way I hope to add to the conversation about the prophets. My goal is to have readers personally connect with prophetic history—both to take pride in our past and to become bearers of our heritage.

These hopes are both professional and personal, and the two are deeply intertwined. My own rabbi, Rabbi Michael Robinson, was a disciple of Rabbi Abraham Joshua Heschel who freely quoted his mentor as well as the prophets. He used the expression "Prophetic Judaism" to describe his faith. He marched, and was arrested, with Martin Luther King Jr.; he protested the Vietnam War; he campaigned for nuclear disarmament; he advocated for Israeli-Palestinian accord; he promoted interfaith dialogue . . . and all this made a deep impression on me. With this work I honor Rabbi Robinson's legacy.

After twenty-five years as a congregational rabbi, I was given the opportunity to lead The Jewish Publication Society (JPS), the nation's oldest Jewish publisher, founded in 1888, but with roots that predate the Civil War. JPS published the great books that brought Heschel to national attention, including *The Prophets* (1963), which was noted by *Time* magazine and the Associated Press. Taylor Branch, the Pulitzer Prize–winning biographer of King and the civil rights era, later remarked in an interview: "[King] becomes like a driven Old Testament prophet . . . all those guys used to carry around Heschel's book *The Prophets*. They really identified with the prophets." With this work I honor the legacy of Martin Luther King Jr. and Abraham Joshua Heschel.

JPS also published *The Holy Scriptures* (1917) and the JPS Tanakh (1985)—the two Hebrew Bible translations that for a century have been the translations of record for the Jewish community and beyond. The latter translation is used for all biblical passages in this book. With this work I honor The Jewish Publication Society.

My sincere appreciation to the staff of The Jewish Publication Society—Carol Hupping, Joy Weinberg, Sarah Segal, Suzanne Selengut, Trisha Lubrant; and to its leadership—David Lerman, Gittel Hilibrand, and the JPS Board of Trustees. Thanks, too, to our publishing partner, the University of Nebraska Press, so ably led by Donna Shear.

I am grateful for the support and understanding of my wonderful synagogue, Congregation Adas Emuno, of Leonia, New Jersey.

My deepest gratitude extends to my wife, Debby, my children, Nadav, Talia, and Noam; and my parents, Barbara and Rudy. The unfailing love of my family makes all things possible.

About This Book

I wrestled with how to capture the prophetic walk, the Bible's ethical legacy, in a compelling, readable way. Much of the classical prophetic books take the form of poetic oracles in archaic language that is challenging to understand. When people try to read the prophets, their eyes glaze over. At other times the biblical account is very sparse or enigmatic, especially when it comes to the prophets' lives. Like the sages who wrote midrash through the generations, one feels the need to fill in the gaps.

My response is to introduce the story of each prophet with a short first-person "historical-fictional" narrative—historical in that it is based on the known facts of the prophet's life, and fictional in my having weaved the narrative together with dialogue that is not recorded in the Bible.

Key Scripture citations form the second, "From the Bible," section of each chapter. Together with the creative retelling, the biblical text conveys the quintessential episode in the lives of our heroes.

I encourage readers to turn to a Bible commentary to fully appreciate the biblical text. Over the centuries Jews have approached the reading of biblical texts through the practice of *pardes*—an acronym that spells the word "orchard" or "garden" (the word "paradise" is derived from it)—and which refers to four levels of interpretation: *peshat* (literal or historical), *remez* (allegorical), *derash* (analogical), and *sod* (mystical). Christians developed a somewhat analogous practice of sacred reading, known as *lectio divina,* that also moves in four steps from explanation to contemplation. Both approaches share the common goal of deep reading and reflection that make Bible study a transformative experience. The "Living the Bible" study guide at the back of this book is designed to support this process.

The third section of each chapter, "The Prophetic Moment," discusses the crucial turning point in the prophet's life, and its ethical import. I attempt to single out the quality of the prophetic spirit that best defines each shining moment and identify the Hebrew term associated with this quality in order to build the ethical vocabulary unique to the prophetic spirit. My special interest is how that ethical insight evolves through Jewish tradition. I trace how this ethical insight evolves over time in Jewish history and thought.

The fourth section of each chapter, "Walking with . . . ," examines how each prophetic moment lives on. I trace the legacy of the prophetic moment and incorporate relevant quotations from Jewish tradition and elsewhere to help us internalize the challenges and triumphs of our forebears.

The final section of the book contains a "Prophetic Glossary" of key Hebrew terms, followed by a chapter-by-chapter "Living the Bible" study guide. Biblical, Rabbinic, and modern sources from the chapter are highlighted with questions to facilitate group discussions. These, in turn, pave the way for sacred study and self-reflections designed to challenge us to wrestle with those sources and make them our own. After all, the true power of Torah is its capacity to simultaneously describe what happened long ago *and* what is happening in our lives right now. To paraphrase Heschel, "What happened once upon a time happens all the time." The deepest level of understanding is attained when we discern that the Bible is describing not only characters of old, but you and me!

The "Living the Bible" study guide often provides broader biblical readings for each chapter for those who want to go beyond the excerpts provided in this book. So, along with a JPS TANAKH or similar Bible, this book can be used for a broad-based Bible study course.

Only one step is missing from the guide—turning study into action. That is the ultimate step each of us must take—the leap of action that comes from a leap of faith.

Preface

Why the Prophets?

Why is this book different from all other books? Because at all other times we read books of political history, but at this time we read a book of prophetic history.

The lens of prophetic history is not power, but justice. The concern of prophetic history is not conquest, but compassion. The focus of prophetic history is not feat, but faith.

The heroes of prophetic history are not kings or generals, but visionaries and dreamers. They are seekers of justice and exemplars of compassion. They are often ordinary people who have moments of extraordinary courage and insight. They are unexpected heroes.

Most histories focus on political supremacy: who ruled and for how long. Far fewer testify to prophetic authority: who bore witness and for what purpose. As Rabbi Abraham Joshua Heschel, one of the twentieth century's outstanding religious thinkers, memorably wrote: "Others have considered history from the point of view of power, judging its course in terms of victory and defeat, of wealth and success; the prophets look at history from the point of view of justice, judging its course in terms of righteousness and corruption, of compassion and violence."

In the wider world, this approach is sometimes called "moral history." There is a long tradition in world literature of presenting history through heroes or heroic themes. But the choice of heroes in a moral history is unconventional. Rather than focus on mighty warriors, moral history spotlights spiritual seekers. These pioneers of the spirit are sometimes called to their vocation from an early age. Others are common folk with uncommon experiences.

The Bible itself is part conventional history, part moral history. It chronicles the political and the prophetic. I believe that it is the latter voice that defines the Bible's essence: the true heart of the Bible. The political voice is concerned with who assumed power, and how they kept command. The prophetic voice is concerned with who challenged power, and how they kept the commandments.

The prophetic voice that courses through Scripture, often as a foil to the political establishment, is unprecedented and unanticipated. No one elected the prophets. We don't know where they came from or how they became so influential. Yet their burning spirit topples kings and unsettles clerics. More quietly, the prophetic spirit heals families and restores faith.

The stakes are very high. Heschel explained it this way: "The prophets' great contribution to humanity was the discovery of the evil of indifference. One may be decent and sinister, pious and sinful." Elucidating further: "The prophets were shocked not only by the acts of injustice on the part of scoundrels, but also by the perversion of justice on the part of the notables." This led to Heschel's famous declaration that in a free society, "few are guilty; all are responsible." No one is exempt from the pursuit of justice. In the words of an old adage, "If you are not part of the solution, you are part of the problem."

Heschel also noted, "To the prophets, a minor, commonplace sort of injustice assumes almost cosmic proportions." As a result, "Tranquility is unknown to the soul of the prophet. The miseries of the world give him no rest." One of Heschel's disciples, Rabbi Michael Lerner, elaborates on this theme:

> For the prophets *it was nothing less than a catastrophe that the Jewish people were using the language of the tradition but missing its essence. Having established a society in which they had power, the ancient Israelites were now acting the way the other nations acted, and had set up a society in which the ordinary evils of other societies appeared. Violence and cruelty were once again becoming regnant realities, and all this supposedly in a society embodying Jewish values! For the prophets*

this was a scandal, and with every ounce of their being they denounced the perversion built into this accommodation with the way the world normally operates.

The prophets took it upon themselves to critique leaders and laymen alike. Many assailed society in the role of gadfly. Yet others were less confrontational and chose (consciously or intuitively) to effect change by more quietly modeling a higher code of ethics.

Some of the prophets dwelt in the public eye. Others lived unobtrusively in their families and clans. In common, they created enough of an impression so as to be remembered in the national saga that became codified as Scripture, what we call the Bible.

Who Are the Prophets?

The prophets are people driven by a higher calling. At crucial moments they act on their ideals for the common good, often with disregard for their own security. Those whom the Bible explicitly designates as prophets are said to speak in God's name and to communicate God's message. This is the classical definition of the prophet (which has little to do with predicting the future—a more modern usage of the word). Indeed, the prophets who fit this definition, such as Isaiah and Jeremiah, Ezekiel, Amos, and Hosea, are often referred to as the "classical" prophets.

The classical prophets criticize, cajole, and comfort. They most often intercede on God's behalf to the people, but sometimes on the people's behalf to God. Isaiah excoriates his people: "*They are drunk, but not from wine; they stagger, but not from liquor. For the Lord has spread over you a spirit of deep sleep, and has shut your eyes, the prophets, and covered your heads, the seers; So that all prophecy has been to you like the words of a sealed document*" (Isa. 29:9–11).

The most common Hebrew word for prophet, *navi*, is found in the Bible more than three hundred times. We first encounter it in an oft-overlooked passage in connection with Abraham. Genesis describes how King Abimelech, who desires to wed Sarah (believing that she is Abraham's sister, not wife) has a dream in which God warns him not marry her, and commands him to restore Sarah to her husband, *"since he is a prophet [navi], he will intercede for you—to save your life"* (Gen. 20:7). Scholars link the word *navi* to the Akkadian *nabu,* "to call"; it signifies, in the words of biblical scholar Nahum Sarna, "one who receives the (divine call) or one who proclaims, a spokesman. The prophet is the spokesman for God to man; but intercession before God in favor of man is also an indispensable aspect of his function."

Other expressions in the Bible point to people who possess prophet-like qualities. While considerably less common than *navi,* these include *ro-eh* (seer), *khozeh* (visionary), and *ish-Elohim* (man of God). A most intriguing passage in the book of Samuel employs these terms in what amounts to a parenthetical insert about how prophecy had evolved in ancient Israel: *"Formerly in Israel when a man went to inquire of God, he would say, 'Come, let us go to the seer'—for the prophet of today was formerly called a seer."* Here's the context: A servant of the young Saul, who is destined to be king, urges him to seek out *"the man of God."* Saul agrees, and the two set out for *"the town where the man of God lived."* Once there, they ask, *"Is the seer in town?"* (1 Sam. 9:8–11).

These multiple terms are juxtaposed in another intriguing passage that concludes the first book of Chronicles. Recording the death of King David after a long and prosperous reign, the biblical author notes: *"The acts of King David, early and late, are recorded in the history of Samuel the seer, the history of Nathan the prophet, and the history of Gad the seer"* (1 Chron. 29:29). Here we are introduced to some of the prophets who have not left us prophetic books. Only glimpses of their missions and excerpts of their words survive in the Bible's historical accounts.

Readers of the Bible will encounter other people who are not explicitly called prophets, but are described as bearing God's spirit. Caleb is one of my favorite examples. While Caleb never formally communicates God's message, his words and actions certainly do:

He is willing to defy his fellow scouts and urge the Israelites to move forward to the Promised Land. So do the brave actions of the "God-fearing" Hebrew midwives, Shiprah and Puah, who risk their lives to deliver Hebrew babies in the face of Pharoah's decree. The same might be said of the oft-overlooked five daughters of Zelophachad, who, wishing to keep their father's name alive, confront Moses and the tribal leaders to rectify what they consider to be an injustice in biblical law.

Other biblical figures may not be prophets in the classic sense, or even described as "filled with the spirit" or "God fearing," but are simply exemplars of the Bible's highest ethical ideals. My broad definition of a prophet (or "child of the prophets," a term I will introduce later) includes all three of these categories. That is why I include Judah and Joseph in addition to the patriarch Abraham. It is why I include Hannah and Ruth from the period of the Judges, in addition to Samuel. It is why I end with Ezra in addition to Elijah and Elisha. If not formally prophets, they are seers, visionaries, people-of-God, or simply heroes in the prophetic mold.

Prophets, heroic as they may be, can nonetheless be difficult people. In fact, Heschel describes the classical prophets as "the most disturbing people who ever lived." He points to their confrontational natures, their stinging rebukes of both the ruling elite and the indifferent masses, and the severity of their grievances.

Yet, as Heschel repeatedly emphasizes, the prophets were concurrently compassionate. They criticized, and consoled, out of love. Much like parents who both chastise and comfort their children for the youngsters' well-being, the prophets of old admonished the children of Israel to turn back to God's way. They urged their people to never despair of God's love. They dreamed great dreams of a world at peace. Heschel brilliantly and beautifully summed up the prophetic spirit as combining "a very deep love, a very powerful dissent, a painful rebuke, with unwavering hope."

Speaking about the prophets' defining characteristics in this way, Heschel was echoing one of the Bible's most celebrated verses. The prophet Micah famously taught that what God ultimately wants from us is: *"to do justly, love mercy, and walk humbly with your God"* (Mic. 6:8).

To me this epitomizes the essence of the prophetic spirit. When I was ordained as a rabbi, a weaver in my very first congregation offered to make me a tallit (prayer shawl) and asked me what verse I would like woven on the collar. I chose Micah, and have worn that precious vestment at every service since.

These qualities of justice, compassion, and faith form the organizing principles of this book. They determine the heroes I chose and the way I analyze their unique contributions to biblical history. I identify the prophetic moment and quality that animates and defines each hero. In doing so, I endeavor to tell an inspiring story, in historical context. At the same time, I introduce the reader to the rich vocabulary of prophetic ethics. In this sense, *Path of the Prophets* is a history book, but at the same time, and perhaps even more so, it is an ethics book. The "history" in it is not value-neutral, but value-laden. To the prophets, theology is the prelude to advocacy. Faith, consummated in doing, is the way of righteousness in the real world.

Now, I present a few caveats. First: Prophetic history is not source-critical history. It does not seek to analyze biblical texts for historical accuracy, but for moral veracity. In this book I do not question, as some biblical scholars do, whether the Bible's detailed accounts are essentially true. Rather, I grant that while events may not always have happened as written, these stories were crafted with wise intent.

A second caveat concerns the clarion call to justice, compassion, and faith that we call the prophetic voice. Within the Bible, this is not an exclusive voice. Not all of what the Torah commands, and not all of what the classical prophets say and do, is consistent with their central message.

Admittedly as well, at times the prophetic voice is also extremist and even fanatical. Moses, Samuel, and Elijah all order the slaughter of opponents or innocents. Rabbi Michael Lerner is especially sensitive to what he calls the two voices of God in Torah: the one just and compassionate, the other "insensitive, chauvinistic, or even cruel." He insists that "the voice of cruelty is not the voice of God."

I make the same assumption in this book. I have chosen to concentrate on the lofty prophetic voice.

In truth, none of the Bible's heroes, prophets very much included, were infallible. As flawed human beings, they did not always practice what they preached. Even worse, they sometimes preached what was wrong.

Rabbi Jonathan Sacks, the former chief rabbi of Great Britain, pointedly notes about the Torah: "No religious literature was ever further from hagiography, idealization and hero-worship. No religion has held a higher view of humanity than the books that tell us we are each in the image and likeness of God. Yet none has been more honest about the failings of even the greatest."

In his study of biblical heroes, scholar Elliot Rabin makes a similar point: "The Bible's main hero is God," he reminds us. "Human beings are distractions at worst, challengers at best. Heroes are able to partner with God, challenge God at times, receive blessings from God, but they must be drawn as utterly distinct." He adds: "Unlike other ancient heroes, in no way can a biblical hero be confused for a deity. For this reason biblical heroes appear remarkably unheroic, unglorified."

Indeed, Scripture is remarkable in its insistence in seeing great leaders as flawed human beings. Is there a more dramatic example than King David? The national saga of the Jewish people portrays its greatest monarch as its greatest sinner—the Bible astonishingly never hiding David's adultery or his commission of a killing.

Genesis introduces us to human grandeur and human foible almost from the moment of our creation. The heroes from Genesis we consider in this book—Abraham, Judah, and Joseph (not to mention others such as Jacob and Laban)—all exhibit morally questionable if not untenable behavior.

In this light, I believe that my picking and choosing from the prophets' teachings is no disservice to the reader, so long as we acknowledge that the reality of the prophets' lives was far messier than the ideal. I have consciously chosen to emulate what elevates us in the quest toward "living the Bible."

The Hero's Secret Strength

A standard dictionary definition of a hero is "a person admired for great acts." The Talmud emphasizes the inner quality of such greatness when it asks, and answers: "Who is a hero? The person who masters one's self." A later commentary to this passage adds: "Who is a hero? The one who turns enemy into friend."

The Rabbinic tradition, influenced by the prophetic, identifies with internal more than external heroism. The secret strength of the hero is not control of others, but control of self. Such inner strength fuels the prophets' passion for justice, compassion, and faith.

The Prophetic Moment

This work concentrates on the prophetic moment—one particular episode that defines these extraordinary individuals and their legacy.

Sometimes, these prophetic moments are downright surprising. Who would have thought that a group of sisters would challenge Moses, or that Judah, who sold his brother Joseph into slavery and failed to protect his daughter-in-law Tamar (by not allowing his son Shelah to marry and protect Tamar after Shelah's brothers had died), was destined for greatness?

These exalted moments also represent one small fraction of their complex and imperfect lives. To be sure, our heroes' ability to surmount personal faults and limitations in order to have their great moment is a large part of what makes them so remarkable.

And so, the question arises: Can a person be judged by one shining moment? Can a legacy be built around triumph rather than failure?

I think an honest answer is, "yes and no." In truth, an accurate legacy should encompass the totality of our acts. On the other hand, often our shining moments have the greatest impact.

The Bible itself seems to go out of its way to acknowledge its unexpected choice of heroes. We know absolutely nothing of Abraham when he is called by God to his history-changing mission. His heir, Isaac, is not his firstborn. Jacob is the younger of Isaac's twins and morally suspect. Judah is the fourth born of Jacob, and Joseph even further down the line; neither gets off to an auspicious start. Moses is essentially raised as an Egyptian. Shiphrah and Puah may not even have been Hebrews themselves, but midwives to the Hebrews. Ruth was certainly not Israelite, but Moabite. Miriam is almost completely eclipsed by her brothers. Tirzah and her sisters are five ordinary daughters without a father. Hannah is first mistaken as a drunk. She gives up her son Samuel for adoption. Caleb is just one of the twelve spies. Jonah is so reluctant a prophet that he takes a ship in the opposite direction of his calling. Jeremiah is depressive and wishes he had never been born.

Why in the Bible is the unexpected hero seemingly the norm? The conventional answer is that God does the choosing and God has reasons. If we expect primogeniture, that the firstborn has special privileges, including becoming head of the family, God intervenes to upend natural law. If we expect superheroes of perfection, God shows up to underscore that no one can do it alone.

But I think there is another powerful lesson here. The Bible's unexpected heroes teach us that no one is beyond hearing the prophetic call. To say that the heroic is unexpected is actually to acknowledge that it can come at any time to any person. One need not be born with prophetic qualities, be raised with special privilege, lead a charmed life, or be free of sin to rise to the heroic.

More often than not, however, the heroism is a long time in coming. The summons may begin in an instant, but the prophetic path continues with a long, winding journey.

Walking the Walk

The lives of the prophets are suffused with imagery of the journey. The summons to that journey likely involves changing one's place, spiritually if not physically. As a rabbi I have always been intrigued by the notion of pilgrimage—and, as an avid hiker, to the idea of sacred treks. So I'm captivated by the biblical metaphor of walking.

Abraham's call to commence his life-changing journey is conveyed in two short, alliterative words: *lech lecha* (go forth) (Gen. 12:1). The words suggest an external and internal journey at the same time, since *lech lecha* can also mean "go to yourself."

Heschel reminds us: "The oldest form of piety expressed in the Bible is walking with God." Abraham's call is soon followed by the explicit command to *"walk in my ways"* (Gen. 17:1). Before Abraham, Noah, too, is said to walk with God (Gen. 6:9). Earlier, a descendent of Adam named Enoch walks in the same way (Gen. 5:24). The verb "to walk" is even used to describe God in the Garden of Eden (Gen. 3:8). Abraham is not only commanded to walk before God, but to *"walk about the land, through its length and its breadth"* (Gen. 13:17).

The spiritual dimension of walking is found in other ancient sources as well. Akkadian documents employ "walking with the lord" as a term for absolute political loyalty to a monarch. Bible scholar Nahum Sarna notes: "In the Bible, to 'walk before God' takes on an added dimension. Allegiance to Him means to condition the entire range of human experience by the awareness of His presence and in response to His demands." Walking becomes an act of devotion.

Jewish law is known by the term *halakhah*, from the very root "to go" or "to walk" that is first used to command Abraham. In the Rabbinic period, the link between walking as following—through *imitatio dei*, the imitation of God's ways—is explicit. A celebrated passage from the Talmud teaches, "You shall walk after the Lord your God—this means that you should imitate God's virtues. Just as God clothed the naked, so, too, you should clothe the naked. Just as the Holy One comforted mourners, so, too, you should comfort mourners. Just as the Holy One buried the dead, so, too, you should bury the dead."

Much later, the Hasidic movement developed a notion of sacred walking called *halicha*—an idea reflected in the view of its founder, the Ba'al Shem Tov, that "traveling from place to place is for sake of purifying the sparks." Elliot Wolfson, a scholar of Jewish mysticism, describes this notion in an article aptly entitled, "Walking as a Sacred Duty."

Henry David Thoreau's wonderful essay *Walking* (1862), touches on this same connection. He recognized the liberating quality of walking, and how it transported one to a new place of opportunity. "Every walk," he wrote, "is a sort of crusade to go forth and reconquer. . . . It requires a direct disposition from Heaven to become a walker. I have met with but one or two persons in the course of my life who understand the art of walking, that is, of taking walks—who had a genius, so to speak, for sauntering."

Thoreau goes on to explain that "sauntering" is derived from people who roved about the country in the Middle Ages, under the pretense of going "à la Sainte Terre," to the Holy Land. Children would exclaim, "there goes a Sainte-Terrer—a saunterer."

Whether we understand the Holy Land as a place or state of being, "they who never go to the Holy Land in their walks, as they pretend, are indeed mere idlers and vagabonds; but they who do go there are saunterers in the good sense, such as I mean." Thoreau adds. "So we saunter toward the Holy Land, till one day the sun shall shine more brightly than ever he has done, shall perchance shine into our mind and hearts."

Interestingly, as I was writing this work I came across recent research that establishes a scientific link between walking and creativity. In his book *The Geography of Genius*, Eric Weiner cites two Stanford University researchers, psychologists Marilyn Oppezzo and Daniel Schwartz, who created a test to measure "divergent thinking," the kind of thinking we employ when we formulate multiple unexpected solutions to problems. Another hallmark is dissent from conventional thought. Divergent thinking is considered key to creativity. Oppezzo and Schwartz discovered that creativity levels were "consistently and significantly higher" for walkers versus sitters. Evidently we do our best thinking when we are on the move.

In their journeys, the prophets, like us, are often mired in the depths. Yet what makes them inspirational is their willingness to embark on a journey to seek new spiritual insight. As scholar and theologian Walter Brueggemann writes in his influential book *The Prophetic Imagination*, the prophet's primary role is "to evoke a consciousness and perception alternative to . . . the dominant culture around us." To get to this countercultural evocation, we must journey to a new vantage point.

Seeking the Prophets

In an interview shortly before his death, Rabbi Heschel explained how writing a book about the prophets changed his life. He was compelled to go beyond the comfort of academia "to be involved in the affairs of man, in the affairs of suffering man." Then he added, "And I would like to say that one of the saddest things about contemporary life in America is that the prophets are unknown. No one knows the prophets."

Heschel wrote his doctoral dissertation about the prophets in Berlin in 1933, on the eve of the Holocaust. In researching the story I learned dramatic details: how the courage and convictions of his ancient forebears inspired him to persevere during the Nazis' rise to power. His acclaimed English version of *The Prophets* was published in 1963, on the eve of America's civil rights era. Once again, the prophets inspired him—this time, to walk hand in hand with Martin Luther King Jr. in Selma.

Rabbi Daniel Polish echoes Heschel's lament about the prophets. "We are, of course, the people of the Book," Polish writes. "But truth be told, the fact that we are 'of the Book' does not mean we necessarily read the Book." He points out that whole parts of Scripture—including prophetic literature—are alien even to those familiar with the Torah. "We regard them as sacred, but they do not fully make sense to us."

It is not as if the prophets have been entirely forgotten. The Reform movement of American Judaism especially has drawn inspiration from the prophets, consistently emphasizing their ethical message since its founding in the mid-nineteenth century. This was true of its first platform, the Pittsburgh Platform (1885), and even more so its second platform, the Columbus Platform (1937), which acknowledges: "The people of Israel, through its prophets and sages, achieved unique insight in the realm of religious truth. We regard it as our historic task to cooperate with all men in the establishment of the kingdom of God, of universal brotherhood, justice, truth, and peace on earth. This is our Messianic goal."

The Columbus Platform goes on to state, in eloquent language that would have made the prophets proud:

> *In Judaism religion and morality blend into an indissoluble unity. Seeking God means to strive after holiness, righteousness and goodness. The love of God is incomplete without the love of one's fellowmen. Judaism emphasizes the kinship of the human race, the sanctity and worth of human life and personality and the right of the individual to freedom and to the pursuit of his chosen vocation. Justice to all, irrespective of race, sect or class, is the inalienable right and the inescapable obligation of all. The state and organized government exist in order to further these ends. Judaism seeks the attainment of a just society by the application of its teachings to the economic order, to industry and commerce, and to national and international affairs. It aims at the elimination of man-made misery and suffering, of poverty and degradation, of tyranny and slavery, of social inequality and prejudice, of ill-will and strife. It advocates the promotion of harmonious relations between warring classes on the basis of equity and justice, and the creation of conditions under which human personality may flourish. It pleads for the safeguarding of childhood against exploitation. It champions the cause of all who work and of their right to an adequate standard of living, as prior to the rights of property. Judaism emphasizes the duty of charity, and strives for a social order which will protect men against the material disabilities of old age, sickness and unemployment.*

The Reform movement's third platform, the San Francisco Platform (1976), though less lofty in its language, acknowledges, "Lawgivers and prophets, historians and poets gave us a heritage whose study is a religious imperative and whose practice is our chief means to holiness."

The latest Pittsburgh Platform (1999) again offers a pointed reference to the prophets' message when it states:

> *We bring Torah into the world when we strive to fulfill the highest ethical mandates in our relationships with others and with all of God's creation. Partners with God in tikkun olam, repairing the world, we are called to help bring nearer the messianic age. We seek dialogue and joint action with people of other faiths in the hope that together we can bring peace, freedom and justice to our world. We are obligated to pursue tzedek, justice and righteousness, and to narrow the gap between the affluent and the poor, to act against discrimination and oppression, to pursue peace, to welcome the stranger, to protect the earth's biodiversity and natural resources, and to redeem those in physical, economic and spiritual bondage. In so doing, we reaffirm social action and social justice as a central prophetic focus of traditional Reform Jewish belief and practice. We affirm the mitzvah of tzedakah, setting aside portions of our earnings and our time to provide for those in need. These acts bring us closer to fulfilling the prophetic call to translate the words of Torah into the works of our hands.*

The activist wing of the Reform movement was so enamored of the prophetic call that it coined the term "Prophetic Judaism" to describe its mission. As Rabbi Walter Jacob explains, the term first broadly stood for the "ethical monotheism" that took precedence over ritual observance; later it became more defined as an activist commitment to the pursuit of social justice. Although the term is used less often today (in part because of the Reform movement's reclaiming of ritual practice), the claim of the prophets remains strong. Rabbi Rick Jacobs, president of the Union for Reform Judaism (URJ), has identified *tikkun olam* (a term meaning "repairing the world" that has become shorthand for the pursuit of social justice) as one of the URJ's three core values.

Interestingly, today the Jewish community as a whole professes a deep allegiance to *tikkun olam*. As Rabbi Sid Schwarz puts it in his book *Judaism and Justice*, "Few commitments unite Jews as much as a commitment to create a more just and equitable society." He cites an oft-quoted 1988 poll that asked Jews to name the "the quality most important to their Jewish identity" in which half of the sample cited a "commitment to social equality," whereas only 17 percent cited religion and 17 percent Israel. Two years later, another poll found that the most important factor determining how American Jews vote for a candidate for public office was—by far—his or her position on social justice.

The Israeli Declaration of Independence (1948) contains the striking phrase, "The State of Israel . . . will be based on freedom, justice, and peace as envisaged by the prophets of Israel." Earlier in the declaration, the founders point with pride to the Jewish people in their homeland who have given the world the "Book of Books." While these founders ranged from secular to Orthodox Jews, they agreed that prophetic values should inform the new Jewish state.

Of course, it was Martin Luther King Jr. who did so much to bring the prophets into the consciousness of America. In his famous "Letter from Birmingham City Jail" (1963) he wrote, "But more basically, I am in Birmingham because injustice is here. Just as the prophets of the eighth century BC left their villages and carried their 'thus saith the Lord' far beyond the boundaries of their home towns . . . so am I compelled to carry the gospel of freedom beyond my own home town." In his iconic "I Have a Dream" speech at the March on Washington of the same year, King quotes the prophet Amos: "No, no, we are not satisfied, and we will not be satisfied until 'justice rolls down like waters, and righteousness like a mighty stream'" (5:24), and Isaiah, "I have a dream that one day every valley shall be exalted, and every hill and mountain shall be made low, the rough places will be made plain, and the crooked places will be made straight, and the glory of the Lord shall be revealed and all flesh shall see it together" (40:4–5).

Perhaps the most stirring words about the prophets in modern times were spoken by King as he addressed the Synagogue Council of America on December 5, 1966:

> *When silence threatens to take the power of decision out of our hands . . . one looks into history for the courage to speak even in an unpopular cause. Looming as ethical giants are those extraordinary of men, the Hebrew prophets. . . .*
>
> *They did not believe that conscience is a still, small voice. They believed that conscience thunders or it does not speak at all. They were articulate, passionate, and fearless, attacking injustice and corruption whether the guilty be kings or their own unrepentant people. Without physical protection, scornful of risks evoked by their unpopular messages, they went among the people with no shield other than truth. . . .*
>
> *The Hebrew prophets belong to all peoples because their concepts of justice and equality have become ideals for all races and civilizations. Today we particularly need the Hebrew prophets because they taught that to love God was to love justice; that each human being has an inescapable obligation to denounce evil where he sees it and to defy a ruler who commands him to break the covenant.*
>
> *The Hebrew prophets are needed today because decent people must be imbued with the courage to speak the truth, to realize that silence may temporarily preserve status or security but to live with a lie is a gross affront to God.*
>
> *The Hebrew prophets are needed today because we need their flaming courage; we need them because the thunder of their fearless voices is the only sound stronger than the blasts of bombs and clamor of war hysteria.*

Yet King himself might have asked the question: Even when we pay homage to the prophets, do we resist their message? Do we recite the ancient words without internalizing their meaning? Heschel asked if we really "know" the prophets. Lerner laments: "The prophets of the past were revered, but those of the present continued to be seen as radicals who were breaking with the "authentic" tradition. . . . So, yes, prophecy was accepted and the prophetic message incorporated, but there was always an attempt to incorporate it in ways that would not too deeply shake up the present. Hence, the prophetic message could be read in synagogues every week, but always kept at an acceptable distance."

Children of the Prophets

When Jews study the prophets, we are reclaiming part of our biblical heritage. Famed German poet and essayist Heinrich Heine called the Bible the "portable homeland" of the Jews. The acclaimed novelist Chaim Potok wrote, "It is a Jew's sense of self, the beginning of it, and the foundation stone of it." Celebrated Israeli author Amos Oz notes: "What kept the Jews going were the books. After the destruction of the Second Temple, only books remained sacrosanct. [Our] scriptures and their progeny are a legacy of collective human greatness. The texts are palatial. Genesis, Isaiah, and Proverbs are our pyramids, our Great Walls, our Gothic cathedrals. Our inheritance is compiled of a few modest geographical markers and a great bookshelf." As such, whatever I can personally do to enhance biblical literacy in general, and the teaching of the prophets in particular, is both an honor and a responsibility.

In his final interview Heschel was asked if he himself was a prophet. He demurred. "Let us hope and pray," he replied, "that I am worthy of being a child of the prophets." In so responding, Heschel was reflecting Hillel's classic teaching that if we Jews are not prophets, then at least we are their disciples. Another Rabbinic source from the talmudic period explains: "When the latter prophets died . . . then the Holy Spirit came to an end in Israel. But even so, they made them hear through an echo [*bat kol*]." This understanding of our tradition is appealing: Though we are not prophets, we try to follow in their ways. We, like Heschel and King, are children of the prophets.

Taking this a step further, Rabbinic scholar Shai Held emphasizes: "The Torah wants us to know that it is not just prophets who must step forward; what is true of Abraham and Moses ought to be true of us as well. Even the children of the prophets . . . must argue for justice and plead for mercy. If, following Abraham's example, [we] are asked to argue with God, how much the more so are we called to speak up in the face of human injustice." The Talmud itself makes this dramatically clear in a remarkable passage: "Whoever is able to protest against the transgressions of his own family and does not do so is held responsible for the transgressions of his family. Whoever is able to protest against the transgressions for the people of his community and does not do so is held responsible for the transgressions of his community. Whoever is able to protest against the transgressions of the world and does not do so is responsible for the transgressions of the entire world."

The prophetic spirit lives on in those who protest the unjust, embrace the compassionate, seek the spirit, study our heritage, and walk in faith. It lives on in those who, as Heschel said, express "a very deep love, a very powerful dissent, a painful rebuke, with unwavering hope." In the process, we too become worthy of being called children of the prophets.

Introduction

The Ethics-Driven Life

The Covenant Call

Our biblical forebears began their journey to Sinai with a dimly remembered, centuries-old call: *"Go forth from your land, and from your birthplace, and from your father's house, to the land that I will show you"* (Gen. 12:1).

The call changed not only Abraham's life forever but the lives of his descendants. Abraham is commanded to leave home and homeland. He must relinquish all that is familiar and comfortable and journey to a new place. The challenge is daunting, physically and emotionally. Imagine the effort required of a well-settled and aging patriarch, and the entirety of his household.

The Torah then reveals the reason for the call: *"And I will make of you a great nation, and I will bless you . . . and all the families of the earth shall bless themselves by you"* (Gen. 12:2–3). In effect, this is the mission statement of the Jewish people. While the wording of Genesis is a declaration, the Jews will understand it as a challenge. The children of Abraham are destined and called to become a purpose-driven people. The mission could not be more consequential—to bring blessing to all humanity.

Isaiah unforgettably reaffirms this mission when he declares, *"I the Lord, in My grace, have summoned you, and I have grasped you by the hand. I created you and appointed you a covenant-people, a light of nations—opening eyes deprived of light, rescuing prisoners from confinement, from the dungeon those who sit in darkness"* (Isa. 42:6–7).

The idea of a sacred covenant between God and a people is the birthright idea of Judaism. It is the cornerstone of the Abrahamic revolution and the Mosaic revelation. The esteemed modern Jewish thinker Eugene Borowitz terms covenant "the first and most formative experience" in Judaism and opines that to this day, "believing Jews live in the reality of the covenant." Noted political philosopher Michael Walzer observes that "Prophecy, in its critical mode, is hard to imagine without the covenant, for the prophets don't invent obligations for the people; they remind the people of the obligations they already have and know they have."

The Hebrew term for covenant, *brit,* is used more than two hundred times in Scripture. This fundamental biblical notion utterly transforms Abraham, his family, and his progeny. While the *content* of this covenant, to become the moral beacon to humanity, is of great significance, the *act* of covenant makes it possible. God and Abraham have entered into a committed relationship. Abraham will stay committed to the arrangement, despite his trials and tribulations. Abraham's faith will serve as a model for his heirs, through their misfortunes; when they obey; when they stray; and when they wrestle with the covenant stipulations. The prophets will uphold the covenant as the measuring stick of our standing before God and each other.

The covenant with Abraham is not God's first promise to humanity. When God announces the intention to flood the earth, God assures Noah, *"I will establish My covenant with you"* (Gen. 6:18), and spares him and his family. After the flood, God extends that covenant to *"every living creature with you, for all ages to come"* (8:10). In the dénouement of the Noah story, the term *brit* is used seven times in the space of ten verses to cement how this notion undergirds God's relationship with the world. The covenant described here is a unilateral and universal pledge of protection; a covenant of God with all humanity.

Isaiah reminds the people that this covenant is built on the unending love of God. When the nation of Israel falls to the Babylonians and the now exiled Jews believe themselves to be scorned by God, he preaches, *"For a little while I forsook you, but with vast love I will bring you back . . . for this to Me is like the waters of Noah: As I swore that the waters of Noah nevermore would flood the earth, so I swear that I will not be angry with you or rebuke you. For the mountains may move and the hills be shaken, but my loving-kindness shall never move from you, nor my covenant of friendship be shaken"* (Isa. 54:7–10).

Rabbinic tradition affirms a Noahide covenant with all humanity. The Talmud and other sources postulate basic commandments from this covenant that are incumbent on every society. Most commonly, the seven "Noahide laws," as they are termed, include prohibitions against murder, stealing, illicit sexual relations, blasphemy, denying God, and eating a live animal as well as the command to establish courts of law to enforce justice.

The highest expression of *brit,* however, manifests in the second covenant, with Abraham and his heirs. The covenant with Noah is unilateral; the *brit* with Abraham is bilateral. The former is universal; the latter is particular. The children of Noah are promised protection; the children of Abraham are promised purpose and prosperity.

Noah's relationship with God requires an initial act of obedience. God summons Noah to build an ark and save humanity—no mean feat. Yet the post-flood narrative gives no evidence that the relationship continues. Indeed, the one further story of Noah hints at a lonely and troubled man, drunk, exposed, and belligerent (Gen. 9:21–29).

Abraham's relationship with God, by contrast, demands continual dialogue, tests, and faith. God summons Abraham to not only undertake a journey but to demonstrate loyalty and to begin building a people. The patriarch will have physical, spiritual, and ethical demands placed upon him. The fulfillment of the covenant will occupy his entire life.

The sign of the covenant with Noah is a rainbow in the sky: *"I have set My bow in the clouds, and it shall serve as sign of the covenant between Me and you . . . and every living creature among all flesh, so that the waters shall never again become a flood to destroy all flesh"* (Gen. 9:13–15). A dramatic and welcomed sign, the rainbow signals the cessation of a storm, the return of light, and the renewal of the divine promise not to flood the earth again.

The sign of the covenant with Abraham, though, is even more dramatic, intimate, and ever present. *"Such shall be the covenant between Me and you and your offspring to follow which you shall keep: every male among you shall be circumcised"* (Gen. 17:10). The *brit* is seared into the flesh. To this day, Jewish males are traditionally circumcised on the eighth day of life in a ceremony referred to as *brit milah*, the covenant of circumcision. Perhaps no other Jewish ritual has so long endured. The Abrahamic revolution is reaffirmed with Jewish male birth (and today with covenant ceremonies of naming for Jewish girls as well). Declaration of the *brit* is the first ritual act of the Jew, sacrificial and irreversible in nature.

Readers of the Bible sometimes overlook a key passage in Genesis that elaborates on the initial charge to Abraham. Intending to destroy Sodom, God says, *"Shall I hide from Abraham what I am about to do, since Abraham is to become a great and populous nation, and all the nations of the earth are to bless themselves by him? For I have singled him out, that he may instruct his children and his posterity to keep the way of the Lord by doing what is just and right, in order that the Lord may bring about for Abraham what He has promised him"* (Gen. 18:17–19). Here, the moral essence of the Abrahamic covenant is made the most explicit: God seeks what is "just and right." Importantly, God, in deciding not to hide the pending destruction of Sodom, seems ready to submit to Abraham's moral scrutiny.

An Echo of the Call

Moses becomes the first prophet to hear an echo of the call to covenant—he hears a voice from amidst a burning bush at the "mountain of God." Astonishingly, not long thereafter, an entire people will be party to that call at the same mountain.

Many biblical scholars have emphasized the unique quality of this epic event. As Jeremiah Unterman expresses it, "In the Jewish Bible, the most important event in the history of the Israelites was God's revelation at Sinai. Indeed, in all of recorded history, only in the Bible do we have the claim of a god's revelation to an entire people. This revelation is a democratization of divine communication which stands in stark contrast to the revelation claimed in the ancient Near East only by an elite—king, priest, or prophet. The undeniable message is that every single Israelite is significant to God." Walzer explains: "Israel was founded twice, once as a family, a kin group, once as a nation, a political and religious community—and both times the founding instrument was a covenant. The covenant was with Abraham . . . the second covenant is with the people of Israel at Sinai . . . the birth model and the adherence model."

The Children of Israel's epic trek to the Promised Land recalls Abraham's journey. Like the patriarch's, it crosses a physical and spiritual wilderness: The Israelites move from enslavement to the false god of Pharaoh to the worthy servitude of the true God of the universe. And just as God spoke directly to Abraham, and to Moses, so God will speak to the people at Sinai. Although Moses may be the mouthpiece, the call is addressed to the people.

There is no better restatement of the call to covenant and the mission statement of the Jewish people than God's first words to Moses when the prophet and the people first reach Mount Sinai: *"The Lord called to him from the mountain, saying: 'Thus shall you say to the house of Jacob and declare to the children of Israel: You have seen what I did to the Egyptians, how I bore you on eagle's wings and brought you to Me. Now then, if you will obey Me faithfully and keep My covenant, you shall be My treasured possession among all the peoples. Indeed, all the earth is Mine, but you shall be to Me a kingdom of priests and a holy nation'"* (Exod. 19:3–6).

While the Exodus constitutes liberation, freedom is not the ultimate purpose of the escape from Egypt. Freedom from human tyranny is certainly a prerequisite to the service of God. But "freedom from" in the Torah is meant for the higher purpose of "freedom to." Freedom is responsibility. Freedom's fulfillment is in the assumption of the Torah covenant, with all its stipulations.

The biblical writers feared that moral autonomy (freedom for its own sake) could lead to moral anarchy. The point of the Exodus is to reach Sinai and revive the call to Abraham. The point of Sinai is to answer the call through the commanded life—the holy life. All the prophets will return to this theme time and again.

As such, the Exodus is the rebirth of a mission-driven people. The promise to Abraham that was lost through centuries of oppression is revived. The turning point comes early in the Exodus saga, when the Torah says, *"God heard their moaning, and God remembered His covenant with Abraham and Isaac and Jacob"* (Exod. 2:24). Long ago Abraham journeyed to a mountain, where he was given a test of faith. So too will the Israelites, who will respond anew to the summons. As God remembers the covenant, so will the people.

Birth imagery suffuses not only the micro-story of Moses, but the macro-story of the Israelites. A suffering but growing clan, once animated by a sense of destiny, is gestated anew in the fertile but ultimately oppressive womb of Egypt. The long gestation is followed by the labor pains of the plagues, the parting of the waters, and finally birth upon the dry land of a new world. Through the painful experience of expulsion from Egypt (the name in Hebrew, *Mitzrayim,* means "narrow straights"—like a birth canal), a people are born. Indeed, it is only when we begin the book of Exodus that the Torah explicitly refers to the Israelites as a people, *am b'nei yisrael* (Exod. 2:9).

Every birth is a beginning . . . but only the beginning. Like a newborn baby, the people of Israel precariously move forward to their *brit.* The covenant ceremony takes place at Sinai. The people hear the terms of the sacred pact between them and their God. They pledge their loyalty. Their pledge is their mark. The description in the Torah, complete with the dashing of blood, is reminiscent of circumcision: *"Then he [Moses] took the record of the covenant and read it aloud to the people. And they said, 'All that the Lord has spoken we will faithfully do!' Moses took the blood and dashed it on the people and said, 'This is the blood of the covenant which the Lord now makes with you concerning all these commands'"* (Exod. 24:7–8).

The Covenant Responsibility

What does it mean for a people in its entirety to witness and accept the covenant? A community has now been created with a defined and urgent sense of both individual and collective responsibility. Unterman spells it out clearly and succinctly:

> For the first time *in the ancient world, the individual is responsible for the fate of the community by his/her behavior. In reality, each individual now has a dual responsibility—as an individual and as a member of the nation. The community whom the Bible addresses is now apprised of the extraordinary importance of each individual. So, the community must take steps to ensure that its individuals obey the law. Additionally, this concern will be reflected in numerous Divine laws that enjoin the community and its members to care for the vulnerable elements of society. For the first time, the community becomes responsible for the fate of the individual. Thus is born the concept of communal responsibility.*

The covenant responsibility is also intergenerational. This deeply embedded sense of mutual responsibility can also be seen as the source of the biblical imperative to educate our children. The most notable expression of this imperative is in Deuteronomy, in a passage that has become central to Jewish liturgy: *"Take to heart these instructions with which I charge you this day. Impress them upon your children. Recite them when you stay at home and when you are away, when you lie down and when you rise up"* (Deut. 6:6–7). Later, Moses reminds the people that they enter into the covenant with *"your children"* and with *"those who are not with us here this day"* (Deut. 29:10,14), traditionally understood to mean future generations. Moreover, recollection and celebration of the Exodus is to be observed *"as an institution for all time, for you and for your descendants,"* and *"When your children ask you, 'What do you mean by this rite?' you shall say . . ."* (Exod. 12:24,26).

Furthermore, at Sinai, the entirety of a people accept the Abrahamic covenant as expressed in a specific array of laws, Torah, that are in effect a national constitution. Sacred scripture and civil law are indistinguishable. Both have their common source, according to the Bible itself and the community of the faithful that follow it, in divinely revealed legislation. As the contemporary philosopher Rabbi David Hartman wrote, "Sinai permanently exposes the Jewish people to prophetic aspirations and judgments. . . . Sinai requires of the Jew that he believe in the possibility of integrating the moral seriousness of the prophet with the realism and political judgment of the statesman. Politics and morality were united when Israel was born as a nation at Sinai."

Hartman then touches on the danger of nationalism divorced from ethics, a theme with relevance throughout Jewish and world history. The prophetic ethic cannot abide by such a separation; indeed, it rails against it with an incessant voice. "The prophets taught us that the state has only instrumental value for the purpose of embodying the covenantal demands of Judaism," Hartman insists. "When nationalism becomes an absolute for Jews, and political and military judgments are not related to the larger spiritual and moral purpose of our national renaissance, we can no longer claim to continue the Judaic tradition."

The Covenant Commemoration

The rebirth of a covenant people and their mission is annually commemorated in the great Jewish festivals of Pesach and Shavuot. Retelling the Exodus from Egypt and the Revelation at Sinai thus becomes living (as well as past) history instruction. However the trials and tribulations of the covenant people may continue, the covenant is alive and well, and needs to be reaffirmed *b'kol dor v'dor,* "in every generation." The Passover seder motif *m'avdut leherut,* "from slavery to freedom," replays itself in every age. There will be suffering, but there will be redemption.

So, too, in every generation the historical memory turns into moral demand: "*You shall not oppress a stranger, . . . having yourselves been strangers in the land of Egypt*" (Exod. 23:9). There is no escaping the journey or the mission.

Crucially, the Exodus-Sinai narrative is woven not only into Pesach and Shavuot, two central holidays of the Jewish year, but also into the weekly fabric of Jewish life. Its means is that uniquely biblical institution called the Sabbath.

So central is the Sabbath that the Torah understands it to be part of God's original plan of creation: "*On the seventh day God finished the work which He had been doing and He rested on the seventh day from all the work which He had done. And God blessed the seventh day and declared it holy, because on it God ceased from all the work of creation which He had done*" (Gen. 2:2–3).

And the Sabbath is embedded in the Sinai story, squarely in the middle of the Ten Commandments. The first commandment introduces God as the one "*who brought you out of the land of Egypt, the house of bondage*" (Exod. 20:1). The fourth commandment expressly orders that on the seventh day "*you shall not do any work—you, your son or daughter, your male or female slave, or your cattle, or the stranger who is within your settlements*" (Exod. 20:9). The Sabbath is a small taste of the radical freedom and equality envisioned by the covenant (even if the reality is much more distant). As the Sabbath prayer over the wine, the *Kiddush*, proclaims, the Sabbath is both "a reminder of the work of Creation" and "a recollection of the Exodus from Egypt."

The Sabbath-Exodus connection is made ever more explicit in the second telling of the Ten Commandments (the Deuteronomy Decalogue), which adds, "*Remember that you were a slave in the land of Egypt, and the Lord your God freed you from there with a mighty hand and an outstretched arm; therefore the Lord your God has commanded you to observe the Sabbath day*" (Deut. 5:5). As Rabbi Ethan Tucker aptly notes, "According to this version of the Ten Commandments, Shabbat is about taking home the lessons of being a slave and making sure that the economically disadvantaged get a chance to rest. Shabbat here emerges from Jewish history. We have firsthand experience of a culture of incessant work; when God redeemed us from that state, we took on a corollary obligation: Never again to create a culture that economically enslaves people without a break."

Recollections of the Exodus-Sinai covenant journey are even present in the Jewish daily liturgy. Every morning and evening service features the singing of a selection from the "Song of the Sea," the *Mi Khamokha* (Exod. 15:11). The prayer continues, "With a new song the redeemed sang Your praise at the shore of the sea" in the morning, and "Your children witnessed Your sovereignty—the sea splitting before Moses" in the evening. Both versions conclude with praise to God "for redeeming Israel." For the observant Jew, not a day is to go by without remembering the liberation and revelation of Exodus and Sinai.

This message is likewise reinforced in a list of "daily miracles" recited early in the morning service. We give thanks to God "who has made me free." We give praise to God "who made me in the image of God." We acknowledge God "who girds Israel with strength" and "crowns Israel with splendor." We are grateful to God "who frees the captive" and "who lifts up the fallen." By reciting these elements of the covenant experience, we perpetuate the journey.

The Covenant Journey Continues

Yet Sinai is not the end of the journey. Holy ground and place of revelation that it is . . . Sinai is nevertheless a stop on the way to the final destination. In fact, according to the Torah, God needs to gently but firmly remind the people of Israel to keep going. God commands the Israelites with the words *lech aleh,* an echo of Abraham's *lech lecha.* Even from the heights of Sinai the people are told to ascend, *aleh*—in effect, to keep climbing. They are instructed to do so *mizeh,* literally "from this place," but also "from this situation" (Exod. 33:1).

One cannot remain forever on the heights of Sinai. Descent is inevitable, but eventually ascent will follow. There are valleys to cross and other mountains to scale. The ultimate destination is not another

Sinai, but Israel, the Promised Land. While this saga describes the Israelites, their journey became the archetype and inspiration for many others (like the Puritans) throughout history.

The long slog through the wilderness may well represent the years of adolescent wandering (why does it take so long to grow up?). You can take the child out of slavery but can you take slavery out of the child? Learning to become a servant of God rather than a slave of Pharaoh is a long road. Slowly, slowly the desert trek will impart the lessons of justice and compassion, of humility and faith, that will mark a people ready for the Promise. The people progress and regress. They often take one step forward and two steps backward. But they march on. At the end of the book of Exodus we are told that the Israelites will set out *"on their various journeys"* but only *"when the cloud lifted"* (Exod. 40:36). Confusion and uncertainty is a constant companion. At their lowest points the people are threatened with a paralyzing despair. The lessons will come slowly, but they will come.

In their moments of clarity, our ancestors sensed that, in the words of esteemed travel writer Bruce Chatwin, "their vitality lay in their movement." The journey must continue. At a critical juncture, when their morale is at its lowest, one of the unexpected and uncelebrated heroes of the Bible steps forward to convey just this message. Caleb is one of the twelve spies Moses sends to scout out the Promised Land. The majority of the spies return with a deeply pessimistic assessment of the people's chances to prevail in their mission and fulfill their destiny. The resulting effect on the community's morale is so deleterious that a near riot ensues, and the tribes rail, *"if only we had died in the land of Egypt . . . or if only we might die in this wilderness,"* and, astonishingly, *"it would be better for us to go back to Egypt! Let us head back for Egypt"* (Num. 14:2–4).

Only Caleb and Joshua dissent from the gloom and doom of the spies. Hushing the people, Caleb urges them to continue on, with the words *aloh na'aleh, "let us by all means go up!"* (Num. 13:30). Here again is an echo of God's words at Sinai, themselves an echo of God's words to Abraham. The language is of ascent. The Hebrew is what scholars call the "emphatic construct," a phrase that repeats the same word in two different forms: "By all means" or "Certainly, we shall ascend." Caleb's next words again employ the emphatic form, *yachol nuchal, "We shall surely overcome!"*

Little more is said about Caleb. He, like some of the other prophets we will observe, is one of those meteors in the night sky. Tellingly, though, the Torah concludes the account of his heroic moment by calling him *"my servant Caleb"* and emphasizing that he was imbued *"with a different spirit"* (Num. 14:24). He has not been counted as one of the classical prophets per se, but Caleb has the prophetic spirit. This spirit gives him the strength to stand against the majority and refuse to abandon the mission.

The prophetic spirit is indeed "a different spirit"—the very spirit that defines the prophets. Ancient Israel's great visionaries, it has often been noted, held no political power or elective office. More often than not they were neither priests nor even members of the religious establishment. Their journey was public but solitary. Their message was loud but unpopular; timely but shunned. An expression arose, *ein navi b'iro*, "there is no prophet in his own city." In the words of theologian Frederick Buechner: "There is no evidence to suggest that anyone ever asked a prophet home for supper more than once."

The late Bible scholar Yohanan Muffs described a prophet, borrowing from the memorable phrase of Ezekiel (22:30), as one summoned to *"stand in the breach"* between God and Israel. The prophets' primary task was to convey God's message to the stiff-necked people who were not inclined to hear it.

Yet, at the same time, the prophets, with Moses at the lead, also found themselves needing to plead with God on behalf of the people. As Rabbi Shai Held explains: "[The prophet] loves God and finds the people's corruption intolerable; but he also loves the people, and cannot abide the thought that they will meet with devastation and desolation." After the people's loss of faith following the spies report, for example, an incensed God wants to wipe out the entire generation of the Exodus, save for Moses' line. *"How long will this people spurn Me, and how long will they have no faith in Me?"* exclaims the exasperated deity (Num. 14:11). Moses must come to the people's defense. The prophet is holding God accountable, as it were, to the same standards of justice and compassion as the people.

Moses is successful, but only to a point. God's response, *"I pardon, as you have asked"* (Num. 14:20), averts an immediate calamity. The Exodus generation will die in the desert as punishment for their sins, but their children will live.

As intercessors from the people to God, the prophets have mixed results. As intercessors from God to the people, the prophets unfortunately succeed to an even lesser extent. Yet if the prophets are often ignored in the short run, their messages persist in the long run. Their stories and teachings are told and retold. Their words are passed down, later written down, and come to occupy a crucial portion of the Hebrew Bible. The prophets' challenge to the conscience of the nation lodges in the collective memory and is not forgotten. Each generation encounters the prophetic path and the opportunity to travel the road less taken.

The Covenant Response: Here I Am

It is no surprise that the Israelites have trouble staying focused on the prophetic call. Genesis teaches that human beings seem to have an almost genetic disposition toward evading responsibility. After Adam and Eve eat the forbidden fruit, Genesis describes God as walking, *mithalech* (or, more idiomatically, "moving about") in the Garden of Eden. The human pair immediately hides: *"They heard the sound of the Lord God moving about in the garden at the breezy time of the day; and the man and his wife hid from the Lord God among the trees of the garden"* (Gen. 3:8). Evidently Adam and Eve know they have done something wrong. When the voice of God comes calling, when the threat of discovery and possible confrontation is looming, their first instinct is to evade.

Why is evasion our first reaction? Perhaps it is hardwired into our brains: flight or fight. When given the opportunity, flight is the response of choice. Our brains are signaling that this is the safest path. Yet, as the first human beings are about to learn, such behavior carries unavoidable consequences. The flight from the ethical will not stand. Our unique humanity as moral beings will depend on overcoming instinct.

God calls out to Adam and Eve with a simple but startling question. It is one word in the Hebrew: *Ayecha? "Where are you?"* (Gen. 3:9).

Heschel teaches us that this is God's first, and eternal, question to humanity, "a call that goes out again and again. Religion begins with a consciousness that something is asked of us. The beginning of religiosity is the feeling of being summoned by a power greater than yourself."

Adam replies, *"I heard the sound of You in the garden, and I was afraid because I was naked, so I hid"* (Gen. 3:10). Adam does not say where he is, but rather what he is doing. He admits to hiding because he is fearful. This is no innocent game of hide and seek . . . something has occurred, and Adam is not proud of it. Adam suggests that his nakedness is the issue, but nakedness is not something to fear, unless one is afraid of exposing something else.

Heeding God's call is never easy for the rest of us, either. Like children, sometimes we plug our ears, hoping the summons may pass us by. We distract ourselves with a million other pursuits. We are like a radio unable to tune in to the right frequency. The signal is beaming but we do not receive the message.

And when we do hear the call, we may choose to ignore or suppress it. Whether out of insecurity or inertia, fear of disquiet or discomfort, we sense the summons but do not respond. The phone rings, and we pretend no one is home. The text message is received, and we press delete. We make a quick mental calculation that we can safely carry on without entering the conversation. Or, we offer a perfunctory response intended to avoid meaningful dialogue.

Adam hears God's question but does not respond admirably. He blames Eve, who in turn blames the serpent. Genuine dialogue does not ensue; acceptance of responsibility does not result. Adam and

Eve will begin a journey, but it is not the prophetic path. The Torah describes an involuntary exile from Eden. There must be a better way.

Just as the prophetic query to humanity is embodied in one biblical word *ayecha* (Where are you?), so too is the response, *hineni* (Here I am!).

The prophets repeatedly use this expression of presence. When Abraham is called by name during his excruciating test of faith, he responds three times with this very word:

To God—"He said to him, 'Abraham,' and He answered, 'Here I am.'" (Gen. 22:1)
To Isaac—"Then Isaac said to his father Abraham, 'Father!' And he answered, 'Here I am, my son.'" (Gen. 22:7)
To the angel—"Then an angel of the Lord called to him from heaven: 'Abraham! Abraham!' And he answered, 'Here I am.'" (Gen. 22:11)

The great medieval biblical commentator Rashi labels this *lashon aniya*, "the language of response." Abraham stands in distinct contrast to the evasive Adam. He is ready to answer the call.

Later in Genesis, Abraham's grandson is also called. Jacob responds like his forebear: *"God called to Israel in a vision by night: 'Jacob! Jacob!' He answered, 'Here I am'"* (Gen. 46:2).

When Moses stands before the burning bush: *"God called to him out of the bush: 'Moses! Moses!' He answered, 'Here I am'"* (Exod. 3:4).

When Samuel is just a boy, his mother takes him to the priest Eli. One night, *"The Lord called out to Samuel, and he answered, 'I'm coming.' He ran to Eli and said, 'Here I am; you called me'"* (1 Sam. 3:4). This happens a second time and then a third, before Eli realizes what is happening and instructs Samuel to speak to God.

Isaiah sees himself among angels: *"Then I heard the voice of my Lord saying, 'Whom shall I send? Who will go for us?' And I said, 'Here I am; send me'"* (Isa. 6:8).

Isaiah later declares of God: *"I said, 'Here I am, Here I am,' to a nation that did not invoke My name"* (Isa. 65:1). Yet Isaiah also envisions the day when God will say definitively *"When you call, the Lord will answer; when you cry, He will say: 'Here I am'"* (Isa. 58:9).

As a rule, the prophets hear the call more keenly than the commoners. Perhaps the most vivid expression of this is Amos's declaration: *"The lion has roared, who can but fear? My Lord God has spoken, who can but prophesy?"* (Amos 3:8). The prophet is describing a calling that shakes him to the core.

Sometimes, the prophets' visions of being called are so powerful, they overcome our all-too-common denial and reluctance. *"I behold my Lord seated on a high and lofty throne,"* says Isaiah. He demurs: *"Woe is me; I am lost! For I am a man of unclean lips, and I live among a people of unclean lips.... Yet my own eyes have beheld the King, Lord of Hosts."* Once an angel touches a live coal to his lips and declares, *"Now that this has touched your lips, your guilt shall depart, and your sin be purged away"* (Isa. 6:1–8), Isaiah knows there is no turning back. His "Here I am; send me" ushers forth.

Jeremiah's prophetic call is even more angst-ridden. He begins his work by acknowledging that he is destined to the prophetic call, saying, *"The word of the Lord came to me. Before I created you in the womb, I selected you; before you were born, I consecrated you; I appointed you a prophet concerning the nations"* (Jer. 1:5). Yet, like his reluctant predecessors—Isaiah claimed *"unclean lips,"* Moses that he was *"slow of speech and slow of tongue"* (Exod. 4:10)—Jeremiah objects. He contends that he is too young: *"Ah, Lord, God! I don't know how to speak, for I am still a boy"* (Jer. 1:6). However, when *"The Lord put out His hand and touched my mouth, and the Lord said to me: Herewith I put My words into your mouth"* (Jer. 1:9), Jeremiah too relents.

More than any other prophet, Jeremiah will suffer physically and emotionally. He will endure imprisonment and exile. He will repeatedly mourn his own birth: *"Woe is me, my mother, that you ever bore me," "Accursed be the day that I was born!"* and *"Why did I ever issue from the womb, to see misery and woe, to spend all my days in shame"* (Jer. 15:10, 20:14,18). Yet, Jeremiah will preach on.

With *hineni*, the prophetic journey is launched. The path will meander and wander, ascend and descend, through trepidation and affirmation, confrontation and cooperation, despair and exaltation, rebuke and consolation, fear and faith. Through it all, a commitment to the covenant mission will sustain us.

The Covenant Goal: Holiness

Recall the mission statement to the Jewish people at Sinai: *"Now then, if you will obey Me faithfully and keep My covenant, you shall be My treasured possession among all the peoples. Indeed, all the earth is Mine, but you shall be to Me a kingdom of priests and a holy nation"* (Exod. 19:3–6). The reward of the covenant, and its goal, is holiness. So Moses declares to the people at the outset of their epic trek through the wilderness, and then again near its end, *"The Lord will establish you as His Holy people, as He swore to you, if you keep the commandments of the Lord your God and walk in His ways"* (Deut. 28:9). In the middle of the Torah we are likewise reminded, *"You shall be holy, for I, the Lord your God, am holy"* (Lev. 19:1).

We best understand covenant holiness as an exalted or sanctified state of being dedicated to a higher purpose—serving God. Interestingly, the first realm that the Bible describes as holy is time—the Sabbath. *"And God blessed the seventh day and declared it holy, because on it God ceased from all the work of creation which He had done"* (Gen. 2:3). One day of the week is elevated above the rest. The Sabbath is distinct and special by virtue of it being a rest day. In Genesis it is a rest day from the divine work of creation. In Exodus it is a respite from the human toil of daily existence.

The second realm the Bible describes as holy is space—the place where Moses meets God. *"And He said, 'Do not come closer. Remove your sandals from your feet, for the place on which you stand is holy ground'"* (Exod. 3:5). One piece of geography is elevated above the rest. The burning bush on the mountain is distinct and special by virtue of its being the locale of human-divine encounter. In this early part of

Exodus holy ground is Mount Horeb, *"the mountain of God."* Later in Exodus, it is Mount Sinai. Still later, it is the Tabernacle in the desert, and, finally, the Temple in Jerusalem, which preserves the memory of the mountain.

The third realm described as holy is humanity—the people when living in covenant with God. *"If you will obey . . . a holy nation . . . a holy people . . . if you keep the commandments . . . you shall be holy"* (Exod. 19:3, Deut. 28:9, Lev. 19:1). The status of one people is elevated above the rest. These people are distinct and special by virtue of their commitment to the ethical life of the covenant. Note the conditional and future-tense language of the text. Holiness is not inherent but latent. The potential is always there, but it takes right behavior to realize holiness.

One might think that human beings are inherently holy based on the Torah's view that we are created in the image of God. Indeed, Moses' cousin Korah expresses such a view, contending that *"all the community is holy, all of them, and the Lord is in their midst"* (Num. 16:1). The esteemed Israeli philosopher Yeshayahu Leibowitz acknowledges these two conceptions, explaining, "The [first concept] of holiness is not a fact, but a goal. In the [second concept] holiness is something granted to us: we are holy."

Nonetheless, throughout his career, Professor Leibowitz advocated for the concept of conditional, rather than inherent, holiness. He saw the latter as dangerous, whether applied to the land or the people of Israel. The land, he argued, is not holy until we sanctify it, and we are not holy unless we are ethically observant.

The connection between holiness and ethics is nowhere more explicit than in the famous "Holiness Code" of Leviticus. As Unterman observes,

> Following the introductory declaration, *"You shall be holy, for I, the Lord your God, am holy," Leviticus 19 enumerates over 60 positive ('Do . . .') and negative ('Don't do . . .') commandments/laws, approximately two-thirds of which belong to (or are associated with) the ethi-*

cal sphere, while the rest belong to the ritual domain. Herein one finds a wide range of moral requirements—on providing food for the poor and stranger, not lying or acting deceitfully, not defrauding or holding back wages, not exploiting the helpless or slandering, not rendering unfair judgment or cheating in business, not standing idly by while your fellow is in danger, and others. Most of these are written in the direct address style that we witnessed in the Ten Commandments. One of the effects of this style is to raise moral statements to legal status.

Unterman further notes:

Only in the Jewish Bible is ethical behavior presented as part of the requirements for holiness. This idea, similarly to the "image of God" of Genesis 1 and 9, represents an emulation of Divinity—imitatio dei. . . . Obviously, the people's obedience to the ethical obligations of holiness is not a precise imitation of Divine ethical behavior—for God does not engage in business, revere parents, etc. Rather, if Israel strives for holiness by behaving ethically, they shall be separated from the nations, as God is separated from His world. So, by following God's rules, the people cannot become God, but they can become Godly.

The Covenant Relationship: Love

Covenant is a relational term. In civil law it implies the reciprocal responsibilities between two parties. In the biblical conception it describes the divine-human encounter. The prophets understood the covenant as God's way of loving us, and obedience to the commandments as our way of loving God.

Our biblical ancestors would not have understood the distinction we draw today between love and law because in the Bible love of God is not a sentiment as much as a way of acting. In a recent study, Harvard professor Jon Levenson cites a variety of biblical passages connecting love with loyalty and obedience and concludes, "If we put all this together, we come up with an identification of the love of God with the performance of commandments. Love, so understood, is not an emotion, not a feeling, but a cover term for acts of obedient service."

In Judaism, actions speak louder than words and, in many cases, louder than feelings as well. The covenantal love of Israel for God is more like the love of children for parents than the romantic love of modern marriages. Deeds over time are what count the most, grounding and proving the relationship. Perhaps this helps us understand the Rabbinic dictum, "Greater is he who has been commanded and does the deed than he who had not been commanded and does the deed." For the prophets, the climactic moment of the covenant relationship may well be when the people as a whole say *na'aseh v'nishma*—literally, *"we will do and we will obey,"* but also translated as *"we will do what we have heard,"* or *"we will faithfully do"* (Exod. 24:7; cf. Exod. 19:8, 24:3). It is as if the entire people are saying *hineni*, "Here I am," to the covenant and its demands.

The Torah memorably commands the love of God, the love of neighbor, and the love of the stranger. If we were to conceive of this love as sentiment, like the Greek notions of *eros* (romantic love) or *philos* (fraternal love), it would be difficult to understand how such a feeling could be commanded. Even if we were to define this love in the more spiritual sense as *agape* (altruistic love), the same challenge ensues. After all, short of the mystical devotion or cleaving to God (known to the kabbalists but not to the prophets), such rarified dedication and zeal is too elusive to attain. However, if we understand the commanded love of the Torah as loyalty and fidelity to the covenant and its commandments, things make more sense. Again, the proof of love is in deeds: in how one treats one's fellow and one's God.

A great talmudic teaching amplifies God's covenantal love for humanity:

> *"Beloved is man for he was created in the image. Extraordinary is the love made known to him that he was created in the image, as it is said, For in His image did God made man" (Gen. 1:27, 9:6). Beloved are*

> *Israel for they were called children of God. Extraordinary is the love made known to them that they were called children of God, as it is said: "You are the children of the Lord, your God" (Deut. 14:1). Beloved are Israel for to them was given a precious implement. Extraordinary is the love made known to them that they were given the precious implement with which the world was created, as it is said: "For I give you a good doctrine, you shall not forsake My teaching." (Prov. 4:2)*

God's creation of humanity in the divine image is a first act of love. Granting our human awareness of this unique creation is another act of love. Offering a covenantal relationship with the children of Israel is a third act of love. Israel's awareness of the covenant is a fourth act of love. Giving the Torah is a fifth act of love. Israel's awareness of the commandments is a final act of love.

The Ethics-Driven Life

Scholars have often dubbed the core prophetic message as "ethical monotheism"—the idea that righteous living is God's primary demand. For the prophets, the ethics-driven life is the heart of it all—our purpose and our task. While the prophets did not employ the term "ethics" per se (a philosophical concept from the ancient Greeks), their central preoccupation was morality. Yet the prophetic call to holiness through ethical living is not generic. While the prophets' soaring oratory was not deficient in ethical generalities, they nonetheless saw themselves in a covenant relationship with God, and the content of that covenant was something quite specific—the Torah. The prophetic message rests on a formidable list of detailed commandments *bein adam l'makom,* between us and God, and *bein adam l'havero,* between us and our fellow.

In the Torah, of course, all kinds of commandments cover every aspect of human life. The sages identified 613 commandments related to everything from food and sex to sacrifices and holidays. The prophets, however, emphasized those commandments that govern how we relate to God and to one another. Micah's great formulation is prefaced by the declaration, *"He has told you, O man, what is good, and what the Lord requires of you"* (6:8). The Hebrew "require," *doresh,* is a strong term that could also be translated as "demand." The God of the prophets is demanding, and the stipulations are clear. While the Torah espouses its ethical principles through stories that are meant to set examples (*aggadah*), it is also very much a legal code of ethics (*halacha*) meant to be followed.

In the course of this book I follow both moral pathways. Recognizing that stories are the best teachers, I emphasize episodes in the prophets' lives that dramatize the ethical principles they espouse. That said, since the prophets themselves would insist upon a commandment-based blueprint for the ethical life, in each chapter I also connect these stories to biblical commandments and Rabbinic teachings that define the prophetic path. We are inspired by biography but guided by law.

In order to appreciate the dictates of the covenant that inform the prophets, I have compiled three sets of the Torah's most important ethical commandments. In the following text I order them according to the same three categories that structure this book: Micah's call to justice, compassion, and faith. These decrees are largely drawn from three sets of biblical commandments in the Torah: the Covenant Code of Exodus, the Holiness Code of Leviticus, and the Justice Code of Deuteronomy.

Justice

The prophetic message of justice is built on the exhortation: *"Justice, justice shall you pursue"* (Deut. 16:20). The call to justice emphasizes the necessity of true impartiality before the law: *"You shall appoint magistrates . . . and they shall govern the people with due justice. You shall not judge unfairly: you shall show no partiality; you shall not take bribes, for bribes blind the eyes of the discerning and upset the plea of the just"* (Deut. 16:18–19; see also Lev. 19:15, Exod. 23:2–3,6–8). Basic rules against murder, theft, and perjury are familiar to us because they are enshrined in the Ten Commandments. Fair treatment of workers and timely payment of their wages is fundamental to a just society: *"You shall not abuse a needy and destitute laborer; whether a fellow countryman or a stranger in one of the communities of your land"* (Deut. 24:14). Also: *"You must pay [a laborer] his wages on the same day, before the sun sets, for he is needy and urgently depends on it"* (Deut. 24:15; similarly Lev. 19:13).

Perhaps the most distinctive feature of the prophetic call to justice is the attention given to the needy and vulnerable: *"You shall not wrong a stranger or oppress him, for you were strangers in the land of Egypt. You shall not ill-treat any widow or orphan"* (Exod. 22:20–21; similarly, Exod. 23:9, Lev. 19:33, Deut. 24:17–18). The prophets recognized the hard truth of the human condition: those who live on the margins of society are easily neglected and oppressed. The heart of the prophetic ethic is a rebuttal of this injustice, and a rebuke to those who abuse power at the expense of the lowly.

Ten Commandments of Justice

1. *"Justice, justice shall you pursue."* (Deut. 16:20)
2. *"You shall appoint magistrates . . . and they shall govern the people with due justice. You shall not judge unfairly; you shall show no partiality; you shall not take bribes, for bribes blind the eyes of the discerning and upset the plea of the just."* (Deut. 16:18–19, Lev. 19:15, Exod. 23:2–3,6–8)
3. *"You shall not abuse a needy and destitute laborer; whether a fellow countryman or a stranger in one of the communities of your land. You must pay a laborer his wages on the same day, before the sun sets, for he is needy and urgently depends on it."* (Deut. 24:14–15, Lev. 19:13)
4. *"You shall not defraud your neighbor."* (Lev. 19:13)
5. *"You shall not stand idly by (or profit by) the blood of your neighbor."* (Lev. 19:16)
6. *"You shall not murder."* (Exod. 20:13, Deut. 5:17)
7. *"You shall not steal."* (Exod. 20:13, Lev. 19:11, Deut. 5:17)
8. *"You shall not bear false witness against your neighbor."* (Exod. 20:13,23:1, Deut. 5:17)

9. *"You shall not wrong a stranger or oppress him, for you were strangers in the land of Egypt. You shall not ill-treat any widow or orphan."* (Exod. 22:20–21, 23:9, Lev. 19:33, Deut. 24:17–18)
10. *"You shall have one law for stranger and citizen alike."* (Lev. 24:22, Num. 15:15)

Compassion

"Love your neighbor as yourself" (Lev. 19:18) has been called the Torah's greatest biblical command. Rabbi Akiva termed it the *k'lal gadol* (great principle), and it is often considered the basis of the "golden rule" as espoused by Hillel and Jesus.

This supreme exhortation of compassion expresses the broadest ideal of compassion. Yet, again, those on the margins of society—the poor, the handicapped, and the stranger—are most frequently and dramatically singled out for special concern:

"You shall not insult the deaf, or place a stumbling block before the blind." (Lev. 19:14)
"You shall rise before the aged and show deference to the old." (Lev. 19:32)
"When you reap the harvest of your land, you shall not reap all the way to the edges of the field, or gather the gleaning of your harvest. You shall not pick your vineyard bare, or gather the fallen fruit of your vineyard; you shall leave them for the poor and the stranger." (Lev. 19:9–10, Deut. 24:19–21)
"Do not harden you heart and shut your hand against your needy kinsman. Rather you must open your hand and lend him sufficient for whatever he needs." (Deut. 15:7–8)
"The stranger who resides with you shall be to you as one of your citizens; you shall love him as yourself, for you were strangers in the land of Egypt." (Lev. 19:34)

Ten Commandments of Compassion

1. *"You shall not insult the deaf, or place a stumbling block before the blind."* (Lev. 19:14)
2. *"You shall rise before the aged and show deference to the old."* (Lev. 19:32)
3. *"You shall not hate a kinsman in your heart."* (Lev. 19:17)
4. *"Reprove your neighbor, but incur no guilt because of him."* (Lev. 19:17)
5. *"You shall not take vengeance or bear a grudge."* (Lev. 19:18)
6. *"Love your neighbor as yourself."* (Lev. 19:18)
7. *"When you reap the harvest of your land, you shall not reap all the way to the edges of the field, or gather the gleaning of your harvest. You shall not pick your vineyard bare, or gather the fallen fruit of your vineyard; you shall leave them for the poor and the stranger."* (Lev. 19:9–10, Deut. 24:19–21)
8. *"Do not harden your heart and shut your hand against your needy kinsman. Rather you must open your hand and lend him sufficient for whatever he needs."* (Deut. 15:7–8, 11)
9. *"The stranger who resides with you shall be to you as one of your citizens; you shall love him as yourself, for you were strangers in the land of Egypt."* (Lev. 19:34)
10. *"When you approach a town to attack it, you shall offer it terms of peace."* (Deut. 20:10)

The refrain about the stranger can be considered a leitmotif of the Torah. According to the sages, it is repeated thirty-six times.

I term this the doctrine of "historical empathy": We know the heart of the stranger because we were once strangers. Historical empathy is arguably the prophets' most important ethical legacy. The Bible bids us to learn from our experience. The moral lesson we draw from the past of our people is never again to perpetrate the oppression that was leveled against us. Even more, it is to replace the hate that can easily fill our hearts with love instead. *"The stranger who resides with you shall be as one of your citizens; you shall love him as yourself, for you were strangers in the land of Egypt"* (Lev. 19:33).

In his careful study of biblical ethics, Jeremiah Unterman discerns seven distinct motivational reasons (or at least variations on the key theme of empathy) for justice and compassion toward the stranger:

> *Appeal to empathy through remembrance of the past in which you were in a similar inferior social situation—"for you were strangers in the land of Egypt." (Exod. 22:20)*
>
> *Appeal to empathy since your identity was affected in a similar fashion due to your similar precarious experience—"for you know the soul of the stranger." (Exod. 23:9)*
>
> *Appeal to the ultimate moral authority, God, who commands the law—"I am the Lord your God." (Lev. 19:34)*
>
> *Appeal to humanitarian impulse—"You shall not abuse a poor and destitute laborer, either from your brethren or from your stranger in your land in your gates. You must pay his wages on that very same day . . . for he is poor and urgently depends upon it." (Deut. 24:14–15)*
>
> *Threat of punishment—"Else he will cry against you to the Lord, and you will incur sin." (Deut. 24:15) Also: "Cursed is he who subverts the justice due to the stranger, orphan, and widow." (Deut. 27:19)*
>
> *Imitation of God's ethics—"(God) loves the stranger . . . so you must love the stranger." (Deut. 10:18)*
>
> *In order to receive reward—"so that the Lord your God will bless you in all that you do." (Deut. 14:29)*

An intriguing archeological footnote to this central Torah teaching: In 2008, an ostracon (writing on a potsherd) was discovered at Khirbet Qeiyafa in the Elah Valley in central Israel. The faded writing is in old (paleo) Hebrew and is very difficult to read. Still, two independent scholars, Gershon Galil and Emile Puech, have noted that the words for justice, widow, and stranger (and, possibly, also orphan and poor) appear. Unterman comments: "As these terms appear for the first time together in the Torah, this ostracon may provide extremely early evidence of the existence of Torah law. Scientific dating of the ostracon in the precise place in which it was found has been very convincingly set at the end of the 11th century or the beginning of the 10th century BCE, i.e., the time of the founding of the Israelite monarchy." The oldest Hebrew inscription ever found deals with justice for the stranger and the needy!

The Bible itself presents two historical events that testify to its preoccupation with ethics. During the reign of King Zedekiah and King Nebuchadnezzar's campaign against Judea (c.588 BCE), the prophet Jeremiah reports that the King ordered the release of all Hebrew slaves. *"But afterward they turned about and brought back the men and women they had set free, and forced them into slavery again"* (Jer. 34:11). This moral outrage prompts Jeremiah to accurately predict the demise of the nation by Babylon.

Several generations later, upon the people's return from the Babylonian exile: *"There was a great outcry by the common folk and their wives against their brother Jews"* (Neh. 5:1). Creditors seized many returnees' lands and possessions—the returnees relinquishing prized belongings to secure immediate funds with which to purchase food (thereby avoiding starvation) and/or pay their taxes. Yet Torah law forbids seizure of land to pay a debt (see Exod. 22:20–25). The people cried out to Nehemiah, their governor, *"Now we are as good as our brother, and our children as good as theirs; yet here we are subjecting our sons and daughters to slavery . . . and we are powerless, while our fields and vineyards belong to others."* To his credit, Nehemiah took control of the situation by castigating the offenders and declaring a jubilee. He is a shining example of turning theory into practice.

During many centuries of internal, self-rule in the diaspora, the Jewish community would practice what it preached by establishing free-loan societies and a variety of other measures intended to aid the disadvantaged.

In our own day, Jewish involvement in the civil rights struggle and other social justice causes realizes the prophetic insistence on justice and compassion. Rabbi Arthur Lelyveld articulated and embodied the love of the stranger when he responded to the call to join the civil rights campaign in Mississippi in 1966 (and was seriously beaten by Southern racists for doing so). "It does not diminish our dignity as Jews," he wrote, "when we seek to achieve the precious ability to feel empathy with Negro bitterness and frustration. The command that we do so comes to us directly out of the Torah: *V'atem y'datem et nefesh hager—You should be able to know the very being of the stranger for you were strangers in the land of Egypt.* And not only in Egypt 3,000 years ago; we were there yesterday."

In one of his last orations, Moses explicitly and remarkably commands, *"Do not hate an Egyptian, for you were a stranger in his land"* (Deut. 23:8). Mercy and compassion are not always natural human responses, especially in the wake of oppression. The prophetic ethic demands sure action against injustice, but at the same time urges us to rise to a most difficult challenge: letting go of hate. *"You shall not hate a kinsman in your heart"* (Lev. 19:17). *"Reprove your neighbor, but incur no guilt because of him"* (Lev. 19:17). *"You shall not take vengeance or bear a grudge"* (Lev. 19:18). The prophetic ethic understands that to achieve true goodness and freedom, we cannot be trapped in the past. As Rabbi Jonathan Sacks comments, "Had the Israelites continued to hate their enemies, Moses would have taken the Israelites out of Egypt, but he would not have taken Egypt out of the Israelites."

Compassion and concern for the lowly in society course through all the classical prophets. Nowhere is this more evident than in Second Isaiah, whose challenging words the sages chose millennia ago to be read in the synagogue on Yom Kippur morning—a practice that continues to this day: *"No, this is the fast I desire: To unlock the fetters of wickedness, and untie the cords of the yoke; to let the oppressed go free; to break off every yoke. It is to share your bread with the hungry, and to take the wretched poor into your home; when you see the naked to clothe him; and not to ignore your own kin"* (Isa. 58:6–7).

The Psalmist also affirms the mandate of social justice. After extolling God as the creator of heaven and earth, he lauds the One *"who secures justice for those who are wronged; gives food to the hungry; sets prisoners free; restores sight to the blind; makes those who are bent stand straight; loves the righteous; watches over the stranger; gives courage to the orphan and widow"* (Ps. 146:6–9).

Ultimately, the prophets were not against religious ritual, but religious hypocrisy. Sacrifice is no substitute for justice. As one biblical scholar, Shalom Paul, puts it, "In sum, the Lord wants right, not rite." Another scholar, Shalom Spiegel, echoes, "God requires devotion, not devotions."

Faith

The final category of commandments relates to faith—what Micah called *"the humble walk."* These commandments address our direct relationship with God and with our families. The first of the Ten Commandments, *"I am Lord am your God who brought you out of the land of Egypt, the house of bondage"* (Exod. 20:2, Deut. 5:6), has long been understood as a command to know that there is a God and to recognize God's active and redeeming presence in the world. Further commandments are insistent that worship of anything but God is idolatry, to be resisted at all cost.

In addition, we are challenged both to affirm God and to love/obey God completely: *"You shall love the Lord your God with all your heart and with all your soul and with all your might"* (Deut. 6:5). The prophets understood that while such devotion was ultimately expressed in outward acts, strength of spirit was also required. Although few commandments relate to inner thoughts, the last of the Ten Commandments is an injunction against jealousy: *"You shall not covet your neighbor's house; you shall not covet your neighbor's wife . . . or anything that is your neighbor's"* (Exod. 20:14, Deut. 5:18). Along these lines, many of the prophets speak about the inner spirit needed to turn from the wayward path to the one of righteous living.

Faithfulness, it should be noted, is built on devotion to God, but more concretely, to family as well. Honoring one's father and mother and refraining from unfaithfulness in marriage are at the core of the Ten Commandments. We are commanded to observe a day of rest, the Sabbath, for ourselves and our family. A great act of faith—"*Teach them to your children*" (Deut. 6:7)—speaks to keeping faith with future generations by imparting our heritage. The prophets often avail themselves of family metaphors to explain unfaithfulness in the people. They understood that people comprehend best what they have experienced in the most intimate settings of family life.

Ten Commandments of Faith

1. "*I the Lord am your God who brought you out of the land of Egypt, the house of bondage.*" (Exod. 20:2, Deut. 5:6)
2. "*You shall have no other gods beside Me.*" (Exod. 20:3, Deut. 5:7, 6:4)
3. "*You shall not make for yourself a sculptured image, or any likeness.*" (Exod. 20:4, Lev. 19:4, Deut. 5:8)
4. "*You shall not swear falsely by the name of the Lord your God (or take God's name in vain).*" (Exod. 20:7, Lev. 19:12, Deut. 5:11)
5. "*You shall love the Lord your God with all your heart and with all your soul and with all your might.*" (Deut. 6:5)
6. "*Remember the Sabbath day and keep it holy.*" (Exod. 20:8, Deut. 5:12)
7. "*Honor your father and mother.*" (Exod. 20:12, Lev. 19:3, Deut. 5:16)
8. "*You shall not commit adultery.*" (Exod. 20:13, Deut. 5:17)
9. "*You shall not covet your neighbor's house; you shall not covet your neighbor's wife . . . or anything that is your neighbor's.*" (Exod. 20:14, Deut. 5:18)
10. "*Teach them to your children.*" (Deut. 6:7)

Walking with the prophets is to acknowledge, as Rabbi Michael Lerner puts it, "that the way things are is not the way things have to be." Nudging the world toward the good is our covenant-demanding purpose. The path of the prophets is audacious. "They saw their task as remaking the social order," Lerner continues. "Justice, justice shall you pursue. And love your neighbor as yourself. Don't oppress the stranger—use one standard for yourself and for the other. Take care of the powerless, the orphan, the widow, and again the stranger. Don't be oppressive to animals. Redistribute the land. Don't withhold wages of those who have done work for you. Make sure the poor have enough to eat. Don't repeat the ways of the oppressor."

The path of the prophets is the road less taken. It spells the disruption of home and comfort. It entails toil and risk. This path was difficult to the point of desperate for Abraham and Moses, for Elijah and Jeremiah. Yet it was exhilarating too, for Tirzah and Miriam, for Ruth and Hannah. It is there before us; beckoning to us, children of the prophets.

PART 1

To Do Justly

1

Abraham's Argument

THE PATH OF PROTEST

I Am Abraham

The three men who came to visit us bore an extraordinary message. Sarah and I had despaired of ever having a child. I was sad and perplexed and almost without hope. I did not understand the voice of God that had repeatedly told me that I would be the father of a great nation, yet we had no children. I had listened to that commanding voice from the time I was told to leave my home and homeland. I heeded that voice when I sealed a covenant with the Lord, promising me a new land, and descendants like the stars in the sky and the sand on the shore. I had attended to that voice when a son was born to me by Hagar, only to be told he would not bear the covenant.

You will excuse Sarah for laughing when the men said that she would give birth in one year. I too had laughed when God first spoke of it. We had done so much and waited so long for this to happen, and it didn't. I don't want to say that I had lost faith in God, but I just did not understand the plan. It was in this state of confusion and perplexity that I reacted so strongly to what happened next, when the men took leave and God revealed to me what was about to happen to Sodom. Not only was Sodom a big city, but it is where my nephew Lot and his family lived. The thought that it could be wiped out in one fell swoop hit me like a thunderbolt.

I hurled the question to my Maker: "Will you sweep away the innocent along with the guilty?" I shouted, "Far be it from You to do such a thing, to bring death upon the innocent as well as the guilty, so that innocent and guilty fare alike! Shall not the Judge of all the earth deal justly?"

There was no turning back from my challenge. "What if there should be fifty innocent within the city, will you then wipe out the place and not forgive it for the sake of the innocent fifty who are in it?" Each time God responded, I pressed my case. What if there are forty, thirty, twenty, ten? And then, just like that, the argument was over, the debate unresolved.

I was shaking, but I knew in my heart I had done the right thing. If God didn't want me to respond, then why had God told me? In fact, in thinking about it I realized that perhaps this was a test, yet another in a series from my inscrutable Creator. Did I pass this text? When God first spoke to me I was led to understand that the people that would issue from my loins would not only be great in number, but great in character. Had not my Lord said, "I will make you a great nation, and I will bless you; I will make your name great, and you shall be a blessing. I will bless those who bless you and curse him that curses you; and all the families of the earth shall bless themselves by you." If that is our destiny, then I, Abraham, must set the example. In every instance of injustice I must speak out, even if it comes from the Almighty himself!

There is much I do not understand of the Eternal One. I know I am but flesh and blood. But my God has given me the ability to know right from wrong. I will speak out. I have challenged the Almighty and lived to tell the story.

Abraham's Argument: From the Bible

The call to Abraham (Gen. 12:1–3):

> [1]*The Lord said to Abram, "Go forth from your native land and from your father's house to the land that I will show you.*
> [2]*I will make of you a great nation,*
> *And I will bless you;*
> *I will make your name great,*
> *And you shall be a blessing.*
> [3]*I will bless those who bless you*
> *And curse him that curses you;*
> *And all the families of the earth*
> *Shall bless themselves by you."*

Abraham's argument with God (Gen. 18:16–33):

> [16]*The men set out from there and looked down toward Sodom, Abraham walking with them to see them off.* [17]*Now the Lord had said, "Shall I hide from Abraham what I am about to do,* [18]*since Abraham is to become a great and populous nation and all the nations of the earth are to bless themselves by him?* [19]*For I have singled him out, that he may instruct his children and his posterity to keep the way of the Lord by doing what is just and right, in order that the Lord may bring about for Abraham what He has promised him."* [20]*Then the Lord said, "The outrage of Sodom and Gomorrah is so great, and their sin so grave!* [21]*I will go down to see whether they have acted altogether according to the outcry that has reached Me; if not, I will take note."*
>
> [22]*The men went on from there to Sodom, while Abraham remained standing before the Lord.* [23]*Abraham came forward and said, "Will You sweep away the innocent along with the guilty?* [24]*What if there should be fifty innocent within the city; will You then wipe out the place and not forgive it for the sake of the innocent fifty who are in it?*

[25]Far be it from You to do such a thing, to bring death upon the innocent as well as the guilty, so that innocent and guilty fare alike. Far be it from You! Shall not the Judge of all the earth deal justly?" [26]And the Lord answered, "If I find within the city of Sodom fifty innocent ones, I will forgive the whole place for their sake." [27]Abraham spoke up, saying, "Here I venture to speak to my Lord, I who am but dust and ashes: [28]What if the fifty innocent should lack five? Will You destroy the whole city for want of the five?" And He answered, "I will not destroy if I find forty-five there." [29]But he spoke to Him again, and said, "What if forty should be found there?" And He answered, "I will not do it, for the sake of the forty." [30]And he said, "Let not my Lord be angry if I go on: What if thirty should be found there?" And He answered, "I will not do it if I find thirty there." [31]And he said, "I venture again to speak to my Lord: What if twenty should be found there?" And He answered, "I will not destroy, for the sake of the twenty." [32]And he said, "Let not my Lord be angry if I speak but this last time: What if ten should be found there?" And He answered, "I will not destroy, for the sake of the ten."

[33]When the Lord had finished speaking to Abraham, He departed; and Abraham returned to his place.

Abraham's Argument: The Prophetic Moment

Abraham came forward and said, "Will You sweep away the innocent along with guilty? . . . Shall not the Judge of all the earth deal justly?" (Gen. 18:23, 25)

Abraham's argument with God is altogether remarkable. Abraham is otherwise portrayed as a man of utter obedience. In response to the call to uproot himself and his family, to journey further and further, to establish a covenant, to circumcise himself and all the males in his household, and even to sacrifice his beloved son, Abraham always submits to God's commands. With nary a word of comment or objection he does what he is told. That the patriarch of unquestioning faith steps forward to question God's actions comes as a shock.

Abraham's argument—how could God, the ultimate Judge, act unjustly by countenancing the killing of potentially innocent people?—is nothing less than a moral challenge to God.

Once the debate begins, Abraham does not let go. While unfailingly polite, he continues to press his point, down to the question of whether God will destroy an entire city if ten innocents be found there. Then Abraham's argument comes to an abrupt and truncated end. *"When the Lord had finished speaking to Abraham, He departed; and Abraham returned to his place"* (Gen. 18:33).

Abraham is a champion of justice because he insists on righteousness even from God. In doing so he initiates the venerable Jewish tradition of disputation and debate in service of a higher purpose. Because God's action weighs heavily on Abraham, he feels compelled to do something about it—to protest, to argue, even with God. He will do so respectfully; the biblical text shows much deference. But Abraham will not back down.

It is imperative to remember on what basis Abraham challenges God. To miss this point is to miss the essence of the patriarch and his signal contribution to Western monotheism. Abraham initiates the prophetic path of protest, but he does so from a place of faith. He protests because he has a relationship with God, an agreement with God, and an expectation of God. That agreement, the *brit* (covenant), is central to both God and Abraham.

Note how and why God feels compelled to disclose to Abraham: *"Shall I hide from Abraham what I am about to do, since Abraham is to become a great and populous nation and all the nations of the earth are to bless themselves by him? For I have singled him out, that he may instruct his children and his posterity to keep the way of the Lord by doing what is just and right, in order that the Lord may bring about for Abraham what He has promised him"* (Gen. 17–19). If not for the covenant, there would be no compelling reason for God to disclose the intended destruction of the city, for Abraham to object, or for God to respond in dialogue.

Nobel Peace Prize–winner and writer Elie Wiesel maintains that this Abrahamic dialectic of protest and faith is at the core of Jewish identity. In his book *A Jew Today* he writes: "To be a Jew means to serve God by espousing man's cause, to plead for man while recognizing his need of God. And to opt for the Creator and His creation, refusing to pit one against the other. Of course man must interrogate God, as did Abraham.... But only the Jew opts for Abraham—who questions and for God-who-is-questioned.... Only the Jew knows that he may oppose God so long as he does so in defense of His creation." Abraham wants God to adhere to the same standard that the Torah will later command us: *"Justice, justice shall you pursue"* (Deut. 16:20).

Abraham's prophetic moment can be appreciated not only against the backdrop of his faith but also his life circumstances and his conscience. The patriarch's life of late has been ... tumultuous. Abraham has journeyed far, far from home. No sooner does he arrive in Canaan then a famine forces him to journey farther to Egypt. There he endures a crisis with his wife. Upon his return, he has to deal with two emergencies regarding his nephew Lot, not to mention hostile neighbors. Moreover, there is no peace in his home. Sarah cannot conceive. When she gives Abraham her maidservant Hagar, and Hagar becomes pregnant, the enmity between the two women intensifies to the point that Abraham heeds Sarah's demand to banish Hagar. She returns, gives birth to Ishmael, and the tensions rise again. Abraham has enough on his plate. The last thing he needs is a run-in with God. But he cannot remain silent.

The reason he can't is because something is bothering him. Today we employ Freudian psychology to say that Abraham is troubled by his conscience. He has an innate sense that the innocent should not be punished with the guilty. Abraham has a moral code. He believes the code should apply to all, even God, who apparently seems willing to violate that code in wholesale destruction of a city.

In ethical theory, the term for the problem that sparks Abraham's indignation is "collective punishment." It is familiar to us each time our son or daughter complains "it's not fair" that their whole class is punished for the mistakes of the few. On a larger scale, it haunts societies that wrestle with issues of noncombatant immunity and proportionality during times of war.

Abraham's prophetic moment of protest ends inconclusively and enigmatically. At first God appears to accept Abraham's argument, but the argument halts at the consideration of ten innocent people. The Torah records that the cities of Sodom and Gomorrah were indeed destroyed. Did God uphold the terms of the debate? Were there fewer than ten innocent people to be found? If Abraham's intention was to save the cities from destruction, he failed (though his nephew was saved). If his intention was to give God pause, to make God rethink before taking action, he may have succeeded. Torah teacher and psychotherapist Naomi Rosenblatt understands the lesson of Abraham's prophetic moment as the "power of one man of integrity to be the conscience of the world."

Walking with Abraham: The Path of Protest

Abraham establishes the extraordinary precedent that, for the sake of justice, even God can be questioned. The Talmud has a unique expression that describes just this attitude: *chutzpah k'lapei shamaya*—boldness, or nerviness, toward heaven (or, as Rabbi Shlomo Carlebach once called it, "holy chutzpah!")

Abraham is the first, but certainly not the last, to display such chutzpah. In his company is none other than Moses, the other paragon of God's faithful servant. While the majority of the time Moses is an advocate for God to his stiff-necked people, at several junctures he feels compelled to side with his stubborn and wayward compatriots (sometimes disparagingly called "riffraff" or "mixed multitude.")

The Torah does not shy away from portraying what appears to be a vengeful God who is not beyond wiping out the people . . . if not for the protest of Moses. The most striking example occurs after the Children of Israel hear the bleak report of the twelve spies (Joshua and Caleb excepted) and break out into a near riot. God is so exasperated and angry—*"How long will this people spurn Me, and how long will they have no faith in Me despite all the signs I have performed in their midst?"*—that God threatens their annihilation: *"I will strike them with pestilence and disown them"* (Num. 14:11–12).

Alarmed, fearing for the Israelites' very existence, Moses immediately takes up his people's defense. Like a lawyer, he tries several lines of argument. First, he appeals to God's reputation: God's ego (to again borrow from Freud). He poses the question, *"What will the Egyptians think if you do such a thing?"* Then he answers his own question to drive his point home: *"If then You slay this people to a man, the nations who have heard Your fame will say, 'It must be because the Lord was powerless to bring that people into the land which He had promised them on oath that He slaughtered them in the wilderness.'"* Then Moses reminds God of the qualities of mercy and kindness that the Lord has previously self-described: *"slow to anger and abounding in kindness; forgiving iniquity and transgression."* Finally, the prophet goes for a direct appeal that references God's past record: *"Pardon, I pray, the iniquity of this people according to Your great kindness, as You have forgiven this people ever since Egypt"* (Num. 14:13–19).

Job also follows in Abraham's legacy of protest—and his dissent before God is as powerful as Abraham's or Moses'. Indeed, "The Book of Job sanctifies defiance of unjust authority," writes author William Safire in *The First Dissident,* his book about Job. "It enshrines dissent and demands moral self-reliance." In his introduction Safire maintains:

> *The moral excitement in the Book of Job is the sufferer's outrage at God's refusal to do justice. . . . Job reaches across the millennia to express modern Man's outrage at today's inequities.*

> *Job cries out: Why does He give light to the sufferer, and life to the bitter in spirit? (3:20) On my part, I will not speak with restraint; I will give voice to the anguish of my spirit. (7:11) Indeed I know that it is so: Man cannot win a suit against God . . . Who can say to Him, "What are You doing?" (9:2, 12)*

I say to God, "Do not condemn me; Let me know what You charge me with. Does it benefit You to defraud, to despise the toil of Your hands, while smiling on the counsel of the wicked?" (10:2–3)

I insist on arguing with God . . . I will have my day, come what may upon me. (13:3, 13) *Why do You hide Your face, and treat me like an enemy?* (13:24)

Why do the wicked live on, prosper and grow wealthy? (21:7)

By God who has deprived me of justice . . . my lips will speak no wrong, nor my tongue utter deceit. Far be it from me to say you are right; until I die I will maintain my integrity. (27:2, 4–5).

The path of protest is likewise carried forward in the Eastern European Hasidic tradition. Two remarkable examples come from Rabbi Levi Yitzhak of Berditchev. In the first, the famous "Lawsuit against God," the Rebbe, although deferential like Abraham, is ready to litigate against God to end the Jewish people's suffering and exile. He argues:

I come to You with a lawsuit from Your people Israel.
What do you want of Your people Israel?
From my stand I will not waver,
And from my place I shall not move,
Until there be an end to this Exile.
Magnified and sanctified is only Thy name.

In the second example, a story is told of a simple tailor who argues eloquently with God on Yom Kippur: "You wish me to repent of my sins, but I have committed only minor offenses. I may have kept left-over cloth, or I may have eaten in a non-Jewish home, where I worked, without washing my hand. But you O Lord, have committed grievous sins. You have taken away babies from their mothers and mothers from their babies. Let us be even. You forgive me and I will forgive you." Rabbi Levi Yitzhak interjects: "Why did you let God off so easily? You might have forced God to save all of Israel!"

On a broader level, the disputations of Abraham, Moses, Job, Levi Yitzhak, and the tailor with God convey the importance of challenging authority when our conscience calls. I'm reminded of the popular television commercial of years ago in which a man is about to evade his moral responsibility when a woman's voice asks, "Joe, this is your conscience calling?" When we heed the call, we can't look the other way. We can't pretend that all is right or claim that we are too occupied or someone else will address the problem.

When we protest, we exemplify the great Torah command: *"Do not stand idly by the blood of your neighbor"* (Lev. 19:16).

When we protest, we embody the all-important Talmudic ethic: "Whoever is able to protest against the transgressions of his own family and does not do so is held responsible for the transgressions of his family. Whoever is able to protest against the transgressions for the people of his community and does not do so is held responsible for the transgressions of his community. Whoever is able to protest against the transgressions of the world and does not do so is responsible for the transgressions of the entire world."

When we protest, we follow the prophetic model of the Rev. Martin Luther King Jr., who once said: "There are some things in our society to which we should never be adjusted. We must never adjust ourselves to racial discrimination and racial segregation. We must never adjust ourselves to religious bigotry. We must never adjust ourselves to economic conditions that take necessities from the many to give luxuries to the few. We must never adjust ourselves to the madness of militarism and the self-defeating effects of physical violence."

The form of protest is also important. Abraham uses words. He expresses his dissent through a dialogue. Some call it a negotiation; I see it as a debate. Abraham engages God in a back and forth to broadly determine if God is acting justly, and to more narrowly decide the minimum number of innocents it will take to save the city. It is another Abrahamic legacy: Dissent through debate will become central to Judaism.

Abraham's protest also embodies what the Talmud coins *mahloket l'shem shamayim*, "an argument for the sake of heaven." Such an argument is a worthy debate; it is for the right reason—to advance a justifiable position. The sages thus distinguish between debates that advance understanding and those made to sow dissension or just for the sake of argument: "Every debate that is for the sake of heaven will make a lasting contribution. Every debate that is not for the sake of heaven will not make a lasting contribution."

The classic example of worthy debate began between two great sages, Hillel and Shammai, and continued for decades among their disciples. "For three years there was a dispute between Beit Hillel and Beit Shammai. . . . Then a voice from heaven announced: both are the words of the living God . . . but the law is in agreement with Beit Hillel." Even though the school of Hillel and his more lenient judicial philosophy prevailed, the Talmud suggests that there is a legitimate place for *Shammai's* dissenting voice. As author Rabbi Joseph Telushkin remarks in a book about Hillel: "It says something about Judaism that both Hillel and Shammai, and many of their followers, remain revered figures . . . even when they embody opposite approaches to the law and life itself. It isn't simply the answer that is prized; it is the argument itself, the culture of disputation, the wrestling with the truth."

The nineteenth-century German Jewish thinker Rabbi Samson Raphael Hirsch, who many consider the father of modern Orthodox Judaism, makes a similar point. While acknowledging that one viewpoint will usually prevail, he writes: "Both views will have permanent value because . . . [they] shed new light on the issue under debate, and will have contributed to the attainment of the proper understanding of the question discussed. They shall be remembered as . . . advancing the cause of the genuine knowledge of truth."

The Hasidic leader Rabbi Nachman of Bratzlav goes even further, calling debate the holiest form of communication. Debate, he boldly asserted, echoes the divine process of *tzimtzum*, "limitation," by making space for the creation of something new. Just as God enters into an act of self-limitation in order to allow for the created world, so worthy debaters restrain themselves in order to make room for opposing viewpoints. A contemporary teacher, Rabbi Or Rose, comments: "When we disagree with one another . . . we create the necessary space for the emergence of new and unexpected ideas. Without *makhloket* . . . the horizon of human discovery would be severely limited."

At a time when there are calls to stifle debate and suppress dissent, it is worth remembering these lessons: Our arguments to advance a justifiable position are for the sake of heaven; out of our differences we are likely to emerge more enlightened; and in the very act of worthy protest we echo the divine!

At times the path of protest may mean joining a picket line. At times it may mean breaking the law (civil disobedience, examined in chapter 2). Often, however, in the model of Abraham, protest means using one's words — to write a letter or an essay, to engage in passionate debate. And just like Abraham's careful words were intended to change God's mind, protest means respectfully advocating for a different course of action.

When we protest, we bear witness. In the wise words of Elie Wiesel: "There may be a time when we are powerless to prevent injustice, but there must never be a time when we fail to protest."

2

Shiphrah's Defiance

THE PATH OF CIVIL DISOBEDIENCE

I Am Shiphrah

I am a midwife. I bring life into the world. I show the panting mother how to lean on the birthstool. I tell her how to breathe and how to push. I speak words of comfort to her. I reach for the crowning head. I pull the baby out. I clear its nose and its mouth. I slap the newborn babe to hear its first cry—the most joyous sound in the world. I cut the cord. I clean up the blood. I place the infant on its mother's bosom. I give thanks to the gods.

This is my work; this is my world. This is what I was chosen to do in life—to give life.

Pharaoh's order stabbed me in my heart. Yes, he is the ruler of all Egypt. Yes, he is the son of the gods. But he is a man who was born in the same way as every baby I deliver. His command to look upon the birthstool and to kill every male Hebrew baby is wrong, wrong, wrong. It is a violation of all that is sacred; it cannot be the will of the gods. I bring life into the world, not snuff it out. I cannot obey.

In my shock and horror I went to old Puah. Side by side we have served together these many years. There is nobody I trust more. She is wise. "Speak to me," I pleaded. "What are we to do? We deliver Egyptian babies. We deliver Hebrew babies. All are the same when they come naked into the world. How can the Pharaoh command death?"

Puah was silent for several heavy moments. Then she spoke, softly but firmly. "The Israelites grow in number even as Pharaoh oppresses them. Their god must be with them. He must be very strong. It is no small thing to defy the king, but defy him we must. And let us hope the god of the Hebrews will protect us."

I had a pit in my stomach. My heart was racing. Puah continued, "The king knows no more than any man of the way of women in birth. When he asks why we have done this thing, we shall tell him that these Hebrew women are different than the Egyptian women. They are like animals: they are vigorous and drop their young before we can get to them. He will believe us."

I was stunned. I embraced Puah. What will happen to us I do not know. All I can say is that I am a midwife. Another mother is crying out and another baby is waiting to be born. It is time to go to work.

Shiphrah's Defiance: From the Bible

The defiance of the midwives (Exod. 1:15–21):

> [15]*The king of Egypt spoke to the Hebrew midwives, one of whom was named Shiphrah and the other Puah,* [16]*saying, "When you deliver the Hebrew women, look at the birthstool: if it is a boy, kill him; if it is a girl, let her live."* [17]*The midwives, fearing God, did not do as the king of Egypt had told them; they let the boys live.* [18]*So the king of Egypt summoned the midwives and said to them, "Why have you done this thing, letting the boys live?"* [19]*The midwives said to Pharaoh, "Because the Hebrew women are not like the Egyptian women: they are vigorous. Before the midwife can come to them, they have given birth."* [20]*And God dealt well with the midwives; and the people multiplied and increased greatly.* [21]*And because the midwives feared God, He established households for them.* [22]*Then Pharaoh charged all his people, saying, "Every boy that is born you shall throw into the Nile, but let every girl live."*

Shiphrah's Defiance: The Prophetic Moment

The midwives, fearing God, did not do as the king of Egypt had told them; they let the boys live. (Exod. 1:17)

Shiphrah and Puah's refusal to obey Pharaoh's order has been called the first act of civil disobedience in recorded history. These two extraordinary women may or may not have been Israelite. The Hebrew can be read as "Hebrew midwives" or "midwives to the Hebrews." Either way, their action is daring and consequential. The Torah notes, *"And God dealt well with the midwives; and the people multiplied and increased greatly. And because the midwives feared God, He established households for them"* (Exod. 1:20–21).

Shiphrah and Puah protest against perceived injustice in the spirit of Abraham. In the course of doing so, they also embody the quality of *ometz lev*, "civic courage." They practice what has come to be known in our day as civil disobedience. Defying Pharaoh could easily have meant death. They break the rules, at great risk, for the sake of a higher purpose. At the same time, they seek to mitigate the potential consequences by offering the king a rationale for their behavior—the Israelites' extraordinary birthrate.

Shiphrah and Puah are exemplars among several remarkable women who play courageous roles in the Exodus story. Yocheved gives birth to Moses at a time when others are refraining from having children in the wake of Pharaoh's decree that all boys should be killed. Miriam has the audacity to approach Pharaoh's daughter, Bat-Pharaoh (daughter of Pharaoh), to suggest that a wet nurse be found for the infant. Disobeying her father's authority, Bat-Pharaoh saves Moses by rescuing him from the Nile, paying Yocheved to nurse him, and then adopting him as a son. Finally, Zipporah, Moses' wife, also rescues Moses during a mysterious episode in which God seeks to harm Moses when he fails to circumcise his son (see Exod. 4:24–26). The Exodus saga calls for courage at every turn, and these six women lead by example. Each woman defies conventional expectation and, in modern parlance, answers the call of conscience.

Shiphrah and Puah's legacy of courageous protest is later embodied by a woman named Rahab, who disobeys authority in part in the name of a higher calling. The Book of Joshua relates that Joshua sends two spies to scout the city of Jericho, and they lodge at Rahab's house. When the king of Jericho finds out, he demands that Rahab turn them in. Instead, Rahab hides them and tells the king's men the spies have set out for the hills. She explains to the spies: *"I know that the Lord has given the country to you . . . for the Lord your God is the only God in heaven above and on earth below"* (Josh. 2:9,11). Echoing the God-fearing midwives, this lowly woman risks her life to protect the scouts. At the same time, Rahab asks them for protection: When the Israelites finally conquer the city, she wants her life and her family's life to be spared. Rahab wants to be on the right side of history.

Better known, but likewise unexpected, is Esther's decisive moment of courage. When Mordecai learns of Haman's plot to annihilate the

Jews of Persia, he sends word to his niece, who has somehow amazingly landed in the king's harem and emerged as queen. While Esther is greatly distressed to hear of the plot, she is initially reluctant to intervene with the king. She sends word back to Mordecai that if any person approaches the king unbidden, *"there is but one law for him—that he be put to death"* (Esther 4:11).

Mordecai delivers a sharp message of rebuke that reminds Esther of her responsibility: *"Do not imagine that you, of all the Jews, will escape with your life by being in the king's palace. On the contrary, if you keep silent in this crisis, relief and deliverance will come to the Jews from another quarter, while you and your father's house will perish. And who knows, perhaps you have attained to royal position for just such a crisis"* (Esther 4:13–14).

Esther's valor is now manifest in her response to Mordecai: *"Go, assemble all the Jews who live in Shushan, and fast in my behalf; do not eat or drink for three days, night or day. I and my maidens will observe the same fast. Then I shall go to the king, though it is contrary to the law; and if I am to perish, I shall perish!"* (Esther 4:15–16). Esther is prepared to defy the prescribed protocol for approaching the king and to expose his powerful, nefarious prime minister. She is willing to risk her life for a higher purpose—solidarity with her people.

King Saul's servants and a band of priests are lesser-known biblical exemplars of civil disobedience. When the increasingly paranoid King Saul is pursuing the young David, he learns that a group of priests have sheltered David rather than turn him over per the King's edict. Enraged, King Saul orders his guards to kill the priests, *"'for they are in league with David; they knew he was running away and they did not inform me.' But the king's servants would not raise a hand to strike down the priests of the Lord"* (1 Sam. 22:17–18). Ultimately, David emerges unscathed and later assumes the throne. The soldiers, however, pay with their lives. The Bible records that Doeg the Edomite, one of Saul's mercenaries, massacres the priests and the entire town.

What do the two midwives, Rahab, Esther, the priests, and the soldiers have in common? All are unexpected heroes who rise to the occasion to defy authority at a moment of crisis. They embody the Torah command to *"not stand idly by"* (Lev. 19:11). They display extraordinary mettle in life-threatening situations. They answer to a higher calling than that of the king—the call of conscience.

Walking with Shiphrah: The Path of Civil Disobedience

Like other religions and cultures, Judaism espouses respect for authority. The biblical examples do not portend a well-developed doctrine of civil disobedience. Yet the greatest of the medieval philosophers and jurists, Moses Maimonides, rules that "A person who negates a king's command because he is occupied with a mitzvah, even a minor one, behold, he is not liable." The pursuit of justice in the defiance of an unjust order may indeed be not just a right, but a responsibility; not merely permissible, but commanded.

Notably, the biblical issue of soldiers disobeying an unjust command has arisen in the modern State of Israel. Upon its founding, the Israel Defense Forces adopted a doctrine of *tohar haneshek*, "purity of arms," that espoused moral conduct in war, including a prohibition against looting and wanton destruction and respect for noncombatant immunity (refraining from harming civilians). During the Sinai Campaign of 1956, some residents of the Arab village of Kfar Kassem, returning late from their fields and unaware of a curfew, were gunned down in the main street. A military court found the commanding officer guilty of giving an illegal order, and his soldiers guilty of obeying an illegal command. The court decried the "black flag of lawlessness" that had raised itself in the incident. Prime Minister David Ben-Gurion observed: "I feel it is my duty to express our profound concern at the fact that such an act has been possible—an act that strikes a blow at the most sacred foundations of human morality drawn from Israel's Torah."

The issue arose again during the Lebanon War of 1982, when Colonel Eli Geva, the respected son of a retired general, shocked the military establishment and the nation by announcing from the field that he would not command the anticipated assault on Beirut. Asked why, Geva replied, "When I look through my binoculars, I see children." Geva was dismissed from active duty and dishonorably discharged, but not before his case aroused impassioned debate. An organization called Yesh Gevul (There is a limit) was formed to assist soldiers who refused to follow what they perceived to be unjust orders.

Ironically, the issue of civil disobedience in the military in Israel remains alive and contentious, sometimes for opposite reasons. Some soldiers refuse to serve in the territories because they think it is wrong, and others refuse to evacuate settlements in the territories because they think that is wrong. The following dialogue between a father and son in David Bezmozgis' novel *The Betrayers* captures the dilemma of the latter:

SON: Tell me why I should do it [evacuate a settlement].

FATHER: You're a soldier in our nation's army. The answer I'll give will be the same as the one you get from your commanders and the minister of defense. However much I disagree with him about this operation, I don't disagree that a soldier's job is to obey orders.

SON: Even immoral orders?

FATHER: No, not immoral orders. But it says nothing in the Geneva Conventions about dismantling your own settlements.

SON: It says it in the Torah.

FATHER: I'm not so sure it says it in the Torah. . . . Like it or not, our country is a democracy. The Torah is very nice, but we don't run the country by it . . .

SON: So that's it? You're saying I should go along with this even if it makes me sick? Even if I believe with perfect faith that it is wrong, a sin against God to give up our land?

FATHER: You ask what I would do in your place. Let me ask you. What would happen to our army and our county if soldiers started to choose what orders they would follow? One believes evicting settlers is wrong, another believes the occupation is illegal.

SON: So instead we should all go against our consciences and wait until the next election? I'm talking about a person's soul. When it screams, no! What are you supposed to do? Ignore it? If you see your country is on the road to ruin, do you not do something about it? Before it's too late.

In the modern era, civil disobedience emerged as an important doctrine in the broader community. The nineteenth-century author and activist Henry David Thoreau famously wrote of one's personal responsibility to disobey unjust laws: "Must the citizen ever for a moment, or in the least degree, resign his conscience to the legislator? Why has every man a conscience, then? I think that we should be men first, and subjects afterward. It is not desirable to cultivate a respect for the law, so much as for the right." His manifesto, "Resistance to Civil Government" (also known as "Civil Disobedience"), profoundly influenced three great exemplars of civil disobedience who changed the world. Mahatma Gandhi's campaign of nonviolent civil disobedience of the British led to independence for India. Martin Luther King Jr.'s defiance of segregation led to a new era of civil rights for African Americans. Nelson Mandela's battle against apartheid led to democracy in South Africa. Each leader showed enormous courage and resilience in standing up to repressive authority. All three were willing to accept the consequences of breaking laws they felt to be unjust. They steadfastly insisted that resistance to oppressive authority must remain nonviolent.

As a religious leader, King referenced the biblical prophets as a source of inspiration. In his renowned "Letter from Birmingham City Jail," King wrote: "I am in Birmingham because injustice is here. Just as the prophets of the eighth century B.C. left their villages and carried their 'thus saith the Lord' far beyond the boundaries of their home towns . . . so am I compelled to carry the gospel of freedom far beyond my own hometown." King addressed his letter to the clergy of Birmingham, who were sympathetic to his cause but had urged him not to disturb the peace and break the law. Noting that "injustice anywhere is a threat to justice everywhere," King went on to explain why he felt compelled to break the unjust law of segregation: "One may well ask: 'How can you advocate breaking some laws and obeying others?' The answer lies in the fact there are two types of laws: just and unjust. One has not only a legal but a moral responsibility to obey just laws. Conversely, one has a moral responsibility to disobey unjust laws."

In America the civil rights movement, the anti–Vietnam War movement, and the nuclear disarmament campaign all advanced with concerted efforts of civil disobedience.

The writer Arthur Koestler once said, "Courage is never to let your actions be influenced by your fears." From the midwives Shiphrah and Puah to Thoreau, Gandhi, King, and Mandela, we are ennobled by all those with the courage of their convictions who stand up and defy authority for the sake of justice.

3

Moses' Encounter

THE PATH OF FREEDOM

I Am Moses

One day when I was a young man I went out from the palace and saw an Egyptian beating a Hebrew. Before I knew it I had struck down that Egyptian and hid his body in the sand. Maybe it was the horror of the beating; maybe it was the oppression of the master over the enslaved; or maybe it was that I knew I had been born a Hebrew—whatever the reason, I could not help myself.

The next day I found two Hebrews fighting and stepped in to break it up. When the offender taunted me, "Do you mean to kill me as you killed the Egyptian?" I knew that the matter was known. I had to flee for my life. I escaped to Midian.

No sooner did I come to a village than I saw shepherds harassing girls at the well. I sent those shepherds packing and helped the girls water their flock. One of them, Zipporah, became my wife. We had a son named Gershom. I too became a shepherd, for the flocks of my father-in-law Jethro. My life became quiet and predictable . . . until one day it did not.

I was deep in the wilderness with my flock when my attention was arrested by a blazing fire. The bush was aflame—yet it was not consumed! And, gazing at this wonder, I beheld God! God was calling my name, consuming my soul, commanding my spirit!

The voice was telling me I had a mission, I was to go back to Egypt and speak to the people. . . . No, this was not the mission for me! I felt caught like a ram in a thicket, like a wrestler in a headlock. I objected: I am not the man You want, for I stammer and I stutter . . . only to be told: Your brother Aaron will help you speak.

So back to Egypt I went. By this time, after so many years, I was no longer a young man. With Aaron I assembled all the elders of my long-suffering brethren. I told them it was our destiny to live free—and to return to the Promised Land. I proclaimed that our God had awakened to our plight. God, I said, has not *forsaken us. God remembers the covenant. God will do great things. God will lead us out with an outstretched arm and carry us on eagles' wings. The elders bowed low in homage.*

With my brother by my side I won an audience with Pharaoh. I proclaimed God's message: "Let My people go, that they may serve Me." But the king of all Egypt could only shake his head. "Who is the Lord that I should heed him and let Israel go? Why do you distract the people from their tasks? The people of the land are already so numerous, and you would have them cease from their labors!"

This Pharaoh's heart became as hard as the bricks he tasked us to make. "You are shirkers, shirkers," he said, and oppressed us even more.

Life became so intolerable that the people began turning against Aaron and me. I spoke of God's deliverance, but the people stopped listening. Pharaoh was determined to crush their spirits, and he succeeded.

But Aaron and I did not relent. Gathering the people, we spoke again and again of the promise and the hope. Again and again we went to Pharaoh. His country was falling apart, plague by plague. But no sooner did it seem that Pharaoh would give in, then the plague was stayed and his heart had stiffened once more. In the end it was only death that penetrated that knot of a heart—the death of every firstborn, including his.

Or maybe it was the dawning fear that our Lord was more powerful than any other.

The blood of the lamb smeared on our doorposts spared us that final plague, and in haste we ran from Egypt. Pharaoh's army pursued us. But our liberation could not be denied. God kept His promise. We are subjects of no king save the King of Kings. We bow not to the mighty but to the Almighty. This is our covenant, our freedom, our destiny.

Moses' Encounter: From the Bible

Moses' encounter with his kinsfolk and Midianites (Exod. 2:11–22):

> [11]*Some time after that, when Moses had grown up, he went out to his kinsfolk and witnessed their labors. He saw an Egyptian beating a Hebrew, one of his kinsmen.* [12]*He turned this way and that and, seeing no one about, he struck down the Egyptian and hid him in the sand.* [13]*When he went out the next day, he found two Hebrews fighting; so he said to the offender, "Why do you strike your fellow?"* [14]*He retorted, "Who made you chief and ruler over us? Do you mean to kill me as you killed the Egyptian?" Moses was frightened, and thought: Then the matter is known!* [15]*When Pharaoh learned of the matter, he sought to kill Moses; but Moses fled from Pharaoh. He arrived in the land of Midian, and sat down beside a well.*
>
> [16]*Now the priest of Midian had seven daughters. They came to draw water, and filled the troughs to water their father's flock;* [17]*but shepherds came and drove them off. Moses rose to their defense, and he watered their flock.* [18]*When they returned to their father Reuel, he said, "How is it that you have come back so soon today?"* [19]*They answered, "An Egyptian rescued us from the shepherds; he even drew water for us and watered the flock."* [20]*He said to his daughters, "Where is he then? Why did you leave the man? Ask him in to break bread."* [21]*Moses consented to stay with the man, and he gave Moses his daughter Zipporah as wife.* [22]*She bore a son whom he named Gershom, for he said, "I have been a stranger in a foreign land."*

Moses' encounter with God at the Burning Bush (Exod. 3:1–10):

> [1]*Now Moses, tending the flock of his father-in-law Jethro, the priest of Midian, drove the flock into the wilderness, and came to Horeb, the mountain of God.* [2]*An angel of the Lord appeared to him in a blazing fire out of a bush. He gazed, and there was a bush all aflame, yet the*

bush was not consumed. [3]*Moses said, "I must turn aside to look at this marvelous sight; why doesn't the bush burn up?"* [4]*When the Lord saw that he had turned aside to look, God called to him out of the bush: "Moses! Moses!" He answered, "Here I am."* [5]*And He said, "Do not come closer. Remove your sandals from your feet, for the place on which you stand is holy ground.* [6]*I am," He said, "the God of your father, the God of Abraham, the God of Isaac, and the God of Jacob." And Moses hid his face, for he was afraid to look at God.*

[7]*And the Lord continued, "I have marked well the plight of My people in Egypt and have heeded their outcry because of their taskmasters; yes, I am mindful of their sufferings.* [8]*I have come down to rescue them from the Egyptians and to bring them out of that land to a good and spacious land, a land flowing with milk and honey, the region of the Canaanites, the Hittites, the Amorites, the Perizzites, the Hivites, and the Jebusites.* [9]*Now the cry of the Israelites has reached Me; moreover, I have seen how the Egyptians oppress them.* [10]*Come, therefore, I will send you to Pharaoh, and you shall free My people, the Israelites, from Egypt."*

Moses' encounter with Pharaoh (Exod. 5:1–5):

[1]*Afterward Moses and Aaron went and said to Pharaoh, "Thus says the Lord, the God of Israel: Let My people go that they may celebrate a festival for Me in the wilderness."* [2]*But Pharaoh said, "Who is the Lord that I should heed Him and let Israel go? I do not know the Lord, nor will I let Israel go."* [3]*They answered, "The God of the Hebrews has manifested Himself to us. Let us go, we pray, a distance of three days into the wilderness to sacrifice to the Lord our God, lest He strike us with pestilence or sword."* [4]*But the king of Egypt said to them, "Moses and Aaron, why do you distract the people from their tasks? Get to your labors!"* [5]*And Pharaoh continued, "The people of the land are already so numerous, and you would have them cease from their labors!"*

Moses' second encounter with God (Exod. 6:2–9):

> [2]*God spoke to Moses and said to him, "I am the Lord.* [3]*I appeared to Abraham, Isaac, and Jacob as El Shaddai, but I did not make Myself known to them by My name* YHVH. [4]*I also established My covenant with them, to give them the land of Canaan, the land in which they lived as sojourners.* [5]*I have now heard the moaning of the Israelites because the Egyptians are holding them in bondage, and I have remembered My covenant.* [6]*Say, therefore, to the Israelite people: I am the Lord. I will free you from the labors of the Egyptians and deliver you from their bondage. I will redeem you with an outstretched arm and through extraordinary chastisements.* [7]*And I will take you to be My people, and I will be your God. And you shall know that I, the Lord, am your God who freed you from the labors of the Egyptians.* [8]*I will bring you into the land which I swore to give to Abraham, Isaac, and Jacob, and I will give it to you for a possession, I the Lord."* [9]*But when Moses told this to the Israelites, they would not listen to Moses, their spirits crushed by cruel bondage.*

Moses' third encounter with God (Exod. 19:1–6):

> [1]*On the third new moon after the Israelites had gone forth from the land of Egypt, on that very day, they entered the wilderness of Sinai.* [2]*Having journeyed from Rephidim, they entered the wilderness of Sinai and encamped in the wilderness. Israel encamped there in front of the mountain,* [3]*and Moses went up to God. The Lord called to him from the mountain, saying, "Thus shall you say to the house of Jacob and declare to the children of Israel:* [4]*'You have seen what I did to the Egyptians, how I bore you on eagles' wings and brought you to Me.* [5]*Now then, if you will obey Me faithfully and keep My covenant, you shall be My treasured possession among all the peoples. Indeed, all the earth is Mine,* [6]*but you shall be to Me a kingdom of priests and a holy nation.' These are the words that you shall speak to the children of Israel."*

Moses' Encounter: The Prophetic Moment

Afterward Moses and Aaron went and said to Pharaoh,
"Thus says the Lord, the God of Israel: Let My people go. . . ."
But Pharaoh said, "Who is the Lord that I should
heed Him and let Israel go?" (Exod. 5:1–2)

Moses and Pharaoh's epic confrontation is a pivotal moment in human history. Throughout the ages, Moses' words have become the rallying cry of freedom for oppressed peoples everywhere. As the poet Heinrich Heine put it, "Since the Exodus, freedom has always spoken with a Hebrew accent."

To fully appreciate the mature Moses, let's contemplate a younger Moses. As a child, he grew up in the Egyptian court. The Torah offers us just three fleeting vignettes of the young adult—yet they are revealing. In each case Moses intervenes: first, when he sees an Egyptian beating a Hebrew; second, when he sees two Hebrews arguing; and, finally, when he sees shepherds harassing women. Clearly, Moses is a man of action—and a person who cannot abide injustice.

The Torah notes that Moses *"turned this way and that and, seeing no one about, he struck the Egyptian"* (Exod. 2:11). One reading of the text is not complimentary—Moses looks around to make sure no one sees him before he kills another man. The Rabbinic read, however, is far more generous: Upon witnessing an Egyptian beating a Hebrew slave, Moses looks around to see if anyone else is present who might intervene instead to end the injustice. In the text, the Hebrew, *ein ish,* "there is no man," implies there is no one else willing to "man-up" to the situation. In other words, Moses is willing to fulfill the Rabbinic dictum "in a place where there is no man, strive to be a man."

Notably, the description of Moses' activism is preceded by the introductory verse, *"when Moses had grown up, he went out to his kinsfolk and witnessed their labors"* (Exod. 2:11). The Hebrew word *achim* means both "kinsfolk" and "brothers." The Hebrew word for "labors" or "toil," *sivlot,* often conveys "suffering." Despite his privileged upbringing in the royal court, Moses remembers who he is, and empathizes with his brethren's plight.

Yet even as he reawakens to his true identity and kinship with his people, Moses' passion for justice is not limited to his own people. His drive and courage to act are rooted in a more universal empathy. His encounters with injustice involve first a Hebrew with an Egyptian, then a Hebrew with a Hebrew, and finally a Midianite with a Midianite. Any human being in need deserves justice.

Another life-changing encounter comes when Moses is deep in the wilderness, body and soul. Moses demonstrates the elemental curiosity to say to himself, *"I must turn aside to look at this marvelous sight: why doesn't the bush burn up?"* (Exod. 3:3). Pointedly, the Torah then remarks that God calls out to Moses *"when the Lord saw that he had turned aside"* (Exod. 3:4). Moses' curiosity and wonder bring him to the burning bush. Moses then responds to the call (some say the burning bush is really his soul, which still remembers Egypt) with the classic prophetic response of presence, *"Here I am."*

God then says: *"Do not come closer. Remove your sandals from your feet, for the place on which you stand is holy ground"* (Exod. 3:5). The Torah is signaling that a transformational moment is in the process of unfolding. Indeed, Moses will receive his prophetic calling on this holy ground at the foot of this holy mountain. Victorian poet Elizabeth Browning wrote of the prelude to this encounter: "Earth's crammed with heaven; and every common bush afire with God! But only he who sees, takes off his shoes." Philosopher Martin Buber observed: "God says to man as he said to Moses: 'Put off thy shoes from off thy feet'—put off the habitual which encloses your foot and you will recognize that the place on which you happen to be standing is holy ground." Rabbi and mysticism master Lawrence Kushner discerns: "Not that ground then. But this ground now. You do not have to go anywhere to raise yourself. You do not have to become anyone other than yourself to find entrances. You are already there. You are already everything you need to be. Entrances are everywhere and all the time."

In the Torah, Moses is uniquely heroic: as liberator, lawgiver, and prophetic messenger. Traditionally he is considered the greatest of the prophets. The Torah concludes, *"Never again did there arise in Israel a prophet like Moses—whom the Lord singled out, face to face"* (Deut. 34:10). He leads his people out from slavery. As the Passover Haggadah says, *dayeinu*—"that would have been enough." He goes on to communicate the grand revelation at Sinai. Again, *dayeinu*. Then, already advanced in years, he leads the Israelites for four more decades, through great trials and tribulations, to the brink of the Promised Land. One is hard pressed to think of another figure in Western civilization whose contribution is so multifaceted and significant.

Here, we focus on Moses' prophetic role as a seeker of *herut*, "freedom." God informs Moses: *"I have marked well the plight of My people in Egypt and have heeded their outcry because of their taskmasters; yes, I am mindful of their sufferings. . . . Come, therefore, I will send you to Pharaoh, and you shall free My people, the Israelites, from Egypt"* (Exod. 3:7–10). Now, convinced that his people must be free, Moses tries to rally them—but his first efforts fall short. *"When Moses told this to the Israelites, they would not listen to Moses, their spirits crushed by cruel bondage"* (Exod. 6:9).

Just as Moses will need repeated appeals to stir his people, the same can be said for his confrontations with Pharaoh. Time and time again, the king's stubborn and vacillating heart impedes progress. Moses' first encounter with Pharaoh, with Aaron at his side, only stirs up Pharaoh's deepest anxiety that *"the people of the land are already so numerous, and you would have them cease from their labors!"* (Exod. 5:5). Indeed, Moses' mission appears to backfire; the conditions of slavery only worsen, and the Israelite foremen complain bitterly to Moses.

Each subsequent encounter with Pharaoh is equally frustrating. No sooner does Pharaoh plead for relief from a plague than his heart grows hard and he changes his mind. Even as the calamities worsen, Pharaoh reneges on his promise to let the people go—and even after he finally, ultimately grants permission, he still tries to pursue the fleeing Israelites.

As the physical process of liberation is long, hard, and complex, so is the emotional emancipation from slavery. Freedom is both political and spiritual: a function of the body and the soul. Moses, it has been said, had to take the Israelites out of Egypt and Egypt out of the Israelites. It would take forty years—two generations—in the desert to accomplish this. The thrill of the Exodus evaporates in the dry desert air with remarkable haste. So does the inspiration of the Sinai epiphany. No sooner do the Israelites break camp than the harsh reality of the wilderness trek sets in.

Yet Moses' prophetic moment of leading the Israelites out of Egypt is never forgotten. Indeed it becomes central to the revelation of the Torah and its ethical foundation. The Exodus is referenced in the very first of the Ten Commandments. The God who speaks self-identifies as *"your God"* and *"who brought you out of the land of Egypt, the house of bondage"* (Exod. 20:2, Deut. 5:6). Note that while God could have been introduced as creator of the world, God is instead presented as liberator of the people. The Torah is surely reminding us that the demanding and commanding God is first and foremost the liberating God. Concurrently, the text is also teaching us that there cannot be revelation without liberation. One cannot serve God if one is serving a Pharaoh. Moses knows that first and foremost he must pursue the fight for freedom; only after the Exodus can the journey to Sinai begin.

The Pharaohs of ancient Egypt saw themselves as godlike—perhaps as gods themselves. This may explain the Second Commandment's prohibition against idolatry, *"You shall have no other gods besides me"* (Exod. 20:3). Even symbolic representations of God (as practiced in Egypt) are unacceptable.

The Fourth Commandment—to remember and observe the Sabbath, and keep it holy—brilliantly reinforces the centrality of freedom. Weekly rest applies to *"you, your son or daughter, your male or female slave, your cattle, and the stranger who is within your settlements"* (Exod. 20:10). And in the second listing of the Ten Commandments, in Deuteronomy, the connection to the Exodus is spelled out: *"Remem-*

ber that you were a slave in the land of Egypt and the Lord God freed you from there . . . therefore the Lord your God has commanded you to observe the Sabbath day" (Deut. 5:15).

These lessons will not be lost on the prophets that follow Moses. Long after Pharaoh and Egypt have become distant memories, the prophets will ask: Have we enslaved ourselves to idolatry in other forms? Are we serving other masters? Are we subverting the rights of our fellows, and in effect robbing them of their freedom?

Walking with Moses: The Path of Freedom

In the Exodus experience, the Jewish people are born. By positing their origins in a liberation-from-slavery event, and retelling that story over and over again (at Passover most prominently, but with reminders at every Sabbath, holiday, and indeed at every prayer gathering), Jews never forgot this lesson. The Maccabean revolt against the Greeks, the first and second revolts against the Romans, and the disproportionate involvement by Jews in freedom movements in our time all testify to the Jewish yearning for freedom. As Elazar ben Yair, the leader of Masada, said (according to the historian Titus Flavius Josephus), "Long since we determined to serve neither Romans, nor any other, save God. Those who fell in battle may fitly be celebrated, for they died defending . . . liberty."

The Israelite redemption from slavery also inspired numerous liberation movements throughout the course of history. The Puritans saw themselves as the Children of Israel fleeing oppression for a new Promised Land. Thomas Paine, on the eve of the American Revolution, referred to King George III as "the hardened, sullen tempered Pharaoh of England." Benjamin Franklin proposed adopting a seal for America that depicted Moses standing at the shores of the sea, with the accompanying words "Rebellion to Tyrants is obedience to God." Ironically, the slaves in America read the same Bible and dreamed of their own liberation. The social reformer Frederick Douglass called the abolitionist William Lloyd Garrison "the man . . . raised up by God to deliver this modern Israel from bondage." In the words of the beloved spiritual: "When Israel was in Egypt's land: Let My people go! Oppressed so hard they could not stand: Let My people go!"

One cannot help but notice the irony embedded in the biblical verses that extol freedom while maintaining the institution of slavery. The scholar Nahum Sarna explains it this way: "Everywhere the attitude to the slave was marked by ambivalence: He was a human being in close daily contact with the master and other members of his family; but he was also an item of property to be assessed in terms of monetary value. Biblical legislation is directed toward enhancing the social and legal status of this human chattel. This humanitarian approach expresses itself in a variety of ways."

Throughout the centuries, many biblical readers—Jewish and Christian—wrestled with the ethical conundrum of a Bible that humanizes slavery but does not abolish it. The prophet Jeremiah castigated his countrymen for re-enslaving fellow Israelites who had been set free after the Torah-mandated maximum six years (Jer. 34:8). During the American Civil War, slave owners and abolitionists quoted from the same Bible. Rabbi Morris Raphall of New York gave a sermon defending slavery that attracted national attention; Rabbi David Einhorn of Baltimore did the same on the other side.

Certainly, the biblical view of freedom is rich in complexity. Moses proclaims *shelach et ami v'ya'avduni, "Let my people go, that they may serve me"* (Exod. 7:36, 9:2, 9:13, 10:3). As political philosopher Michael Walzer astutely notes, "True freedom, in the rabbinic view, lies in servitude to God. The Israelites had been Pharaoh's servants; in the wilderness they become God's servants. The Hebrew word *(avadim)* is the same. . . . [Moses transformed them] not merely by breaking their chains but also by . . . giving them laws. He brought them what is currently called 'positive freedom,' that is not so much (not at all!) a way of life free from regulation but rather a way of life to whose regulation they could, and did, agree."

This understanding of freedom is consequential. Freedom is not simply the opportunity to act with impunity—it requires responsibility. The Exodus, after all, is not an end in and of itself. The Exodus culminates in Sinai—liberation is capped by Revelation. The mission is predicated on a covenant, and covenant implies obligation.

Radical freedom can lead to anarchy. Responsible freedom leads to blessing.

Rabbi Nachum Amsel emphasizes the decidedly spiritual dimension of biblical freedom: "The highest type of freedom in Judaism is *herut*. This implies spiritual freedom, not merely a cessation from work. That is why Passover is called *Zeman Herutainu*, the holiday of freedom. This is not merely the freedom from bondage of Egypt but . . . the Jewish people becoming a people. Pesach is a celebration of spiritual freedom." Indeed, the Passover Haggadah instructs: "God took us out from slavery [*avdut*] to freedom [*herut*], from despair to joy, from mourning to celebration, from darkness to radiance, from enslavement to redemption."

Note how the Haggadah says "us." This line is prelude to the key verse: "In every generation each person should see him or herself as if he or she personally went forth from Egypt." In the eyes of Jewish tradition, each of us was in Egypt and at Sinai some three thousand years ago. How so? Without resorting to outright mysticism, we might call it "corporate memory." We are part of a people who remembers everything. We connect to a collective experience. As Heschel memorably expresses it, "We are a people in whom the past endures; in whom the present is inconceivable without moments gone by. The Exodus lasted a moment, a moment enduring forever. What happened once upon a time happens all the time."

This crucial line from the Haggadah does admit, however, that you and I were not physically present at Sinai. It inserts the key phrase, *k'ilu*: act "as if" you were there. Use your imagination—your moral imagination. Put yourself in your ancestors' shoes. Don't forget your roots, your origins, where you came from, what you went through. It explains what you are made of, who you are. By remembering and imagining, we come to what Rabbi Shai Held calls the "central project of the Torah—turning memory into empathy."

Time and again, the Torah repeats the clarion call to understand the demand of freedom as the demand of ethics. In Exodus, God commands: *"You shall not oppress a stranger"* (*v'atem yadatem et nefesh hager*), for you know the *nefesh* (the soul), the deepest feelings, of the stranger, *"having been strangers yourselves in the land of Egypt"* (Exod. 23:9). In Leviticus: *"When a stranger resides with you in your land, you shall not wrong him. The stranger who resides with you shall be to you as one of your citizens; you shall love him as yourself, for you were strangers in the land of Egypt"* (Lev. 19:33). In Deuteronomy: *"For the Lord your God . . . upholds the cause of the orphan and the widow, and befriends the stranger. . . . You too must befriend the stranger, for you were strangers in the land of Egypt"* (Deut. 10:17–19).

Toward the end of the Torah, Moses, and God, go one remarkable step further. We are commanded not only to aid the marginalized among us—represented by the orphan, the widow, and the stranger—but to reconcile with the agents of our oppression: *"Do not hate an Egyptian, for you were a stranger in his land"* (Deut. 23:8). As Rabbi Jonathan Sacks writes, "So what is Moses saying? He is telling the Israelites: You have left the physical Egypt. Now you must leave the mental experience of Egypt. You have to let go of hate, because otherwise you will never be free. Had the Israelites continued to hate their enemies, Moses would have taken the Israelites out of Egypt, but he would not have taken Egypt out of the Israelites."

The Torah had been building the case for responsible freedom from day one. Every human being is created in the image of God—yet we make bad choices. We are called to imitate God to insure that our moral choices are the right ones. Like God, we are to love the stranger, the other, the one most unlike us. This serves as the highest expression of our freedom.

The thesis of the Torah and Haggadah remains provocative and radical. The Italian writer and antifascist advocate Ignazio Silone offers this penetrating insight: "You can live in a dictatorship and be free—on one condition: that you fight the dictatorship. The man who thinks with his own mind, and keeps it uncorrupted, is free. But you can live in the most democratic country on earth, and if you're lazy, obtuse or servile within yourself, you're not free. Even without any violent coercion, you're a slave. You can't beg your freedom from someone. You have to seize it."

The prophetic path of freedom is a never-ending journey to our highest selves.

4

Tirzah's Challenge

THE PATH OF EQUALITY

I Am Tirzah

I am the youngest of five children, all of us sisters. Our father's name was Zelophehad, of the Manasseh clan. Even though he is dead, everyone calls us "Zelophehad's daughters." But we each have names. My sisters, from oldest to youngest, are Mahlah, Noah, Hoglah, and Milcha. I am Tirzah.

We loved our father, and he loved us. But I always knew he was disappointed that he did not have a son. Well, maybe not disappointed so much as concerned. Our father worried that without a son there would be no one to inherit his land, no one to share his wealth, and no one to perpetuate his name.

One day not too long after our father died I blurted out to my sisters, "We should take our case to Moses. Why shouldn't we inherit our father's share to pass it on to our children and to perpetuate his name?" My sisters looked at me, dumbfounded. "Stop talking foolishness, little sister," they said at first. But I did not relent. Over and over I reminded them that this was for the sake of our father's name. Finally, they conveyed a message to Moses requesting an audience. We were shocked when it was granted.

We stood before Eleazar the priest, the tribal elders, and Moses himself—all of us at the entrance to the Tent of Meeting. Mahlah, the oldest, spoke for us. She said, "Our father died in the wilderness. He was not of the rebellious faction of Korah that banded together against the Lord. Our father died for his own sin.

He left no sons. Let not our father's name be lost to his clan just because he had no son! Give us a holding among our father's kinsmen."

A murmur went up among the elders. It did not feel antagonistic, just surprised. Moses promised to consult the Lord.

In a few short days we reconvened. Moses announced, "The plea of Zelophehad's daughters is just. We should give them a hereditary holding among their father's kinsmen, transferring their father's share to them. And, from now on: If a man dies without leaving a son, we shall transfer his property to his daughter. If he has no daughter, we shall assign his property to his brothers. If he has no brothers, we shall assign his property to his father's brothers. If his father has no brothers, we shall assign his property to his nearest relative in his own clan, and he shall inherit it. This shall be our law in accordance with what the Lord has commanded."

We cried from happiness. Our father would have been proud of us. We were honoring his name, and keeping it alive.

But we celebrated a little bit too soon. This was not quite the end of the story. Not long after Moses' ruling, some of our Manasseh tribal kin appealed the decision to Moses and the assembly. They said, "The Lord commanded my lord to assign the share of our kinsman Zelophehad to his daughters. Now, if they marry persons from another Israelite tribe, their share will be cut off from our ancestral portion and be added to the portion of the tribe into which they marry. Thus our allotted portion will be diminished."

In all honesty, we hadn't thought about this scenario, since we were young and not yet married. But the time for betrothal was fast approaching for us; in fact it was past due for my older sisters. We understood the argument our uncles were making. We had no desire to diminish our tribe.

Moses said, "The plea of the Josephite tribe is just. This is what the Lord has commanded concerning the daughters of Zelophehad: They may marry anyone they wish, provided they marry into a clan of their father's tribe. No inheritance of the Israelites may pass over from one tribe to another, but the Israelites must remain bound each to the ancestral portion of his tribe. Every daughter among the Israelite tribe who inherits a share must marry someone from a clan of her father's tribe, in order that every Israelite may keep his ancestral share. Thus no inheritance shall pass over from one tribe to another, but the Israelite tribes shall remain bound each to its portion."

I suppose this is a small price to pay for keeping our father's share in the family. I might like to marry a man from another tribe—I wouldn't say it aloud, but some are better looking than the men of our tribe!—but I know I won't have that choice. Maybe my daughters or their daughters will . . . someday.

Tirzah's Challenge: From the Bible

The challenge of the daughters of Zelophehad (Num. 27:1–11):

> [1]*The daughters of Zelophehad, of Manassite family—son of Hepher son of Gilead son of Machir son of Manasseh son of Joseph—came forward. The names of the daughters were Mahlah, Noah, Hoglah, Milcah, and Tirzah.* [2]*They stood before Moses, Eleazar the priest, the chieftains, and the whole assembly, at the entrance of the Tent of Meeting, and they said,* [3]*"Our father died in the wilderness. He was not one of the faction, Korah's faction, which banded together against the Lord, but died for his own sin; and he has left no sons.* [4]*Let not our father's name be lost to his clan just because he had no son! Give us a holding among our father's kinsmen!"*
>
> [5]*Moses brought their case before the Lord.*
>
> [6]*And the Lord said to Moses,* [7]*"The plea of Zelophehad's daughters is just: you should give them a hereditary holding among their father's kinsmen; transfer their father's share to them.*
>
> [8]*"Further, speak to the Israelite people as follows: 'If a man dies without leaving a son, you shall transfer his property to his daughter.* [9]*If he has no daughter, you shall assign his property to his brothers.* [10]*If he has no brothers, you shall assign his property to his father's brothers.* [11]*If his father had no brothers, you shall assign his property to his nearest relative in his own clan, and he shall inherit it.' This shall be the law of procedure for the Israelites, in accordance with the Lord's command to Moses."*

The response of the tribes and the compromise decision (Num. 36:1–12):

> [1]*The family heads in the clan of the descendants of Gilead son of Machir son of Manasseh, one of the Josephite clans, came forward and appealed to Moses and the chieftains, family heads of the Israelites.* [2]*They said, "The Lord commanded my lord to assign the land to the Israelites as*

shares by lot, and my lord was further commanded by the Lord to assign the share of our kinsman Zelophehad to his daughters. [3]*Now, if they marry persons from another Israelite tribe, their share will be cut off from our ancestral portion and be added to the portion of the tribe into which they marry; thus our allotted portion will be diminished.* [4]*And even when the Israelites observe the jubilee, their share will be added to that of the tribe into which they marry, and their share will be cut off from the ancestral portion of our tribe."*

[5]*So Moses, at the Lord's bidding, instructed the Israelites, saying: "The plea of the Josephite tribe is just.* [6]*This is what the Lord has commanded concerning the daughters of Zelophehad: They may marry anyone they wish, provided they marry into a clan of their father's tribe.* [7]*No inheritance of the Israelites may pass over from one tribe to another, but the Israelites must remain bound each to the ancestral portion of his tribe.* [8]*Every daughter among the Israelite tribes who inherits a share must marry someone from a clan of her father's tribe, in order that every Israelite may keep his ancestral share.* [9]*Thus no inheritance shall pass over from one tribe to another, but the Israelite tribes shall remain bound each to its portion."*

[10]*The daughters of Zelophehad did as the Lord had commanded Moses:* [11]*Mahlah, Tirzah, Hoglah, Milcah, and Noah, Zelophehad's daughters, were married to sons of their uncles,* [12]*marrying into clans of descendants of Manasseh son of Joseph; and so their share remained in the tribe of their father's clan.*

Tirzah's Challenge: The Prophetic Moment

And the Lord said to Moses: The plea of Zelophehad's daughters is just: you should give them a hereditary holding among their father's kinsmen; transfer their father's share to them. (Num. 27:6)

The "Tale of the Five Daughters" deserves to be better known than it is. Mahlah, Noah, Hoglah, Milcha, and Tirzah are hardly household names, even to people who know their Bible. Yet these brave young women effect a major change in biblical inheritance law, and in doing so ask us to reconsider the status of women in our communities.

Note that the entire course of events is set in motion by the daughters' concern for the memory and legacy of their father. They point out that Zelophehad was not one of the rebels who participated in the uprising led by Moses' own cousin, Korah. They desire to see his name perpetuated, and they have the temerity to approach Moses and the elders and express what they view as an injustice: *"Let not our father's name be lost to his clan just because he had no son! Give us a holding among our father's kinsmen!"* (Num. 27:3.4). At heart, they are observing the fifth of the Ten Commandments, *"Honor your father and mother"* (Exod. 20:13, Deut. 5:16), even after their father's death.

Evidently at this early point in the evolution of Jewish law there was no provision for passing down a father's inheritance to his children if he did not have sons. Any such inheritance would instead be passed to the husband's family. Zelophehad's daughters want to perpetuate their father's inheritance in addition to his name. As daughters (unless they married into the extended family), they probably would not have received anything at all.

When the daughters "go public," bringing their case to the leadership, the end result is nothing less than a daring ruling that represents a bold change in biblical inheritance law. A legal loophole is closed.

The ruling also survives a challenge from the sisters' own tribal elders. Given that these women's inheritance will pass on to their husbands' tribes when they marry, diminishing the collective holdings of their tribe if they marry outside their clan, a condition to the new law is attached: the daughters must marry within their tribe. Yet the basic ruling remains intact, as the Bible itself later records: *"So in accordance with the Lord's instructions, [the daughters] were granted a portion among their father's kinsmen"* (Josh. 17:4).

In a distant age when the status of women was radically different than today, these biblical women were champions of justice. Judged by the standards of their time, their pioneering quest for *mishpat echad*, "equal rights," won them a significant victory in the battle for equality. To be sure, judged by today's standards, the sisters won only a partial victory. The case did not grant daughters the right to inherit when there were also sons in the family. Further, the daughters were now restricted as to whom they could marry. One can even argue that the women did not win true inheritance rights, only the ability to serve as placeholders until the next generation of male heirs could take over. Nonetheless, they still established a far-reaching precedent.

The seeds of equality in the Torah are planted early and deep (even if they take much time to germinate). All human beings are created in God's image, and *"male and female God created them"* (Gen. 1:27). To be sure, much of what is in the Bible reflects its patriarchal society. But as biblical scholar Jeremiah Unterman puts it, "So, even if the Jewish Bible itself did not advocate a socioeconomic revolution in women's rights, it created the foundation for such a revolution in the future. In similar fashion, Jefferson's 'all men are created equal' in the Declaration of Independence would be eventually understood to encompass all humans."

Unterman also emphasizes, as have other scholars, that the Torah creation account of that unique institution called the Sabbath, portraying divine rest and mandating it for all humans (and animals), is likewise part of the biblical foundation of equality. "This concept of the Sabbath rest had a democratizing influence upon society," he writes. "All were equal for one full day a week (and on certain holidays) and no one could require anybody else to work on that day. Even the king could not ask his lowliest servant to work on that day! The effect of such a desideratum on society cannot be minimized. Here the Bible establishes a weekly rest period as the first labor law—human rights for all members of society, along with the limitation of government."

The Torah does not have an exact expression for "equal rights" as we understand the term today. But *mishpat echad*, an expression meaning "one law" or "standard," comes close. The Torah emphasizes that one law should apply to all residents of Israel: *"You shall have one standard [mishpat echad] for stranger and citizen alike"* (Lev. 24:22). The Torah later repeats: *"There shall be one law for you and for the resident stranger; it shall be law for all time throughout the ages. You and the stranger shall be alike before the Lord; the same ritual and the same rule shall apply to you and to the stranger who resides among you"* (Num. 15:15–16). As biblical scholar Baruch Levine explains, "The same rules apply whether the offender or the victim are Israelites or resident non-Israelites. This stipulation must be made explicit because of the practice, in certain legal systems, of judging resident aliens by a different law." Other biblical scholars do point out that these noted single laws serving different groups of people are linked to specific contexts and thus do not necessarily signify a blanket statement of equal rights. However, they do provide a foundation for moving in that direction.

Rabbinic literature also repeatedly praises the daughters of Zelophehad for the way in which they advocated for equality regarding inheritance rights. In the Talmud they are extolled as "wise" (*chachamot*), "insightful" (*darshanyiot*), and "pious" (*rachmanyiot*): "wise" because they knew when and where to speak; "insightful" because they understood why their case was just; and "pious" because they agreed that they should not marry men outside their tribe. Their actions could have been confrontational and threatening, but instead they were able to effect change cooperatively and gracefully.

Absorbing these and other ideas of equality embedded in the Torah, the classical prophets are all the more disturbed by the economic and political inequalities they witness. Although their concerns tend toward the parochial—critiquing Israelite society—they occasionally express sentiments encompassing the equality of all human beings. Malachi says, *"Have we not all one Father? Did not one God create us?"* (Mal. 2:10). Amos says *"To me, O Israelites, you are just like the Ethiopians"* (Amos 9:7). Isaiah envisions the time when *"My house shall be called a house of prayer for all peoples"* (Isa. 56:7). Equality begins at home, but does not end there.

Walking with Tirzah: The Path of Equality

We know from history that the path of equality does not suddenly open up before us. It is not an all-or-nothing proposition. Equality is hard won by ever expanding the circle of inclusion. In America, for example, the equality bestowed by the founding declaration of inalienable rights to all men only gradually and painfully came to include people of color and women. In our own day, in many communities the circle of inclusion is expanding to include other minorities. Each broadening of the circle seems to set the stage for future efforts.

Little could the biblical sisters know that the inclusion of women in Judaism would radically change, but only after three millennia! This is not to say that individual women did not accomplish great achievements in the long saga of the Jewish people, but by and large women's voices and leadership roles in the community were marginalized. By traditional Jewish law (*halakhah*), women were not allowed to serve as rabbis, cantors, judges, or witnesses. They were not counted in a minyan (a quorum of ten required for communal worship). Nor could they lead a public worship service, read from the Torah in that setting, or be called to the Torah for an *aliyah* (blessing of the Torah). Historically, women also received considerably less Jewish and general education than men, and, not surprisingly, men authored almost all the important works of Jewish literature.

Finally, in mid-nineteenth-century Germany, the pioneers of Reform Judaism laid the groundwork for a dramatic move toward women's equality. Ahead of his time in many ways, in 1837 Rabbi Abraham Geiger passionately argued: "Let there be from now on no distinction between duties for men and women . . . no assumption of the spiritual inferiority of women, as though she were incapable of grasping the deep things in religion; no institution of the public service, whether in form or content, which shuts the doors of the temple in the face of women." Nine years later, Reform rabbis throughout Germany, gathering in Breslau, declared: "It is a sacred duty to express most empathically the complete religious equality of the female sex."

It would take more than another half century for these radical sentiments to be translated in reality. In 1922, Judith Eisenstein, daughter of the pioneering thinker Mordecai Kaplan, became the first bat mitzvah. In 1935, Regina Jonas received private ordination by a liberal rabbi. (Her life and work were forgotten when she perished in the Holocaust, but rediscovered several decades later.) In 1972, the Reform Movement's seminary, Hebrew Union College-Jewish Institute of Religion, ordained the first woman, Sally Priesand, ushering in a sea change in women's religious roles. The Reconstructionist Rabbinical College followed suit in 1974 with the ordination of Sandy Sasso, and the Jewish Theological Seminary (Conservative Judaism) ordained Amy Eilberg in 1985. By then women had begun assuming Jewish leadership positions—among them synagogue, federation, and JCC presidents—in force. In the span of one generation, certainly inspired by the feminist revolution in the greater world, the circle of inclusion had expanded with astounding speed. Today the decided majority of new cantors and nearly half of the new rabbis in the liberal movements are female. Synagogue presidents and board members are as likely to be female as male.

The path of equality is primarily about equal opportunity in the workplace, in the boardroom, and in the voting booth. It is about parity of compensation and recognition of accomplishment. Yet true and lasting equality is also about changing hearts and minds—freeing ourselves from prejudices of the past, opening ourselves to new ways of thinking. As such, the feminist revolution challenged the Jewish community to summon past voices that had been suppressed, to read history with new sensitivity, and to contemplate ritual and tradition in novel ways. Answering that call, the scholar Judith Plaskow wrote *Standing Again at Sinai: Judaism from a Feminist Perspective* (1990), a trailblazing book in which she challenged Jewish women to "reclaim Torah as our own." Plaskow exhorted: "We must render visible the presence, experience, and deeds of women erased in traditional sources. We must tell the stories of women's encounters with

God and capture the texture of their religious experience. We must expand the notion of Torah to encompass not just the five books of Moses and traditional Jewish learning, but women's words, teachings, and actions hitherto unseen. To expand Torah, we must reconstruct Jewish history to include the history of women, and in doing so alter the shape of Jewish memory." Since then, an entire body of Jewish feminist work has appeared; the same is true of the Christian community as well.

In the last two decades, perhaps no issue of inclusion and equality has been as transformational in society at large and the Jewish community in particular as that of gays and lesbians. In 1992, the small Reconstructionist movement became the first Jewish denomination to declare that "All people deserve dignity, integrity and equality. Therefore, we accord the same treatment both to homosexuals and heterosexuals that we now apply regardless of gender, age, disability, and birth religion." Furthermore, the statement acknowledged the holiness of gay and lesbian relationships on a parity to heterosexual ones. "As we celebrate the love between heterosexual Jews, so too do we celebrate the love between gay and lesbian Jews. As we affirm that heterosexual marriages embody *kedushah* [holiness], so do we affirm that *kedushah* resides in committed relationships between gay or lesbian Jews."

The Reform Movement soon followed suit. The Central Conference of American Rabbis (CCAR), the official body of Reform rabbis, had called for legislation decriminalizing homosexual acts in 1977. In 1990 the Hebrew Union College-Jewish Institute of Religion endorsed a change of admissions policy under which gay and lesbian students could openly apply to its rabbinical school. In 1996 the CCAR resolved to "support the right of gay and lesbian couples to share fully and equally in the rights of civil marriage."

The big question for the Reform Movement, however, was whether to endorse religious marriage, thereby acknowledging the holiness of gay and lesbian marriage. One CCAR committee concluded in 1998 that "*kedusha* may be present in committed same gender relationships," while another found that "homosexual relationships, however exclusive and committed they may be, do not fit within this legal category; they cannot be called *kiddushin*." The stage was set for a major debate.

Finally, in March 2000 the CCAR resolved that "the relationship of Jewish, same-gender couples is worthy of affirmation through appropriate Jewish ritual." Although the resolution went on to recognize the diversity of opinion on the issue and the right of rabbis to officiate or not officiate at such weddings, the path to full equality was now open in a major Jewish religious denomination.

The path toward equality for gays was even more controversial within the Conservative Movement, which adheres to Jewish law (*halakhah*) even though it admits to cautious evolutionary change within that law. In 1992 the all-important Committee on Jewish Law and Standards (CJLS) affirmed its traditional prohibition against homosexual conduct, same-sex unions, and the ordination of openly gay clergy. After about a decade and a half of increasing debate, in 2006 the CJLS approved contradictory rulings on the subject. Two responsa (Jewish legal rulings) argued for maintaining the bans on ordaining gay men or lesbians and on performing Jewish commitment ceremonies. However, a third responsum, grounded in the Talmud's reiteration that the honor due all human beings trumped any Rabbinic enactments, opened the door for equality. That same year, the Conservative seminaries (Ziegler School of Rabbinic Studies at American Jewish University and the Jewish Theological Seminary) changed their ordination policies, over the protest of some faculty and rabbis in the field. In 2012 the CJLS went on to approve same-sex marriage ceremonies and to offer texts for same-sex ceremonies of covenant on its website, although it should be noted that these are not identical to traditional *kiddushin* ceremonies, nor has this decision been accepted by all the Conservative Movement's international communities.

Tirzah and her sisters challenged their generation to move toward greater gender equality. So too did Abraham Geiger and the early Reform pioneers. In turn, they inspired leaders in our own generation.

Indeed, because of prophetic teachings, historic leaders, and great social movements (feminism, civil rights, gay and lesbian rights), in the twenty-first century we see dramatic progress toward full equality and inclusion.

Even so, we still have far to go to achieve full inclusion and equality in Judaism, and in our society as a whole. Tirzah's challenge resounds yet today.

5

Samuel's Warning

THE PATH OF REBUKE

I Am Samuel

Before I was born my mother Hannah made a promise: If she gave birth, she would dedicate her child to God's service. I was named Samuel because God heard what my mother asked. Mother was good to her word, and I was not yet five when she took me to live with the priest Eli at Shiloh. It was old Eli who raised me. I was like a new son to him. Eli had grown ones of his own, but they were nothing like him. In fact, they caused him only grief.

One night Eli was asleep in his room, and I was asleep in the temple near the ark, when I heard a voice calling my name. I ran to Eli and said, "Here I am; you called me." But Eli answered, "I didn't call you; go back to sleep." I went back and lay down. Again a voice called, "Samuel!" I ran back to Eli and repeated, "Here I am; you called me." Again Eli told me to go back to sleep. When it happened a third time, Eli knew that the Lord was calling. He told me to listen to God's message. I did, and even though I was young, I understood that Eli's house would fall, and that God would ask of me big things.

I grew up by Eli's side. His sons did not follow in their father's way. But the Lord was with me, and by His grace I became priest and prophet and judge.

For many long years I led Israel. I judged the most challenging cases; I decided the most difficult matters. The Philistines repeatedly tried to attack us, but each time we survived—only because we listened to the Lord. It was God who saved us, not me. I am only God's servant who speaks His word.

Eventually I aged in years, and just like Eli and his sons, my sons caused me grief. One day the elders of Israel assembled and approached me at Ramah. "You have grown old," they said, "and your sons have not followed your ways. Therefore, appoint a king for us, to govern us like all other nations."

I was dumbfounded. I was hurt. I felt betrayed. I was distressed for my sake and for the sake of my people and country. There was good reason why we had never had a king. God is our king!

I prayed to God to know what to do. God said to me, "Heed the demand of the people in everything they say to you!" I was astounded, but God continued, "For it is not you that they have rejected; it is Me they have rejected as their king. Heed their demand; but warn them solemnly, and tell them about the practices of any king who will rule over them."

That is what I did. I warned them that the king would take their sons as his charioteers and horsemen. I warned them that the king would make them plow his fields, reap his harvest, and forge his weapons. I warned them that the king would take their daughters as his cooks and bakers and perfumers. I warned them that the king would seize their fields and vineyards and olive groves. "You shall become his slaves," I said, "and you will cry out."

But the people were of no mind to listen to me. "No," they said, "We must have a king over us, that we may be like the other nations. Let our king rule over us, and go out at our head and fight our battles."

So I found them a king. I gave them one last warning. And then I let it be.

Samuel's Warning: From the Bible

The demand for a king and Samuel's warning (1 Sam. 8:4–22):

[4]All the elders of Israel assembled and came to Samuel at Ramah, [5]and they said to him, "You have grown old, and your sons have not followed your ways. Therefore appoint a king for us, to govern us like all other nations." [6]Samuel was displeased that they said "Give us a king to govern us." Samuel prayed to the Lord, [7]and the Lord replied to Samuel, "Heed the demand of the people in everything they say to you. For it is not you that they have rejected; it is Me they have rejected as their king. [8]Like everything else they have done ever since I brought them out of Egypt to this day—forsaking Me and worshiping other gods—so they are doing to you. [9]Heed their demand; but warn them solemnly, and tell them about the practices of any king who will rule over them."

[10]Samuel reported all the words of the Lord to the people, who were asking him for a king. [11]He said, "This will be the practice of the king who will rule over you: He will take your sons and appoint them as his charioteers and horsemen, and they will serve as outrunners for his chariots. [12]He will appoint them as his chiefs of thousands and of fifties; or they will have to plow his fields, reap his harvest, and make his weapons and the equipment for his chariots. [13]He will take your daughters as perfumers, cooks, and bakers. [14]He will seize your choice fields, vineyards, and olive groves, and give them to his courtiers. [15]He will take a tenth part of your grain and vintage and give it to his eunuchs and courtiers. [16]He will take your male and female slaves, your choice young men, and your asses, and put them to work for him. [17]He will take a tenth part of your flocks, and you shall become his slaves. [18]The day will come when you cry out because of the king whom you yourselves have chosen; and the Lord will not answer you on that day."

[19]But the people would not listen to Samuel's warning. "No," they said. "We must have a king over us, [20]that we may be like all the other nations: Let our king rule over us and go out at our head and fight our battles." [21]When Samuel heard all that the people said, he reported it

to the Lord. [22]And the Lord said to Samuel, "Heed their demands and appoint a king for them." Samuel then said to the men of Israel, "All of you go home."

Samuel's further warning about the king (1 Sam. 12:1–5,13–15):

[1]Then Samuel said to all Israel, "I have yielded to you in all you have asked of me and have set a king over you. [2]Henceforth the king will be your leader.

"As for me, I have grown old and gray—but my sons are still with you—and I have been your leader from my youth to this day. [3]Here I am! Testify against me, in the presence of the Lord and in the presence of His anointed one: Whose ox have I taken, or whose ass have I taken? Whom have I defrauded or whom have I robbed? From whom have I taken a bribe to look the other way? I will return it to you." [4]They responded, "You have not defrauded us, and you have not robbed us, and you have taken nothing from anyone." [5]He said to them, "The Lord then is witness, and His anointed is witness, to your admission this day that you have found nothing in my possession." They responded, "He is!"

[13]"Well, the Lord has set a king over you! Here is the king that you have chosen, that you have asked for.

[14]"If you will revere the Lord, worship Him, and obey Him, and will not flout the Lord's command, if both you and the king who reigns over you will follow the Lord your God, [well and good]. [15]But if you do not obey the Lord and you flout the Lord's command, the hand of the Lord will strike you as it did your fathers."

The warning about future kings in the Torah (Deut. 17:14–20):

[14]If, after you have entered the land that the Lord your God has assigned to you, and taken possession of it and settled in it, you decide, "I will set a king over me, as do all the nations about me," [15]you shall be free to set a king over yourself, one chosen by the Lord your God. Be sure to set as king over yourself one of your own people; you must not set a

foreigner over you, one who is not your kinsman. [16]*Moreover, he shall not keep many horses or send people back to Egypt to add to his horses, since the Lord has warned you, "You must not go back that way again."* [17]*And he shall not have many wives, lest his heart go astray; nor shall he amass silver and gold to excess.*

[18]*When he is seated on his royal throne, he shall have a copy of this Teaching written for him on a scroll by the priests.* [19]*Let it remain with him and let him read in it all his life, so that he may learn to revere the Lord his God, to observe faithfully every word of this Teaching as well as these laws.* [20]*Thus he will not act haughtily toward his fellows or deviate from the Instruction to the right or to the left, to the end that he and his descendants may reign long in the midst of Israel.*

Samuel's Warning: The Prophetic Moment

"But if you do not obey the Lord and you flout the Lord's command, the hand of the Lord will strike you as it did your fathers. . . . if you persist in your wrongdoing, both you and your king shall be swept away." (1 Sam. 12:15,25)

For nearly two centuries after the deaths of Moses and Joshua, ancient Israel was a tribal confederacy. A council of elders led the nation. There was no permanent leader. Certain leaders would rise to a position of national leadership, especially during times of crisis. These leaders, called judges, were sometimes military figures, like the better-known Gideon and Samson, and the lesser-known Othniel and Ehud.

Other judges seemed to be more political or prophetic in nature. One such judge was, remarkably, a woman—and arguably the first political leader in Jewish history. Deborah is introduced to us as a prophetess, and then described as sitting under the "Palm of Deborah" where *"all the Israelites would come to her for decisions"* (Judg. 4:5). Under her guidance, her commanding general Barak scores an important military victory over the Canaanites, celebrated in a long poem often called the Song of Deborah. But that is all we know of Deborah; the text moves on to the next crisis and the next judge.

The intriguing and enigmatic Deborah is part judge, part commander, and part prophet. This eclectic combination appears once more in the last of the judges, who is also the first of the classical prophets. His story is so important that it is the subject of a separate biblical book called Samuel.

We know from Samuel's annunciation story (see chapter 15 in this volume about his mother, Hannah) that he was destined to be a unique leader of Israel. The Bible emphasizes that Samuel possesses prophetic powers from an early age. He is chosen to convey God's message while serving as the political leader of the tribes. Yet even Samuel cannot foresee what will happen in his lifetime.

As the conflict with the Philistines and internal strife among the tribes worsens, the people sense that their leadership is failing them. They demand to have a king like the surrounding nations do. The Israelite nation fears that Samuel has grown too old to protect them and that his sons are not up to the task. They do not mince words: *"All the elders of Israel assembled and came to Samuel at Ramah, and they said to him, 'You have grown old, and your sons have not followed your ways. Therefore appoint a king for us, to govern us like all other nations'"* (1 Sam. 8:4).

Samuel takes it personally. He lashes out at the people, *"Here I am! Testify against me, in the presence of the Lord and in the presence of His anointed one: Whose ox have I taken, or whose ass have I taken? Whom have I defrauded or whom have I robbed? From whom have I taken a bribe?"* (1 Sam. 12:3).

God attempts to reassure him that the people are not rejecting him, but the Lord. And despite his personal feelings of betrayal, Samuel responds to the people's request. He finds a tall, young warrior named Saul from the tribe of Benjamin who seems to have great promise, and anoints him king.

Still, Samuel remains gravely concerned that the presence of a king is contradictory to the Israelites' pledge to serve only the King of Kings. The memory of Israel's long enslavement to the Egyptian pharaohs remains fresh in his mind.

As the first in a long line of prophets who warn against the abuse of power liable to ensue under a monarchy, Samuel becomes a champion of justice. He protests against the Israelites becoming enslaved yet again—this time to a king of their own choosing.

Samuel's rebuke is quite explicit. He warns that a king will level what people everywhere still fear from monarchs or authoritarian regimes: the draft, taxes, and eminent domain (seizure of property). The king will need soldiers for his army. He will need servants for his administration. He will need land for his estates. All of this will require huge taxes. Once this power grab is put into motion, no one will be able to stop it. *"The day will come,"* Samuel admonishes, *"when you cry out because of the king whom you yourselves have chosen; and the Lord will not answer you on that day"* (1 Sam. 8:18).

Perhaps because of his deep ambivalence about kingship, his own personal hurt, and his reluctance to cede power himself, Samuel has an early falling out with Saul. When the young king is poised to counter a Philistine attack and prematurely offers sacrifices before Samuel has arrived (though he waits a full seven days), the prophet offers a blistering castigation: *"You acted foolishly in not keeping the commandments that the Lord your God laid upon you! Otherwise the Lord would have established your dynasty over Israel forever. But now your dynasty will not endure. The Lord will seek out a man after His own heart, and the Lord will appoint him ruler over His people, because you did not abide by what the Lord had commanded you."* (1 Sam. 13:13–14).

Fairly or not, Samuel's merciless criticism repeats itself a short time later when Saul achieves an important victory over the dreaded Amalekites but spares, apparently against the prophet's orders, the foreign king and the choicest spoils. *"Because you rejected the Lord's command, He has rejected you as king,"* Samuel acidly responds. When Saul admits wrong and begs for forgiveness, Samuel again shuns him: *"I will not go back with you; for you have rejected the Lord's command, and the Lord has rejected you as king over Israel."* The Bible relates that as

Samuel turns to leave, Saul seizes the corner of Samuel's robe, and it tears. Samuel turns again to face Saul and says, *"The Lord has this day torn the kingship over Israel away from you and given it to another who is worthier than you"* (1 Sam. 15:23,26,27).

The rift between prophet and king never heals. The Bible reports that Samuel never sees Saul again until the day of his death, and adds that *"Samuel grieved over Saul, because the Lord regretted that He had made Saul king over Israel"* (1 Sam. 15:35).

The Bible relates that immediately thereafter God guides Samuel to a family in Bethlehem and tells him to secretly anoint the youngest son, David. Though at this point he is just a young shepherd, *"the spirit of the Lord gripped David from that day on"* (1 Sam. 16:13). By contrast, *"the spirit of the Lord has departed from Saul, and an evil spirit from the Lord began to terrify him"* (1 Sam. 16:14). Saul declines into mental illness, but continues to rule for many years, until he is killed in battle.

Then David ascends the throne. He attains greatness, but, sure enough, he exhibits some of the very abuses Samuel warned about—taking many wives and slaves, and imposing taxes.

Samuel's prophetic moment will live on in the figure of Nathan (see chapter 6), who must confront David, and in many other prophets who must admonish their leaders. For despite the rocky start, kingship is here to stay. After Saul comes David. After David comes David's son Solomon.

After Solomon's death, the nation splits into two kingdoms: North (Israel) and South (Judah). At this juncture, the Bible's books of Kings appear to validate Samuel's worst fears. Whether in the North or the South, king after king is described as straying into idolatry and injustice. Internal weakness and unwise alliances lead to the destruction of the Northern Kingdom of Israel by the Assyrians in the eighth century BCE and the destruction of the Southern Kingdom of Judah by the Babylonians in the sixth century BCE. One can almost say: Twice the number of kings, twice the trouble.

Amidst all the misfortune come the self-proclaimed prophets, raising an unprecedented moral protest at great personal risk—for a challenge to the king always carried with it a prison sentence, if not a death sentence. Fortunately, the compilers of the Bible deemed the prophetic voices worthy of preservation and inclusion in ancient Israel's sacred library. As Rabbi Jonathan Sacks puts it, "[Judaism is] a religion that will not worship power and the symbols of power—for that is what idols really were and are. . . . Judaism is a sustained critique of power. That is the conclusion I have reached after a lifetime of studying our sacred texts."

Walking with Samuel: The Path of Rebuke

The prophetic critique of power runs so deep, and the particular wariness of kingship is so strong, that a severe warning about it is embedded in the first part of the Torah. In context the following passage occurs long before kingship became a reality in ancient Israel, though some scholars see it as a later insertion into the Torah based on the negative experience of kingship. The passage echoes Samuel's warning about a king's potential abuse of power by means of amassing riches: *"Moreover, he [the king] shall not keep many horses or send people back to Egypt to add to his horses, since the Lord has warned you, 'You must not go back that way again.' And he shall not have many wives, lest his heart go astray; nor shall he amass silver and gold to excess"* (Deut. 17:16–17).

The biblical text goes on to make a striking demand: An Israelite king must have a written copy of the Torah by his side at all times. The scroll is not just for show; the king is to read the Torah, the ever-present reminder of God's law, *"all his life."* Deuteronomy then tells us that it is not for the king to *"act haughtily"* or to deviate from the Torah *"to the right or to the left"* (Deut. 17:20)—that is, in any way that negates or distorts the law.

These rules were intended to instill a reverence for God and observance of Torah law—and to serve as an antidote to monarchs' natural inclinations to haughtiness. As biblical scholar Jeffrey Tigay notes, "In [Mesopotamia] the king was the lawgiver. . . . In Egypt, the king was believed to be a god, and he was the law. These ideas had few echoes in Israel." Indeed, in Israel, the message was clear: No one, not even the king, is above the law.

In later generations, following Samuel's example, other remarkable prophets rebuke their kings. An unnamed "man of God" confronts King Jeroboam at the altar of Bethel where he is committing idolatry, declaring: *"This altar shall break apart, and the ashes on it shall be spilled"* (1 Kings 13:3). The king does not learn his lesson, and so another prophet, Ahijah, delivers this message to him through his wife: *"You have acted worse than all those who preceded you; you have gone and made for yourself other gods and molten images to vex Me; and Me you have cast behind your back"* (1 Kings 14:9).

Several generations later, the prophet Elijah repeatedly confronts King Ahab. When Ahab taunts him, *"Is that you, you troubler of Israel?"* Elijah retorts, *"It is not I who has brought trouble on Israel but you and your father's house, by forsaking the commandments of the Lord and going after the Baalim"* (1 Kings 18:17–18). Later, after an especially egregious incident in which Ahab, under the influence of his exceedingly wicked wife Jezebel, frames and puts an innocent man to death and then steals his prime vineyard, the king and prophet have an even sharper exchange. *"So you have found me, my enemy?"* says Ahab. *"Yes, I have found you,"* Elijah replies. *"Because you have committed yourself to doing what is evil in the sight of the Lord, I will bring disaster upon you. I will make a clean sweep of you . . . all of [your] line shall be devoured by dogs"* (1 Kings 21:20–24).

Decades later, the prophet Isaiah (see chapter 17 of this volume) first criticizes King Ahaz for widespread corruption and an unholy alliance with Assyria, and then King Hezekiah, for the same with Egypt. The prophet Jeremiah (see chapter 11) too has problems with more than one monarch, but especially with King Jehoiakim. He must force the king to face truths he would rather not see, pointing out how Jehoiakim is leading the nation to ruin. The task is never easy.

Nor is rebuke easy—or reserved solely for prophets confronting kings. A key teaching of the Holiness Code is: *"You shall surely rebuke your kinsman; incur no guilt because of him"* (Lev. 19:18). Ordinary people, in everyday situations, are also called upon to rebuke. The Torah is not commending criticism for its own sake but for preventing wrongdoing. We often see others erring. The safe and easier way is to say nothing, keep our mouths shut. The harder way is to get involved and speak up.

This verse from Leviticus has been the subject of considerable Rabbinical comment. Does the word "kinsman" (*amit*), which can also be rendered more generally as "neighbor" or most generally as "fellow," refer just to someone you know or also to someone you don't know? (A similar debate concerns the word *re'ah,* generally rendered as "neighbor," in the conclusion of the verse from Leviticus 19:18, *"Love your neighbor as yourself."* Should you love your family as yourself? A relative? A neighbor? Or any fellow?) The consensus seems to be that we have a responsibility to rebuke others with whom we have a relationship that may have caused us harm, but likewise to rebuke those we do not know, when we see something wrong occurring. In other words, the command can be understood as a means of helping ourselves and helping others, be they friend or stranger.

In what sense does rebuking another help one's self? The sages place the verse in its biblical context, noting that the preceding verse in Leviticus commands, *"Do not hate your brother in your heart,"* while the subsequent verse reads, *"Do not seek revenge or bear a grudge against anyone among your people, but love your neighbor as yourself"* (Lev. 19:17–18). As Maimonides teaches, "When one person wrongs another, the latter should not remain silent and despise him. . . . Rather, he is commanded to make the matter known and ask him: Why did you do this to me? Why did you wrong me regarding this matter? If afterwards, [the person who committed the wrong] asks to forgive him, he must do so." Maimonides suggests that explaining that one feels wronged to the person who committed the wrong is the way to let go of hate, resentment, or revenge.

Nachmanides, while often at odds with Maimonides, here makes the same basic point. His commentary to Leviticus 19:17 concludes: "He admonishes him so that he is to erase his fellow's sin and transgression against him from his heart. Following that admonition, God commanded that he love him as himself." Rabbi Jonathan Sacks explains this psychological dynamic further: "He may apologize and seek to make amends. Even if he does not, at least you have made your feelings known to him. That in itself is cathartic. It will help you to avoid nursing a grievance." The path of rebuke thus serves two purposes: to help the sinner and the sinned against. Both are in need of assistance to continue in the right direction.

In the very next paragraph of his code, Maimonides extends the command of rebuke beyond the personal, stating, "It is a mitzvah for a person who sees that his fellow has sinned or is following an improper path to correct his behavior and to inform him that he is causing himself a wrong by his bad deeds." He goes on to state that the rebuke should preferably be conducted in private, done patiently and gently, and communicated out of concern for his fellow's welfare. If necessary, a rebuke can be repeated a second or third time, or until one's fellow says that he will not listen. Maimonides ends this paragraph on a striking note: "Whoever has the possibility of rebuking [sinners] and fails to do so is considered responsible for that sin, for he had the opportunity to rebuke them."

Another classic Rabbinic commentary offers an intriguing model of rebuke so gentle that it is hardly discernable as criticism. The Talmud calls Aaron, brother of Moses, a man of peace and urges us to "be of the disciples of Aaron, loving peace and pursuing peace." How did Aaron himself accomplish this? With the most tender of words, the commentary says:

> *If two people were feuding, Aaron would walk up to one, sit down next to him and say, "My child, don't you see how much your friend is tearing her heart out and rending her clothes?" The person would then say to himself: "How can I lift up my head and look my friend in the face? I would be ashamed to see her because it is I who treated her foully."*
>
> *Aaron would remain at his side until he had removed all rancor from his heart. Afterwards, Aaron would walk over to the other person,*

sit down next to her and say: "Don't you see how much your friend is eating his heart out and tearing his clothes?" And so this person, too, would think to herself: "Woe unto me! How can I lift up my head and look my friend in the face? I would be ashamed to see him because it is I who treated him foully."

Aaron would sit with this person until she, too, had overcome the rancor in her heart. And finally when these two friends met, they would embrace and kiss each other. That is why it is said [that when Aaron died], "And they wept for Aaron thirty days, the entire House of Israel." (Num. 20:20)

Idealized though it may be, Aaron's example does highlight that there is a way to speak up that does not alienate and is likely to yield positive results. After all, if nobody is willing to speak up, how do we learn from our mistakes? Perhaps this is why the thirteenth-century sage Rabbi Yonah Gerondi gives us the challenging advice to: "Love your critics and hate your flatterers." Our inclination is to do just the opposite. But to become better people, it behooves us to perceive the truth our critics are revealing. If we can adopt the perspective that the critic is actually doing us a favor by accomplishing the difficult task of speaking out, we may be more receptive to the messenger and the message.

The path of rebuke is reinforced by a little noticed but extraordinary verse that brings us back full circle to the story of Samuel. Recall that the sons of the high priest Eli, who raised Samuel, did not follow in their father's ways. According to the Bible, it seems that Eli himself may bear part of this responsibility. How could this be so? *"And I declare to [Eli the high priest] that I sentence his house to endless punishment for the iniquity he knew about—how his sons committed sacrilege at will—and he did not rebuke them"* (1 Sam. 3:13).

Parents certainly have a responsibility to rebuke and discipline their children when they go astray. I have told my own children that unconditional love does not mean uncritical love! The term for "parent" in Hebrew, *horeh,* is related to *moreh,* "teacher." Both share the same root, meaning "to instruct," as does the word *torah*, "teaching," in its broadest meaning. Parents are teachers: teachers of Torah.

Another teaching is inherent in a Rabbinic text that discusses why the repetitive term *hokeach tokhiach* (you shall surely rebuke) is given in Leviticus 19, when one simple command of *hokeach* (rebuke) would have sufficed. A linguist might answer that this is the biblical emphatic construct; the Hebrew Bible commonly emphasizes an action by using two forms of the same verb together. The sages, however, understood the repetition differently—as indicating the imperative to rebuke repeatedly. The Rabbis ask Raba, one of their colleagues, if "repeatedly" means "twice," since the verb is used two times. Raba replies, "No, even a hundred times."

Raba further explains that another reason for the repetitive wording has nothing to do with the number of times one should rebuke, but to teach that the law is reciprocal. "Had there been only a single verb, I would have known that the law applies to a master reproving his disciple. How do we know that it applies even to a disciple reproving his master? From the phrase, *hokeach tokhiach*, implying, under all circumstances."

An important principle, instituted here, contributes to Judaism's well-established and expansive culture of dissent. Despite Judaism's veneration of teachers, disciples may reprove their masters if they see them doing something wrong. Citizens may rebuke their leaders; friends their colleagues; children their parents. The duty of responsible rebuke applies to parents, children, teachers, students, colleagues, friends . . . which means, at one time or another, to all of us.

Rabbi Sharon Brous tells a story about how she once chanced upon a book by Abraham Joshua Heschel at a library sale. When she got home and opened the volume, papers tumbled out—including a hand-typed letter from Heschel dated October 20, 1972 (just two months before his death). The "Dear Colleague" letter reads:

> *The forthcoming election confronts every one of us as American citizens and as Jews with a truly momentous decision. Our country today is in*

a state of profound moral and political crisis. In a free society, some are guilty—all are responsible. At this serious moment of American history, I feel a deep sense of responsibility for the moral decline and confusion in our sense of priorities. If the prophets Isaiah and Amos were to appear in our midst, would they accept the corruption in high places, the indifferent way in which the sick, the poor, and the old are treated? Would they condone the indifference to gun control legislation that has allowed some of our finest . . . to be shot dead? Surely it is the duty of any religious leader to help change a society that tolerates [this].

Heschel seized the moment to rebuke his colleagues, albeit in dignified language. He understood that he could not keep silent. Samuel and the prophets teach us that in the face of wrongdoing, we must speak up against king or commoner or colleague.

6

Nathan's Parable

THE PATH OF RIGHTEOUSNESS

I Am Nathan

From the time I met David I felt the Lord was with him. That my teacher Samuel anointed David only confirmed what I knew in my heart.

When David became king over all Israel and asked me to join him in Jerusalem I agreed. When David was finally granted respite from his enemies and built himself a palace I rejoiced. When David said, "Here I am dwelling in a house of cedar, while the Ark of the Lord abides in a tent!" and asked if he could build a temple, I consented. I said to David, "Go and do whatever you have in mind, for the Lord is with you."

But later that night, when I could not sleep, the word of the Lord came to me. The next day I felt compelled to tell David the misgivings that God was expressing through me. I pointed out that God had never once asked for a house, and I questioned whether David was the one to change that. Then I paused to see David's reaction. I could see that he was crestfallen. I know his intentions were for the best. It was necessary to endure this moment of humility for what I had to say next.

I further told David that although God did not want a house for himself, God wanted a house for David. A house: meaning a dynasty. God had granted the wish of the Israelites for a king; now the future kings of Israel would issue from David. He would become the father of the nation.

David was overcome with emotion. We sat down and prayed to our Lord. David prayed for blessing for himself and his children. What a glorious moment!

And then from the heights came the depths. How could a man who had ascended so high stoop so low? Did he think that his affair with Bathsheba could be kept a secret? Did he think that his plot to make Uriah disappear would go unnoticed? Did he think that all could be hush-hush before God if not man?

I knew I would have to confront the mighty king by trapping him with his own words. I started with a report of a rich man who steals from a poor man. When David flew into a rage against the rich man, yelled that he deserved to die, and ordered him to pay four times over . . . I pounced. "You are the man!" I exclaimed. I berated the king of Israel because he had betrayed the King of Kings. I disclosed the sordid details. I proclaimed his punishment.

The King of Israel was stunned and speechless. To his credit, the first words out of his mouth were, "I stand guilty before the Lord." That saved his life, and his kingship.

But David would never know a day of peace again. I told him that just as he had ruined a family, his family would be ruined. Just as he had stolen a wife, his wives would be stolen. Just as he had taken a life, so a life would be taken.

This gave me no pleasure. David was the elect of God. I was his friend, but now, his foe. I was his confidant, but now his accuser.

I have no choice but to speak truth to power. That is what God demands of me.

Nathan's Parable: From the Bible

Nathan on David's misdeeds (2 Sam. 12:1–14):

But the Lord was displeased with what David had done,[1]and the Lord sent Nathan to David. He came to him and said, "There were two men in the same city, one rich and one poor. [2]The rich man had very large flocks and herds, [3]but the poor man had only one little ewe lamb that he had bought. He tended it and it grew up together with him and his children: it used to share his morsel of bread, drink from his cup, and nestle in his bosom; it was like a daughter to him. [4]One day, a traveler came to the rich man, but he was loath to take anything from his own flocks or herds to prepare a meal for the guest who had come to him; so he took the poor man's lamb and prepared it for the man who had come to him."

[5]David flew into a rage against the man, and said to Nathan, "As the Lord lives, the man who did this deserves to die! [6]He shall pay for the lamb four times over, because he did such a thing and showed no pity." [7]And Nathan said to David, "That man is you! Thus said the Lord, the God of Israel: 'It was I who anointed you king over Israel and it was I who rescued you from the hand of Saul. [8]I gave you your master's house and possession of your master's wives; and I gave you the House of Israel and Judah; and if that were not enough, I would give you twice as much more. [9]Why then have you flouted the command of the Lord and done what displeases Him? You have put Uriah the Hittite to the sword; you took his wife and made her your wife and had him killed by the sword of the Ammonites. [10]Therefore the sword shall never depart from your House—because you spurned Me by taking the wife of Uriah the Hittite and making her your wife.' [11]Thus said the Lord: 'I will make a calamity rise against you from within your own house; I will take your wives and give them to another man before your very eyes and he shall sleep with your wives under this very sun. [12]You acted in secret, but I will make this happen in the sight of all Israel and in broad daylight.'"

[13]David said to Nathan, "I stand guilty before the Lord!" And Nathan replied to David, "The Lord has remitted your sin; you shall not die. [14]However, since you have spurned the enemies of the Lord by this deed, even the child about to be born to you shall die."

Nathan's Parable: The Prophetic Moment

And Nathan said to David: That man is you! (2 Sam. 12:7)

While the term "speaking truth to power" is of relatively recent coinage, it perfectly sums up the prophetic confrontation with kingship. No such confrontation in the Bible is more dramatic than Nathan's before David. The scene of the fearless man of God humbling the great monarch resonates through the ages.

Nathan is not some stranger to David, which might have made his task easier. He is a trusted member of the royal court. The first recorded interaction of the prophet and potentate testifies to this relationship. Even as Nathan tells David he is not the one to build a temple for God, the prophet pronounces an even more important promise: David will give rise to a dynasty that will rule Israel forever. *"The Lord declares to you that He, the Lord, will establish a house for you. When your days are done and you lie with your fathers, I will raise up your offspring. Your house and your kingship shall ever be secure before you; your throne shall be established forever"* (2 Sam. 7:11–12,16). Nathan clearly believes that David is the elect of God. He is apparently as much a devotee of David as anyone.

But above all Nathan is a prophet, one of the unelected moral voices who, as an unwavering champion of justice, is compelled to communicate the message of God. So when David commits the serious sin of adultery, and then even more egregiously, murder, Nathan risks his relationship, if not his life, to confront David. Nathan's simple parable of injustice snares the impulsive yet calculating king into an admission of his own guilt. To Nathan's unforgettable accusation, *"That man is you!"* David can only reply, *"I stand guilty before the Lord"* (2 Sam. 12:13).

The story begins with a whiff of perplexity—one small but potentially ominous note. It is the turn of the year, *"the season when kings go out [to battle],"* yet David inexplicably *"remained in Jerusalem."* While his soldiers are fighting on the front, *"Late one afternoon David rose from his couch and strolled on a roof of the royal palace; and from the roof he saw a woman bathing"* (2 Sam. 11:1–2). David makes inquiries about her, then sends messengers to summon the beautiful Bathsheba. He lays with her; a short time after, she sends word that she is pregnant. That announcement sets a nefarious plot in motion.

David orders Bathsheba's soldier husband Uriah to return from battle on the pretext of receiving a war report; then he tells Uriah to return home before returning to the front. He is of course hoping that Uriah will sleep with his wife. Ever the loyal soldier, however, Uriah instead sleeps at the entrance to the royal palace with other officers. When David questions him about not returning home, Uriah's reply is remarkably pointed: *"The Ark and Israel and Judah are located in Succoth, and my master Job and Your Majesty's men are camped in the open; how can I go home and eat and drink and sleep with my wife? As you live, by your very life, I will not do this!"* (2 Sam. 11:11).

The next night David gets Uriah drunk; still the soldier will not go home.

David is now desperate to insure a cover-up. When Uriah returns to battle, David instructs his commanding general Joab to put the dutiful warrior on the front lines and in the most vulnerable spot of the battle. There Uriah dies.

After the period of mourning, Bathsheba is brought to the palace, and David marries her. She bears him a son. *"But the Lord was displeased with what David had done, and the Lord sent Nathan to David"* (2 Sam. 12:1).

Why is it that David is allowed to remain in office after such grievous sins? The question of whether David was morally fit to continue as king continues to resonate in an age when we debate whether leaders who commit adultery and worse misdeeds should be impeached.

Perhaps, in David's case, it is his swift admission of guilt. Perhaps it is the promise of the dynasty Nathan had previously pronounced.

In any event, David does not go unpunished. Although he holds on to office, David is unable to hold on to his own family. In truth, "*the sword shall never depart from your House*" comes true in his tumultuous family life, and that of his heirs. David witnesses the deaths of three of his sons. His unnamed son from the adulterous union with Bathsheba dies in a matter of days from an unspecified illness. His son Absalom kills his brother Amnon after Amnon rapes their sister Tamar. David's general Joab kills Absalom after Absalom rebels against his father; and a fourth son, Adonijah, suffers a very similar fate after David's death when he is killed under suspicion of rebellion. Ironically it is David's second son with Bathsheba, Solomon, who prevails.

In his prophetic moment, as he calls David to task for his sins, Nathan amplifies one of Scripture's dominant themes: Our actions always have consequences. Every moral choice, every deed defines us. Each constantly steers us closer to the path of blessing or the path of curse.

Moreover, no one, not even a king, is above the law. No one is free from the consequences of breaking the law. Regardless of whether one is convicted in a court, there is accountability before God. The call to righteous living is not discretionary but mandatory. Fundamentally, it is a matter of justice. Given human nature, the tireless pursuit of justice is the only safeguard against the descent into injustice—be one king or commoner.

Walking with Nathan: The Path of Righteousness

I was teaching the story of David and Nathan to teens in my confirmation class when news of President Bill Clinton's liaison with Monica Lewinsky broke. We debated whether the president's transgressions constituted an impeachable offense. Some argued that his private misbehavior was offense enough—a leader must be held to a high moral standard. Others contended that the real problem was his lying to the public and to a court about the affair—and, furthermore, that this legal wrong met the constitutional standard of impeachable "high crimes and misdemeanors."

Those who came to the president's defense pointed out that adultery was no longer a criminal offense, though it might be religiously sinful. Others maintained that lying about a sexual relationship, even under oath, did not constitute a serious enough crime to be removed from office (and that the president should not have been compelled to testify on this matter while in office).

Clinton is just one such example in recent history. This problem of the moral accountability of leaders is regrettably timeless and universal. If, in the words of Lord Acton, "absolute power corrupts absolutely," then there may be a special problem of accountability among leaders. And if so, it is all the more reason that the challenge of advocating for moral accountability belongs to each and every person.

The premise that we should embrace the moral way, but will have trouble doing so, is rooted in the Jewish conception of human free will against the backdrop of our propensity for evil. Already in the opening portion of Genesis the Torah establishes two primary truths—first, that human beings have the ability to *"know good and bad"* (Gen. 3:22), and second, that *"Sin crouches at the door; its urge is toward you; yet you can be its master"* (Gen. 4:7). The latter foundational statement appears in the story of Cain and Abel, when God issues a warning to Cain before his act of fratricide. That Cain was warned and yet to no avail only highlights the Torah's rather grim view of human nature.

Indeed, the first story of humanity evinces disobedience and evasion of responsibility. The second features an exponentially graver example of both. First, God asks Adam, *"Where are you?"* to which Adam says he is afraid and hides. Second, God asks Cain, *"Where is your brother?"* to which Cain first lies, *"I do not know"* and then memorably hurls back the challenge, *"Am I my brother's keeper?"* (Gen. 4:9).

Any doubt about the human inclination to do wrong is dispelled within a generation of man's creation: It is confirmed as endemic to our species when we read in the prelude to the Noah story, *"The Lord saw how great was man's wickedness on earth, and how every plan devised by his mind was nothing but evil all the time"* (Gen. 6:5).

Yet Genesis also teaches that we are the noble creature made *"in the image of God"* (Gen. 1:27); that we are planted in the garden *"to till it and tend it"* (Gen. 2:15); and that Abraham's descendants have a special responsibility *"to keep the way of the Lord by doing what is just and right"* (Gen. 18:19).

The sages sought to comprehend the yawning chasm between human potential and reality, and the apparent conundrum of an omnipotent God allowing evil. They postulated, in the classic statement of Akiba, that "All is foreseen, yet freedom of choice is granted." God is the master of creation, but gives humans the opportunity to transcend the laws of nature by exercising moral choice.

In short, the Torah believes that we have the ability to define and pursue the good, and avoid the bad. As such, to the debate about whether our actions are influenced by nature (genetics) or nurture (environment), Judaism would add a third element: human will. We can be held accountable because moral standards and commandments exist, and we have not just the ability, but the responsibility, to uphold them.

This worldview is memorably summarized in one of Moses' final narrations, when he reminds his fellow Israelites: *"Surely, this Instruction which I enjoin upon you this day is not too baffling for you, nor is it beyond reach. No, the thing is very close to you, in your mouth and in your heart, to observe it. See, I set before you this day life and prosperity, death and adversity. . . . Choose life"* (Deut. 31:11,14–15,19).

The sages speak clearly and unequivocally concerning free will and moral responsibility. Maimonides best sums it up: "Free will is bestowed on every human being. If one desires to turn to the good way and be righteous, he has the power to do so. If one wishes to turn toward the evil way and be wicked, he is at liberty to do so.

Every human being may become righteous like Moses our teacher, or wicked like Jeroboam; merciful or cruel, miserly or generous, and so with all other qualities."

The prophetic demand of righteousness and accountability is uncompromising—and, upon reflection, empowering as well. Judaism readily acknowledges that we have an evil inclination (*yetzer harah*). That inclination does battle with our good inclination (*yetzer hatov*). As the Talmud well puts it: "At first the Evil Impulse is like a passer-by, then he is called a guest, and finally he becomes a master of the house." Remaining on the moral high road is not easy. Temptation is all around; what is more, it is our nature to stray. Yet, as the Talmud also reminds us: "Who is a hero? He who subdues his Evil Impulse." The opportunity to exert control over the impulses that rage within us is omnipresent.

Above the ark in the synagogue I serve, an inscription reads: "Know before whom you stand." This Rabbinic dictum is found in so many synagogues around the world that it can be considered one of Judaism's watchwords. In its original context the verse speaks of standing before God. Others may understand the teaching as standing before ourselves (our conscience) or standing before our community. All of them point to the path of accountability. Nathan reminded David that while he acted in secret, the consequences would be made public. In truth there is no secret and no hiding. We will be called to account before God and the community.

When Nathan is compelled to confront David over his abuses of power, the prophet resorts to a simple "rich man, poor man" parable. The root of the injustice in the story is economic, as is so often the case in real life. Exploitation of the vulnerable is a constant temptation; the weak are an easy target. Such exploitation can also take many forms—outright theft or deceit, as was the case with David; or, perhaps more commonly and subtly, willful or even unintended neglect of one's duty to the needy.

It is no accident that the word for "charity" in Hebrew, *tzedakah*, shares the same root with the word for "justice," *tzedek*, and that both convey the biblical idea of righteousness. *Tzedakah* may be better translated as "economic justice," rather than "charity," in the sense that it is considered obligatory. While the Bible does mention instances of discretionary giving when the heart so moves you, the numerous biblical laws of justice and compassion that address other human beings, and especially those concerning the poor, do not fall into this category. Contrary to the popular bumper sticker, "Practice random acts of kindness," Judaism might retort, "Observe regular acts of justice."

The commandments that spell out righteous behavior are specific and numerous. Consider how many David broke:

≈ *"You shall not murder."* (Exod. 20:13)
≈ *"You shall not commit adultery."* (Exod. 20:13)
≈ *"You shall not steal."* (Exod. 20:13)
≈ *"You shall not bear false witness against your neighbor."* (Exod. 20:13)
≈ *"You shall not covet . . . your neighbor's wife."* (Exod. 20:14)

While David's story is a stern warning about leaders' propensity toward heightened abuses, the prophets remind us that it is also a cautionary tale for us all. Our tradition speaks of two ways we fail to live up to our responsibilities: sins of commission and sins of omission. At times we do wrong; at other times we don't do enough right. The path of righteousness is both the avoidance of evil and the embrace of good. The prophets demand that we examine the negative commandments that we have broken and the positive commandments we have neglected.

The prophets also ask our agrarian ancestors if they have lived up to the covenant in terms they could understand: Have you left the corners of your field for the poor? Have you tithed properly? Have you paid an honest and timely wage? Have you set up courts of law and judged fairly? Have you lived up to your family obligations?

We may not be farmers, but the same questions apply to us. We may not have sinned on David's scale, but Nathan's parable and declaration that *"You are the man!"* demand that we question whether we are as righteous as we may think. To what extent are we complicit in the injustices around us? To what extent are we less than philanthropic than we give ourselves credit for?

The contemporary storyteller Noah benShea offers a provocative parable that relates to Nathan's:

> *A rich man came to Jacob and sought his advice. Why must I give to the poor?*
>
> *Because they are responsible for your freedom, said Jacob.*
>
> *The man was astonished. How does giving to the poor bring about my freedom?*
>
> *You see, said Jacob, either the key to a man's wallet is in his heart, or the key to a man's heart is in his wallet. So, until you express your charity, you are locked inside your greed.*

Are we essentially ruled by an impulse toward the just and the generous? Or are we controlled by other ego-driven impulses, or worse? As the children of Abraham, the *"just and the right"* is the challenge before us.

PART 2

To Love Mercy

7

Judah's Step Forward

THE PATH OF REPENTANCE

I Am Judah

I am the fourth and last-born child of Jacob and Leah. My mother felt unloved by my father; that is no secret. But by the time she had me I think she had reconciled herself to her fate, for my name means "thanks." Either that or maybe my father had shown her some of the care and affection she deserved.

Joseph was my half-brother by my father's beloved Rachel. When he was but seventeen, my other brothers, wild men, cast him in a pit, intending to let him die there. As we sat eating, a caravan of Ishmaelites came through on their way to Egypt. I said to my brothers, "What do we gain by killing our brother and covering up his blood? Come let us sell him to the Ishmaelites, but let us not do away with him ourselves. After all, he is our brother, our own flesh." So we sold him . . . and we did not see Joseph again for twenty years.

Meanwhile my life took a tragic turn, terrible and prolonged. I married a Canaanite woman named Shua, and we had three sons. My firstborn, Er, married a girl named Tamar, and died without an heir. As is the law, I gave my second-born, Onan, to her, so his brother's name could be perpetuated. But Onan died too, with Tamar still childless. I told Tamar to wait until my third son, Shelah, grew up. But when he was grown, I never gave him to Tamar. I was afraid she was bad luck and he too would die.

After my wife died and I finished the period of mourning, I went up to the sheep shearing in Timnah, and there I slept with a woman I thought was a prostitute. As a pledge for payment I left my seal, cord, and staff with her. Sometime later I was told that Tamar was pregnant. I was outraged and humiliated; she was not married. I ordered her burned, but as she was being brought out, she produced my seal and cord and staff! I knew right away that Tamar was right and I was wrong. I had withheld Shelah from her. I had done wrong, and Tamar had set it right. The Lord saw fit to give her a baby through me—two actually—she had twins!

I had made three great mistakes in my life: selling Joseph into slavery (even though I saved his life), lying about it to my father, and wronging Tamar. So years later, when the famine came and my brothers and I were in Egypt pleading for food, and the viceroy of Egypt wanted to take our youngest brother Benjamin away, I knew I must speak up at all costs. I had promised my father that no harm would come to little Benjamin. I could not let tragedy strike our family again. I had to tell the truth.

I stepped forward and poured out my heart to the Egyptian.

Judah's Step Forward: From the Bible

Judah's betrayal of Joseph (Gen. 37:25–28):

> [25]*Then they sat down to a meal. Looking up, they saw a caravan of Ishmaelites coming from Gilead, their camels bearing gum, balm, and ladanum to be taken to Egypt.* [26]*Then Judah said to his brothers, "What do we gain by killing our brother and covering up his blood?* [27]*Come, let us sell him to the Ishmaelites, but let us not do away with him ourselves. After all, he is our brother, our own flesh." His brothers agreed.* [28]*When Midianite traders passed by, they pulled Joseph up out of the pit. They sold Joseph for twenty pieces of silver to the Ishmaelites, who brought Joseph to Egypt.*

Judah's confession to Tamar (Gen. 38:24–26):

> [24]*About three months later, Judah was told, "Your daughter-in-law Tamar has played the harlot; in fact, she is with child by harlotry." "Bring her out," said Judah, "and let her be burned."* [25]*As she was being brought out, she sent this message to her father-in-law, "I am with child by the man to whom these belong." And she added, "Examine these: whose seal and cord and staff are these?"* [26]*Judah recognized them, and said, "She is more in the right than I, inasmuch as I did not give her to my son Shelah." And he was not intimate with her again.*

Judah's promise to Jacob (Gen. 43:8–10):

> [8]*Then Judah said to his father Israel, "Send the boy in my care, and let us be on our way, that we may live and not die—you and we and our children.* [9]*I myself will be surety for him; you may hold me responsible: if I do not bring him back to you and set him before you, I shall stand guilty before you forever.* [10]*For we could have been there and back twice if we had not dawdled."*

Judah's plea to Joseph (Gen. 44:18–34):

> [18]*Then Judah went up to him and said, "Please, my lord, let your servant appeal to my lord, and do not be impatient with your servant, you who are the equal of Pharaoh.* [19]*My lord asked his servants, 'Have you a father or another brother?'* [20]*We told my lord, 'We have an old father, and there is a child of his old age, the youngest; his full brother is dead, so that he alone is left of his mother, and his father dotes on him.'* [21]*Then you said to your servants, 'Bring him down to me, that I may set eyes on him.'* [22]*We said to my lord, 'The boy cannot leave his father; if he were to leave him, his father would die.'* [23]*But you said to your servants, 'Unless your youngest brother comes down with you, do not let me see your faces.'* [24]*When we came back to your servant my father, we reported my lord's words to him.*
>
> [25]*"Later our father said, 'Go back and procure some food for us.'* [26]*We answered, 'We cannot go down; only if our youngest brother is with us can we go down, for we may not show our faces to the man unless our youngest brother is with us.'* [27]*Your servant my father said to us, 'As you know, my wife bore me two sons.* [28]*But one is gone from me, and I said: Alas, he was torn by a beast! And I have not seen him since.* [29]*If you take this one from me, too, and he meets with disaster, you will send my white head down to Sheol in sorrow.'*
>
> [30]*"Now, if I come to your servant my father and the boy is not with us—since his own life is so bound up with his—*[31]*when he sees that the boy is not with us, he will die, and your servants will send the white head of your servant our father down to Sheol in grief.* [32]*Now your servant has pledged himself for the boy to my father, saying, 'If I do not bring him back to you, I shall stand guilty before my father forever.'* [33]*Therefore, please let your servant remain as a slave to my lord instead of the boy, and let the boy go back with his brothers.* [34]*For how can I go back to my father unless the boy is with me? Let me not be witness to the woe that would overtake my father!"*

Judah's Step Forward: The Prophetic Moment

Then Judah stepped forward and said . . . For how can I go back to my father unless the boy is with me? Let me not be witness to woe that would overtake my father! (Gen. 44:18, 34)

Judah is one of the unsung heroes of Genesis. He achieves this status largely because of his self-transformation. He has the ability and willingness to recognize his mistakes and take responsibility for his actions. All of this leads to his shining moment.

By devoting special attention to Judah's travails, the Torah teaches that Judah's leadership did not come out of nowhere. It is the result of painful lessons and a sharp learning curve with far-ranging consequences.

Judah is the fourth-born son of Jacob and Leah. We first meet him when he convinces his brothers to sell their loathed younger sibling, Joseph, rather than kill him. "*What do we gain by killing our brother and covering up his blood . . . after all, he is our brother, our own flesh*" (Gen. 37:26–27). Judah must be credited with saving Joseph's life (although Reuven also tries to steer his brothers away from their murderous intent). Judah has witnessed the violent nature of his siblings when they slaughtered the men of Shechem after their sister Dinah was raped. He may have participated in the killing and plunder. Now he sees their violent nature turning against one of their own: their younger brother. He regrets what is unfolding . . . and he intervenes. It is doubtful, however, that Judah walks away with a clear conscience. Judah colludes not only in selling Joseph into slavery but in lying about it to their father.

The Book of Genesis then interrupts the tale of Joseph to give us an entire chapter devoted to an often-forgotten episode in Judah's life. Tragedy again strikes Judah (his sister was raped, his brother sold into slavery) when Er, his firstborn son, dies, followed not long after by Onan, his second-born. By custom, Judah gives Tamar, the wife of Er, to Onan to provide offspring. But when the younger sibling meets the same fate as the older, Judah takes this—and Tamar herself—as a sign of bad luck. Perhaps understandably from a father's protective point of view, he withholds Tamar from his third and last son, Shelah, sheltering him from the perceived dangers of fraternal duty.

Bereft of husband and children, Tamar disguises herself as a prostitute and sleeps with Judah. When Judah learns about her pregnancy he is outraged. He is ready to kill his daughter-in-law because of the dishonor she has brought as an unmarried widow... until he is confronted with the evidence that he is the father. Then Judah immediately recognizes his wrongdoing, admitting *"she is more right than I"* (Gen. 38:26).

Judah's true prophetic moment comes two decades later, when he approaches the Egyptian who, unbeknownst to him, is really his long-lost brother. The way Judah bares his soul about his responsibilities to his youngest brother Benjamin and to his aged father—amidst an undercurrent of regret for what he has done to Joseph—moves Joseph to tears.

Judah's step forward opens the path to this family's reconciliation.

Notably, Judah is the first exemplar of repentance in the Torah. (While it is true that Jacob affects a degree of reconciliation with his brother Esau, it is not clear that he admits wrongdoing and seeks forgiveness.). Judah's transformation is clearly bound up in compassion—for a father and a brother, and earlier, for a daughter-in-law.

The tribe of Judah will go on to play a pivotal role in Israelite history. From Judah's line David will be born, and the Davidic dynasty will rule Israel for nearly five hundred years. Judah is the forerunner of kings. These kings, like their progenitor, will be punished for their misdeeds and rewarded for their repentance. Such is the worldview of the biblical writer and a provocative thesis for us to consider.

Walking with Judah: The Path of Repentance

"To err is human," Alexander Pope reminds us. Upon reflection, this is not surprising. From Adam to Judah, Genesis reveals how deeply embedded our human flaws are. We are told, *"Sin crouches at the door . . . yet you can be its master"* (Gen. 4:7). The Torah testifies to our power to abstain from wrong, but we often fail. Even the great King David, the Lord's anointed, sinned grievously (see chapter 6). Time and again the prophets emphasize that we need a way to return to the right path—one that restores our relationship with God and with each other. Repentance is that way of return and restoration.

The Bible never uses the word "repentance" (*teshuva*) to describe Judah's actions; in fact, the root word (*shav*) does not appear until Deuteronomy. Yet Judah's confessions of wrongdoing exemplify this doctrine that is introduced later in the Torah and expanded upon in the Prophets. In Moses' first oration to the Israelites, he urges them to *"return to the Lord your God"* after having forsaken God *"when you are in distress"* (Deut. 4:30). Moses returns to the same theme in his final oration: *"When all these things befall you . . . and you return to the Lord your God . . . then [I] will restore your fortunes and take you back in love"* (Deut. 30:1–3).

How are we to understand the implications of *shav*, literally "turning around" or "returning"? The noted biblical scholar Jeffrey Tigay writes, "The Hebrew term does not refer only to contrition but to a change of behavior . . . something that occurs after punishment has taken place. The prophets called upon the people to repent before it is too late, and to thereby avert punishment altogether." Another esteemed scholar, Jacob Milgrom, makes a similar point: "This root combines in itself both requisites of repentance: to turn from evil and to turn to good. The motion of turning implies that sin is not an eradicable stain but a straying from the right path and that by the effort of turning, a power God has given all men, the sinner can redirect his destiny."

Of the many prophets who follow Judah's legacy, it is Jeremiah above all who stresses the need to repent. His repeated refrain, "Return, O Israel," echoes through his prophecies:

≈ *"If you return, O Israel—declares the Lord—If you return to Me; if you remove your abominations from My presence and do not waver, and swear, 'As the Lord lives,' in sincerity, justice, and righteousness—nations shall bless themselves by you." (Jer. 4:1–2)*

≈ *"Turn back . . . only recognize your sin; for you have transgressed against the Lord . . . turn back." (Jer. 3:12–14)*

≈ *"Mend your ways and your actions, and I will let you dwell in this place. . . . if you really mend your ways and your actions; if you execute justice between one man and another; if you do not oppress the stranger, the orphan, and the widow; if you do not shed the blood of the innocent in this place; if you do not follow other gods, to your own hurt—then only will I let you dwell in this place, in the land that I gave to your fathers for all time." (Jer. 7:3–7)*

Note how Jeremiah frames repentance: as a return to the true terms of the covenant through acknowledgment of sin and its replacement by right behavior.

In a later passage, Jeremiah employs a vivid artistic metaphor to convey God's involvement with the creation of humanity and the influence repentance can have on the divine will. After visiting a potter, Jeremiah likens God to a potter shaping clay upon a wheel, for the potter can build up or tear down his creation at any time: *"At one moment I may decree that a nation or a kingdom shall be uprooted and pulled down and destroyed; but if that nation against which I made the decree turns back from its wickedness, I change My mind concerning the punishment I planned to bring on it"* (Jer. 18:7–8). The power of repentance lies not only in its ability to change the sinner but the one sinned against.

Rabbinic Judaism continued the intense focus on repentance but shifted its emphasis from the communal to the individual. Among the numerous Talmudic teachings on this theme is "One hour of repentance and good deeds in this world is more beautiful than all the life in the world to come." In another teaching, Rabbi Eliezer instructs, "Repent one day before your death." His disciples ask, "But does a person know what day he [or she] is going to die?" Rabbi Eliezer replies, "All the more reason therefore to repent today, lest one die tomorrow."

During the Rabbinic period in the early centuries of the Common Era, Yom Kippur, the Day of Repentance, grew in stature to the holiest day of the year. Much of its liturgy, rendered in the first-person plural, emphasizes both the personal and collective need to repent of our sins: "*Al het shehatanu* . . . For the sins that we have committed." The list of sins is long and specific, including a half-dozen ways we err through our words alone. A special section called *Vidui* (confession) also contains an acrostic of sins using every letter of the alphabet. The form may be stylized, but the point is serious: We are all guilty of sins, whether sins of commission or sins of omission, or both.

The prayer book incorporates an important teaching from the Mishnah often recited before the *Kol Nidrei*, the prayer that seeks forgiveness for vows we are unable to fulfill. "For transgressions against God, the Day of Atonement atones; but for transgressions of one human being against another, the Day of Atonement does not atone until they have made peace with one another." Prayer is helpful in orienting a person toward the soul-searching that is a necessary prelude to repentance, but it is no substitute for the hard work of repairing a relationship with one who has been wronged. Ritual transgressions may be righted by the rites of repentance; ethical transgressions require apology and action.

The same High Holiday liturgy contains a crucial verse after the famous "Who shall live; who shall die" section that speaks of repentance as one of the three means (along with prayer and charity) of "tempering the severe decree." While God's judgment is being referred to here, repentance may also induce human forgiveness as well.

These transformations are external, following as a consequence of a prior, internal change. "Who is a hero?" asks the Mishnah. "The one who overcomes his evil inclination," is the reply. It is an echo of the well-known verse from Genesis: *"Sin crouches at the door; its urge is toward you, yet you can be its master"* (Gen. 4:7).

Even earlier in Genesis we are taught that the distinguishing characteristic of human beings is the ability to distinguish right from wrong. *"But God knows that as soon as you eat of it your eyes will be opened and you will be like God, who knows good and bad"* (Gen. 3:5). Soon after, God repeats the statement before exiling Adam and Eve. *"Now that the man has become like one of us [k'echad memenu], knowing good and bad"* (Gen. 3:22). Maimonides adroitly notes that the Hebrew phrase "like one of us" can also mean "from within himself." He likewise comments that "one" can mean "unique" and that "Adam" can mean "person." And so, with a slight change of punctuation and translation, Maimonides renders the verse, "Now each person is unique—from within himself he knows right from wrong." With this unique knowledge we can choose repentance; a quintessentially human act.

Given this understanding, it makes sense that the sages chose the Book of Jonah to be read on Yom Kippur afternoon. After all, the book contains a remarkable example of repentance, by the "enemy" no less. The people of Nineveh are the Assyrians, who will go on to destroy the Northern Kingdom of Israel and nearly conquer the Southern Kingdom of Judah as well. Jonah is commanded to proclaim judgment upon them, *"for their wickedness has come before me"* (Jon. 1:2). But the book also describes how the people of Nineveh heeded Jonah's warning—fasting, putting on sackcloth and ashes, crying out to God. The king himself even prays, *"Let everyone turn back from his evil ways and from the injustice of which he is guilty."* The repentance has its desired effect: *"God saw what they did, how they were turning back from their evil ways. And God renounced the punishment He had planned to bring upon them, and did not carry it out"* (Jon. 3:8–10).

How are we to achieve true repentance? Saadia Gaon, one of the first systematic Jewish theologians, wrote of "four steps to repentance: confession, remorse, asking forgiveness/repairing damage, and accepting responsibility to never repeat the sin." He likely influenced Maimonides, the best-known medieval philosopher, whose teaching on the subject is popularly summarized as the three "Rs" of repentance: remorse, restitution, resolve.

Both thinkers stress that repentance begins with a true feeling of remorse that prompts a verbal confession. Words, however, are not enough. Real action must be taken to right the wrong, or at least to compensate the aggrieved as much as possible. The final stage of complete repentance is the resolve never to do it again. Maimonides teaches that one can never be sure of such resolve until one is faced with the same situation and successfully resists the temptation to sin again.

In his "Laws of Repentance," Maimonides specifies some of the ways to achieve repentance: "Among the paths of repentance is for the penitent to: a) constantly call out before God, crying and entreating; b) perform charity according to his potential; c) separate himself far from the object of his sin; d) change his name, as if to say, I am a different person and not the same one who sinned; e) change his behavior in its entirety to the good and the path of righteousness; f) travel in exile from his home. Exile atones for sin because it causes a person to be submissive, humble and meek of spirit."

Rabbi and best-selling author Joseph Telushkin recalls seeing a cartoon that showed a father examining his son's report card, which was filled with Ds and Fs. As the father scowled, the boy asked: "What do you think it is, Dad, heredity or environment?" Telushkin comments, "Judaism insists on a third factor that influences human behavior: the soul." The moral discernment and free will that are part of our uniquely human souls make us accountable. At the same time, like Judah's step forward, the freedom to make moral choices can also make the experience of repentance truly transformational. The path of repentance is always before us—and we have the power to pursue it.

8

Joseph's Cry

THE PATH OF FORGIVENESS

I Am Joseph

When I was seventeen my father Jacob gave me a coat of many colors. It was as beautiful as the rainbow. I wore that coat everywhere. After that my brothers could barely exchange a civil word with me.

I had a dream, and I told it to my brothers: "We were binding sheaves of wheat in the field, when suddenly my sheaf stood up and your sheaves bowed down." My brothers growled, "Do you mean to reign over us? Do you mean to be our ruler?"

I had another dream, and I again told it to my brothers: "I saw the sun and the moon and eleven stars and they all bowed down to me." This time, even my father got angry. He retorted, "Are we to come, your mother and your brothers and I, and bow to you?"

Not long after that, my brothers sold me into slavery in Egypt. I ended up in prison along with the king of Egypt's butler and baker. The butler told us his dream: Three branches of grape blossoms had ripened into grapes. I interpreted that in three days he would once again be pouring wine for Pharaoh . . . and it came to pass. Then the baker told me his dream: Birds were eating three baskets of food. I interpreted that in three days Pharaoh would sentence him to death . . . and it came to pass.

After that, Pharaoh had two dreams. During the first night, seven fat cows were eaten by seven thin cows, and the next night, seven full ears of grain were swallowed up by seven lean ears of grain. No one in the kingdom could interpret the dream. It was then that the butler remembered that both my dream interpretations had come true and brought me to Pharaoh.

I said to the king, "God has sent you the dream; God is sending you a message. Seven years of plenty shall be followed by seven years of famine." I further told Pharaoh that he would do well to find a man of discernment and wisdom to prepare the country for the coming famine . . . hoping he would choose me.

The king indeed recognized my gifts and appointed me his viceroy. Can you believe that he actually said to his courtiers, "Can we find another like him, a man in whom is the spirit of God"? I became the second-most powerful man in all the land. I made sure to properly gather and store grain during the years of plenty and to ration wisely during the years of famine. When the crops failed there was hunger throughout the lands, but here in Egypt we had bread. Every day, starving people would approach me for food.

One day a group of Hebrews from Canaan came begging—and when I looked up, I saw my brothers! I wiped my eyes; this was no dream. My heart went cold, and I accused them of being spies. I gave them food, and I sent them home, but not before demanding that the one brother who was not with them be brought to me: the youngest; my full brother, Benjamin. I had to see him again; he was but an infant when I had left. So I commanded that Simeon be kept hostage until Benjamin be brought from Canaan to see me.

When I finally saw my little brother Benjamin, my heart started to soften.

Yet I needed to further test my brothers. I contrived to have Benjamin framed for theft.

That is when my brother Judah came forward and everything changed. He spoke about what my brothers had done to me. He told me about the anguish this had caused our father, and how the brothers could not see him suffer the loss of another son. And so, Judah offered to take Benjamin's place in captivity.

By this point I could no longer contain my emotions. I ordered all my attendants to leave the room, and I began sobbing. I cried out to my bothers: "I am Joseph."

In the hours, days, and months that followed I told my dumbfounded brothers over and over what I truly believed. "It was to save life that God sent me ahead of you. God used me to insure our survival. You intended me harm; God intended it for good." I reassured my brothers that they had nothing to fear. I told them we would live again as a family. I told them, "I am Joseph, your brother."

Joseph's Cry: From the Bible

Joseph forgives his brothers (Gen. 45:1–8):

[1]Joseph could no longer control himself before all his attendants, and he cried out, "Have everyone withdraw from me!" So there was no one else about when Joseph made himself known to his brothers. [2]His sobs were so loud that the Egyptians could hear, and so the news reached Pharaoh's palace.

[3]Joseph said to his brothers, "I am Joseph. Is my father still well?" But his brothers could not answer him, so dumfounded were they on account of him.

[4]Then Joseph said to his brothers, "Come forward to me." And when they came forward, he said, "I am your brother Joseph, he whom you sold into Egypt. [5]Now, do not be distressed or reproach yourselves because you sold me hither; it was to save life that God sent me ahead of you. [6]It is now two years that there has been famine in the land, and there are still five years to come in which there shall be no yield from tilling. [7]God has sent me ahead of you to ensure your survival on earth, and to save your lives in an extraordinary deliverance. [8]So, it was not you who sent me here, but God; and He has made me a father to Pharaoh, lord of all his household, and ruler over the whole land of Egypt.

Joseph reiterates his promise (Gen. 50:15–21):

[15]When Joseph's brothers saw that their father was dead, they said, "What if Joseph still bears a grudge against us and pays us back for all the wrong that we did him!" [16]So they sent this message to Joseph, "Before his death your father left this instruction: [17]So shall you say to Joseph, 'Forgive, I urge you, the offense and guilt of your brothers who treated you so harshly.' Therefore, please forgive the offense of the servants of the God of your father." And Joseph was in tears as they spoke to him.

[18]His brothers went to him themselves, flung themselves before him, and said, "We are prepared to be your slaves." [19]But Joseph said to them, "Have no fear! Am I a substitute for God? [20]Besides, although you intended me harm, God intended it for good, so as to bring about the present result—the survival of many people. [21]And so, fear not. I will sustain you and your children." Thus he reassured them, speaking kindly to them.

Joseph's Cry: The Prophetic Moment

Now, do not be distressed or reproach yourselves because you sold me hither; it was to save life that God sent me ahead of you. (Gen. 45:5)

Joseph's cry is among the most dramatic scenes in the Bible. From the beginning of Genesis there is palpable tension between siblings—Cain and Abel, Ishmael and Isaac, Jacob and Esau, and now Joseph and his brothers. Since Joseph's brothers sell him into slavery, one might think that, here, forgiveness and reconciliation would never be possible.

When circumstances conspire to bring Joseph and his brothers back together, Joseph's old feelings of bitterness and resentment resurface. He conceals his identity and puts his brothers to a test. In time, Judah demonstrates that the brothers are genuinely sorry for the tragedy they caused—stirring Joseph's heart. He is ready to reveal who he is, to pardon the past, and to reconcile with his family.

Joseph is a hero, a child of the prophets, because he embodies the value of *selicha*, "forgiveness." This is the first explicit instance of repentance and forgiveness in the Torah (Jacob's meeting with his brother Esau comes close—but does Jacob actually repent?). When Judah expresses remorse, Joseph is able to hear and accept it.

Joseph ultimately "sees past his past" and "lets bygones be bygones" because of his willingness to understand what happened to him in a larger context. At some point Joseph becomes convinced that his fall and rise, his suffering and triumph, is God's plan. Having said as much when he first reveals himself to his brothers, Joseph repeats it moments later: *"God has sent me ahead of you to insure your survival on earth, and to save your lives in an extraordinary deliverance. So, it was not you who sent me here, but God"* (Gen. 45:7–8).

Much later, when Jacob dies, Joseph perceives that his brothers still doubt his forgiveness. Worried about how Joseph will react to news of their father's death, and hoping to protect themselves, they say to him: *"Before his death your father left this instruction: So shall you say to Joseph, 'Forgive, I urge you, the offense and guilt of your brothers for treating you so harshly.' Therefore, please forgive the offense of the servants of the God of your father"* (Gen. 50:16–18). The Torah gives us no indication that Jacob actually left these instructions.

More importantly, Joseph plaintively responds by again emphasizing the big picture: *"Have no fear! Am I a substitute for God? Besides, although you intended me harm, God intended it for good. . . . And so, fear not. I will sustain you and your children"* (Gen. 50:19–21). Leaving no doubt of Joseph's sincerity, the Torah concludes: *"He reassured them, speaking kindly to them"* (Gen. 50:21).

That said, some biblical commentators do share the brothers' doubt of Joseph. A close reading of the text might also suggest that while Joseph is able to move beyond recrimination and revenge, his theological understanding of all that transpired leaves actual forgiveness up to God. Each of the three times Joseph placates his brothers, he emphasizes that everything was God's plan. Joseph never explicitly says, "I forgive you." Perhaps he simply suspended judgment about his brothers.

If in fact he did hold back, does this constitute stopping short of forgiveness, or is this the first step of forgiveness?

Twice, in consecutive sentences (Gen. 50:17), when the brothers speak to Joseph they use the expression *sa na.* Literally, the Hebrew word means "lift up" or "bear" the offense, though it has been simply and widely translated as "forgive." The choice of a colloquial expression for forgiveness conveys the metaphorical sense that the brothers are asking for their burden to be lifted.

This Joseph seems able and ready to do. He tries to allay their concern and bear the (both weighty and liberating) burden of forgiveness, even if full reconciliation with his brothers is somewhat more complicated and elusive.

The Rabbinic literature refers to Joseph as *Yosef Hatzadik*, "Joseph, the righteous one." In its original context, the sages seem to be referring to Joseph's sexual restraint with Potiphar's wife, but the case can also be made for his capacity for forgiveness and faith.

While it is true that Joseph let many years go by without contacting his family (as the powerful Egyptian viceroy he had the means to do so) and possibly would never have "phoned home" had his brothers not come to Egypt out of desperation, nonetheless, when the family reunites, Joseph summons the will and faith to move from fury to forgiveness.

Still, a sophisticated view of the Joseph story admits another troubling complexity. From his youthful arrogance to his adult prominence, Joseph is not without his flaws. Joseph's prophetic quality of taking the moral high ground in his personal life does not prevent him from taking a morally questionable course in his professional life. As modern commentators especially have pointed out, Joseph saves the Egyptian people, but also enslaves them ("saving and enslaving" in the words of biblical scholar Jon D. Levenson). Through his wisdom and planning Joseph averts starvation and gives the people bread (Gen. 47:15). Yet at the same time he is serving Pharaoh, and he demands their horses and flocks (47:16–17). Eventually Joseph takes the people's land and freedom 47:18–25), rendering them as serfs.

The Torah does not criticize Joseph for his actions; it simply reports what transpired. The text does indicate that Joseph did not so act for his personal gain, but for Pharaoh's. Joseph may not have had a choice in the matter; after all, he was in the service of the king. Alternatively, Joseph may have responded as he did in the belief that it was the only way to save the people. In any event, there is a double irony here: The one who was enslaved becomes the enslaver. And Joseph's enslavement of the Egyptians will eventually come back to haunt the Israelites when the Egyptians turn against Joseph's descendants and make them slaves.

Joseph's prophetic moment enables the Book of Genesis to end on a high note of family reconciliation, or at least a reunification and peaceful coexistence—that has otherwise remained elusive through the history of warring brothers Cain and Abel, Isaac and Ishmael, Jacob and Esau. Yet the book's final words hint at gathering storm clouds in the otherwise sunny sky. The Torah reports that Joseph and his family "remained in Egypt," yet the sojourn was supposed to be temporary—and living in the foreign realm of Egypt rather than returning home is fraught with danger. Joseph lives to see the third generation of his sons, but consider his parting words: *"I am about to die. God will surely take notice of you and bring you up from this land. . . . When God has taken notice of you, you shall carry up my bones from here"* (Gen. 50:22–25). Joseph intimates that something bad will happen and that God will take notice. He understands that his true resting place should be Israel and that one day his bones will be moved. The last sentence of Genesis relates that when Joseph dies he is embalmed and placed in a coffin in Egypt. Unlike his father, he is not buried in the Jewish way. Nor does he join his father, grandfather, and great-grandfather within their ancestral plot in Israel.

Moreover, four hundred years of slavery will ensue. A Pharaoh will arise *"who knew not Joseph"* (Exod.1:8). He sees the Israelites as a demographic threat to Egypt and plots their subjugation. Joseph's triumph is prelude to tragedy.

Even though Joseph's forgiveness cannot avert future tragedy, his prophetic moment of compassion endures in the memory of the people. It is possible that this memory adds to the character of a people that will emerge from a clan. Just perhaps, Joseph's story will help a fractured family to evolve into a people that can withstand the calamity to come—and remain spiritually intact enough to embrace freedom when it arrives.

Walking with Joseph: The Path of Forgiveness

A careful reading of Joseph's story reveals that forgiveness is neither automatic nor easy. It is a long process. Joseph's change of heart does not happen upon his first re-encounter with his brothers. He is not willing to reveal his identity. He puts his brothers to a test. It is only after Judah steps forward and demonstrates repentance—and in the process reminds Joseph that he can reunite with his long-lost family that includes his father and little brother—does his heart open up.

Note that while on the path to forgiveness, Joseph does not forget what had happened. In fact, Joseph is not above reminding his brothers of their past actions on several occasions. When he first reveals himself, he says, *"I am your brother Joseph, he whom you sold into Egypt"* (Gen. 45:4). In the next sentence, he says, *"Now, do not be distressed or reproach yourselves because you sold me"* (Gen. 45:5). Later he says: *"for you intended me harm"* (Gen. 50:20). Joseph does not forget what happened. Rather, he offers a new interpretation of the experience that frees the family from the awful burden of the past.

Joseph also needs to see that his brothers understand the consequences of their actions and are remorseful. He needs proof of their repentance. In other words, his forgiveness is conditional. In this way, the story offers a realistic perspective that the process of forgiveness often begins with a perpetrator's expression of remorse. Today, juries and judges tend to temper punishments when the wrongdoer demonstrates some degree of regret.

Moreover, Joseph needs to find room in his heart to forgive. He is able to do so by attributing greater purpose to his suffering.

When it comes to our own forgiveness, some of us, like Joseph, may be able to enlarge our vantage point and understanding of the circumstances out of faith in a divine plan. Others, however, may simply desire to be liberated from the rancor and estrangement that can imprison us or stunt our growth. In his autobiography, Bill Clinton tells the story that when he was governor of Arkansas, he propped up his young daughter Chelsea in front of the kitchen

TV to watch Nelson Mandela's historic release from prison. Later, president-to-president, Clinton asked Mandela how he was able to forgive his captors after so many years in prison. Mandela replied, "I wanted to be free, so I let it go." Nelson Mandela had won his physical freedom, but to win his emotional freedom he knew he would have to forgive.

A parable from the Zen Buddhist tradition also speaks to the liberating power of forgiveness:

Two monks on a pilgrimage come to the ford of a river. There they see a girl dressed in all her finery who doesn't know what to do, for the river is high and her clothes may be spoilt. Without much ado, one of the monks takes her on his back, carries her across, and puts her on dry ground. Then the monks continue on their way. The other monk is pensive. "What is on your mind?" the first monk asks. The second speaks up. "Surely it is not right to touch a woman. It is against the commandment not to have close contact with a woman." He continues, "How can you go against the rules? You have sinned." The monk who carried the girl replies, "I set her down by the river, but you are still carrying her."

Another story, from the Persian tradition:

Two fast friends named Nagib and Moussa are travelling through the dangerous mountains of Persia. One day Moussa loses his footing and falls into a swirling river—and just in time Nagib leaps in and saves him. The grateful Moussa carves these words into a nearby rock: "Wanderer! In this place Nagib saved the life of his friend Moussa." Months later the two friends get into a violent quarrel. Nagib slaps Moussa across the face. The pained Moussa takes a stick and writes these words in the nearby sand: "Wanderer! In this place Nagib broke the heart of his friend Moussa." When one of Moussa's companions asks why he did this, Moussa replies, "I will remember the courage of my friend in stone, and his unkindness in sand."

Alexander Pope famously said, "To err is human; to forgive, divine." Indeed, the Bible provides a vivid example of God's forgiveness. In the Book of Jonah, forgiveness comes to a people with a very bad history (the Assyrians) because of their apparently genuine repentance. *"God saw what they did, how they were turning back from their evil ways. And God renounced the punishment He had planned to bring upon them, and did not carry it out"* (Jon. 3:5–10). Isaiah explains that while God punishes (which helps explain the calamities of the Jewish people), God forgives by not forsaking the people despite their sins. He expresses this ethic of forgiveness best when he declares in God's name: *"For a little while I forsook, but with vast love I will bring you back. In slight anger, for a moment, I hid my face from you. But with kindness everlasting I will take you back in love—said the Lord your redeemer"* (Isa. 54:7–8).

But sometimes even God has a hard time forgiving, at least according to the Torah. When the Israelites are in the desert, for example, God threatens to wipe out the people for rebelling against Moses. It is not until Moses pleads for his own people—*"Forgive, I pray, the iniquity of this people according to Your great kindness, as You have forgiven this people ever since Egypt"*—that God says *"I forgive, as you have asked"* (Num. 14: 19). (Notably, during the Yom Kippur evening service, these words follow the recitation of the *Kol Nidrei* prayer, which itself is a plea for forgiveness for unkept vows.)

Frequently overlooked, however, is the biblical text's continuation with a verse that complicates God's forgiveness. *"Nevertheless . . . none of the men who . . . disobeyed Me shall see the land that I promised on oath to their fathers; none of those who spurn Me shall see it"* (Num. 14:21–23). As biblical scholar Jacob Milgrom points out, "The Hebrew *salach* [here meaning pardon] implies not the absolution of sin but the suspension of anger." In other words, the Israelites' transgressions are neither forgotten nor absolved. There will be consequences for their actions. God has forgiven to the extent that the Israelites will not die immediately, or completely. The Exodus generation will be allowed to live long enough to raise their children. These children, rather than their parents (with the exception of Joshua and Caleb), will be the ones to enter the Promised Land.

This nuanced situation highlights not only the difficulty of granting forgiveness, but the reality that it is often not an all-or-nothing proposition. Forgiveness divorced from accountability is problematic. We want justice served . . . as well as mercy. This dilemma is noted in the masterful medieval commentator Rashi's comment to the very first line of scripture: "At first God intended to create the world by justice alone, but then God realized that the world could not endure and therefore gave precedence to mercy, allying it with justice."

In the Jewish view, forgiveness follows, rather than precedes, repentance or the administration of justice. In this regard it differs from Christian views, which see forgiveness as unconditional.

On June 17, 2015, Dylann Roof massacred nine Bible study participants in a Charleston, South Carolina, church. Within thirty-six hours of the killings, some family members of the fallen spoke of forgiveness during the arraignment in the county courthouse. One daughter, Nadine Collier, said, "I forgive you. You took something very precious away from me. I will never get to talk to her ever again—but I forgive you, and have mercy on your soul. You hurt me. You hurt a lot of people. If God forgives you, I forgive you." Many people were moved by this declaration. "Instead of war, Charleston erupted in grace," *Time* magazine wrote in its cover story, "How Do You Forgive a Murder?" President Obama praised this grace and in his own eulogy broke out into a rendition of "Amazing Grace."

Yet others, including Collier's own family members, objected to what they perceived as a premature or inappropriate expression of forgiveness. The magazine also quoted Rabbi Heschel upholding the view that the crime of murder is unforgivable because the victim is gone, and only the person who has been hurt has the power to forgive. "No one can forgive crimes committed against other people," he wrote. "Even God himself can only forgive sins committed against himself, not against man."

Nonetheless, when considered on the level of the psyche, forgiveness, however challenging, may be necessary for our personal well-being. Echoing Mandela, one of the Charleston survivors who lost her son said, "If you don't [forgive], you're letting evil into your heart. You're the one suffering. You're the one hating. You have to forgive. For you." The husband of another victim said, "When I forgave him, my peace began. I'm done with him. He doesn't have control of me."

A remarkable passage in the Talmud asks, "What does God pray?" The sages would have thought long and hard about the answer, for to imagine the divine mind is no small matter. Finally they reply that God prays, "May it be My will that My compassion overcomes My anger, and that it may prevail over My justice when My children appeal to Me, that I may deal with them in mercy and in love." Here our wise teachers admit that our greatest challenge, and our greatest need, is to find the place of compassion that ennobles us and enables us to be loving and forgiving.

Rabbi Jonathan Sacks beautifully articulates the legacy of repentance that is Judah's and the legacy of forgiveness that is Joseph's. "Repentance establishes the possibility that we are not condemned endlessly to repeat the past," he says. "When I repent I show I can change. The future is not predestined. I can make it different from what it might have been. Forgiveness liberates us from the past. Forgiveness breaks the irreversibility of reaction and revenge. It is the undoing of what has been done. Humanity changed the day Joseph forgave his brothers. When we forgive and are worthy of being forgiven, we are no longer prisoners of our past."

9

Ruth's Vow

THE PATH OF KINDNESS

I Am Ruth

As a Moabite woman I never expected to marry an Israelite man. I never expected that he would die not even ten years later. And I never expected that it would be my mother-in-law, Naomi, who would change my life.

In the country of Moab, where we lived, tragedy was never far from Naomi. It struck the first time when she lost her husband, Elimelech. It struck a second time when she lost a son—my husband, Mahlon. It struck a third time when she lost her other son, Chilion, who was married to Orpah.

Because she was left utterly bereft, is it any wonder that Naomi wanted to go home? Moab to her was cursed; it held no future.

Naomi started on the long road back to Judah. Orpah and I accompanied her. We had grown to love our bereaved mother-in-law. We were three widows: a sisterhood of grief.

One day Naomi turned to us and said, "Turn back, each of you, to your mother's house. May God deal kindly with you, as you have dealt with me. You are young; you will marry again. Find security in the house of a husband."

Orpah and I broke out weeping. We told Naomi we could not leave her; we all had suffered too much together. But she said, "Turn back, my daughters. Why should you go with me? Have I any more sons in my body who might be husbands for you? Turn back, my daughters."

We kept crying, and Naomi kept talking, her voice, and my heart, breaking. "Turn back, my daughters, for I am too old to be married again. Even if I thought there was hope for me, even if I were married tonight, and I also bore sons, should you wait for them to grow up? Should you on their account refrain from marrying? Oh no, my daughters. My lot is bitter, far more than yours. You have a future. I do not. Turn back, for the hand of the Lord has struck out against me."

In tears, Orpah nodded and kissed Naomi farewell. She started down the road. But I clung to Naomi and would not let go.

Naomi said to me, "See, your sister-in-law has returned to her people. Go follow her."

The vow I made right then came pouring out of my heart. "Do not urge me to leave you, to turn back and not follow you. For wherever you go, I will go; wherever you lodge, I will lodge; your people shall be my people, and your God my God. Where you die, I will die, and there I will be buried."

Naomi stood in stunned silence. I too was breathless, my heart thumping in my chest. "Thus and more may the Lord do to me if anything but death parts me from you," I whispered.

Without another word Naomi took my hand and we went on to Bethlehem.

There in Bethlehem the Lord took notice of us. Naomi told me to glean in the fields of Boaz, a kinsman on her husband's side. Boaz spotted me. I told him I was Naomi's daughter-in-law. He knew our story. He was kind to me. He provided for us. I came to him and he took me as a wife.

When I gave birth to a son, the light returned to Naomi's soul. She smiled when the elders prayed for me, "May the Lord make you like Rachel and Leah, both of whom built up the House of Israel." She laughed, yes she laughed, when the town's women whooped in celebration and said to her, "Blessed be the Lord, who has not withheld a redeemer from you today! May his name be perpetuated in Israel! He will renew your life and sustain your old age; for he is born of your daughter-in-law, who loves you and is better to you than seven sons."

Naomi took the baby and held him to her chest. Then she drew me in a tight circle. We were three generations, a family of joy, a promise fulfilled.

Ruth's Vow: From the Bible

Ruth's vow to Naomi (Ruth 1:1–19):

> [1]*In the days when the chieftains ruled, there was a famine in the land; and a man of Bethlehem in Judah, with his wife and two sons, went to reside in the country of Moab.* [2]*The man's name was Elimelech, his wife's name was Naomi, and his two sons were named Mahlon and Chilion—Ephrathites of Bethlehem in Judah. They came to the country of Moab and remained there.*
>
> [3]*Elimelech, Naomi's husband, died; and she was left with her two sons.* [4]*They married Moabite women, one named Orpah and the other Ruth, and they lived there about ten years.* [5]*Then those two—Mahlon and Chilion—also died; so the woman was left without her two sons and without her husband.*
>
> [6]*She started out with her daughters-in-law to return from the country of Moab; for in the country of Moab she had heard that the Lord had taken note of His people and given them food.* [7]*Accompanied by her two daughters-in-law, she left the place where she had been living; and they set out on the road back to the land of Judah.*
>
> [8]*But Naomi said to her two daughters-in-law, "Turn back, each of you to her mother's house. May the Lord deal kindly with you, as you have dealt with the dead and with me!* [9]*May the Lord grant that each of you find security in the house of a husband!" And she kissed them farewell. They broke into weeping* [10]*and said to her, "No, we will return with you to your people."*
>
> [11]*But Naomi replied, "Turn back, my daughters! Why should you go with me? Have I any more sons in my body who might be husbands for you?* [12]*Turn back, my daughters, for I am too old to be married. Even if I thought there was hope for me, even if I were married tonight and I also bore sons,* [13]*should you wait for them to grow up? Should you on their account debar yourselves from marriage? Oh no, my daughters! My lot is far more bitter than yours, for the hand of the Lord has struck out against me."*

[14]They broke into weeping again, and Orpah kissed her mother-in-law farewell. But Ruth clung to her. [15]So she said, "See, your sister-in-law has returned to her people and her gods. Go follow your sister-in-law." [16]But Ruth replied, "Do not urge me to leave you, to turn back and not follow you. For wherever you go, I will go; wherever you lodge, I will lodge; your people shall be my people, and your God my God. [17]Where you die, I will die, and there I will be buried. Thus and more may the Lord do to me if anything but death parts me from you." [18]When [Naomi] saw how determined she was to go with her, she ceased to argue with her; [19]and the two went on until they reached Bethlehem.

Ruth's Vow: The Prophetic Moment

For wherever you go, I will go; wherever you lodge, I will lodge; your people shall be my people and your God my God. Where you die, I will die and there I will be buried. (Ruth 1:16–17)

Ruth's words are among the most beautiful and memorable in all the Bible and literature. And she herself is an extraordinary example of a woman who is willing to forsake her home and homeland for the sake of another whom she has grown to love.

From time immemorial, people have been compelled to leave their homeland. Famine strikes Abraham and Sarah soon after they arrive to Canaan. Jacob and his clan descend to Egypt for the same reason. So do Elimelech and his wife Naomi, who take up residence in neighboring Moab.

After she loses her husband and her two sons, a bereft Naomi, lacking any means of support, is compelled to return to her native Bethlehem of Judah. On the journey, accompanied by her two daughters-in-law, she insists that they remain in their own country, where hopefully they will eventually remarry. One daughter-in-law, Orpah, reluctantly bids Naomi farewell. We expect the other daughter-in-law, Ruth, to do the same—but instead Ruth defies convention and follows her mother-in-law into an unknown world.

Traditionally Ruth has been seen as the first convert to Judaism. For centuries, those making the brave decision to become Jews by choice have repeated her stirring declaration. After all, Ruth not only pledges to follow Naomi, but also to adopt her faith and peoplehood, and indeed Ruth goes on to embrace Naomi's "people" and "God."

Even more broadly, Ruth is a hero. She is a true *eshet hayil*, "woman of valor"—the only woman in the Bible to be so called (in Ruth 3:11) by this distinguished epithet (from Proverbs 31:10).

Why Ruth? Because she embodies the value of *hesed*.

This key word of the Jewish lexicon is variously translated as "love," "kindness," "compassion," "mercy," or "loving-kindness." *Hesed* evokes the loyalty that comes from love and the behavior that emanates from that fealty and compassion toward another. Ruth loves Naomi. She refuses to abandon her. She is willing to change her life for the sake of her love. The ancient sage Rabbi Zeira teaches, "Ruth was written to teach about *hesed* and its rewards." The contemporary scholar Tamara Eskenazi writes: "Ruth delineates a theology of *hesed*—generosity that goes beyond the call of duty."

The word itself appears three times in the Book of Ruth. In the first instance, as Naomi urges her daughters-in-law to turn back from accompanying her on the road back to Judah, she prays that the Lord *"will deal kindly [ya'aseh hesed] with you, as you have dealt with the dead and with me"* (1:8). This verse makes the link that will serve as the leitmotif of the tale: human love manifests God's love. In the words of the late Bible scholar Tikvah Frymer-Kensky, "the characters in the Book of Ruth themselves act to fulfill the blessing that they bestow on one another in God's name."

After Ruth brings her food gleaned from the fields of Boaz, Naomi says to her daughter-in-law, *"Blessed be he of the Lord, who has not failed in His kindness [lo azav hesed] to the living or to the dead"* (2:20). Again we see a link between the *hesed* of people and that of God. Naomi seems to be referring to the kindness of her kinsman Boaz (*"he of the*

Lord"), who has ordered that the "foreign girl" working in his field not be harassed and be given gleanings to take home to her. Then Naomi invokes Boaz's kindness as testimony to divine favor and praises God. She sees God's hand in everything that happens in her life: Here the good is brought about by Boaz's basic compassion, and that in turn emanates from God.

The third use of *hesed* emphasizes the loyalty that is intrinsic to love. When Ruth comes to Boaz at night, seeking his protection and expressing her willingness to marry him, he exclaims, *"Be blessed of the Lord, daughter. Your latest deed of loyalty [hesed] is greater than the first"* (3:10).

The sages deliberate over what precisely constitute Ruth's former acts of "kindness" here. Remember that the word *hesed* does not have an exact English equivalent and has a range of meanings that sometimes point to kindness or loyalty or love.

Is Boaz referring to Ruth's decision to accompany her mother-in-law to Judah? Ruth, like her sister-in-law, could have gone on to rebuild her life in Moab—but she felt so attached to Naomi, she could not bear to be separated. Perhaps she feared for Naomi's well-being as a lonely and aged widow. Perhaps she realized that Naomi had become her closest companion. Perhaps she wanted Naomi to know what was in her heart—a desire to cast her lot with Naomi and her people. Each and all of these motivations convey *hesed.*

Might Boaz be referring to her kindness to Naomi in seeking to glean in his fields?

When Ruth goes to Boaz's field to glean she is demonstrating her loyalty, both by taking the initiative and following her mother-in-law's wish. Ruth proposes, *"I would like to go to the fields and glean."* Naomi responds, *"Yes, my daughter, go"* (2:2).

When she takes the much greater step of pledging herself to Boaz, Ruth not only passes up the opportunity to marry a younger man (as Boaz acknowledges, *"you have not turned to younger men, whether poor or rich"* (3:10), but makes the commitment that any children will be of Naomi's extended family. Indeed, when Ruth gives birth to a son, the Bible goes out of its way to portray it almost as if Naomi has given birth again. We read this remarkable passage: *"And the women said to Naomi, 'Blessed be the Lord, who has not withheld a redeemer from you today! . . . He will renew your life and sustain your old age; for he is born of your daughter-in-law, who loves you and is better to you than seven sons.' Naomi took the child and held it to her bosom. She became its foster mother, and the women neighbors gave him a name, saying, 'A son is born to Naomi!'"* (Ruth 4:14–17).

Boaz's actions also exemplify a variety of commandments that will be codified in the Holiness Code of Leviticus. Ruth's bond with her mother-in-law Naomi embodies reverence of parents, *"You shall each revere his mother and his father"* (Lev. 19:3), and, more broadly, the ethic of respect, *"You shall rise before the aged and show deference to the old"* (Lev. 19:32). Boaz's permission to Ruth to glean in the field, and his protective order instructing his field hands to watch over her, recall the commandment to leave the corners and dropped gleanings *"for the poor and the stranger"* (Lev. 19:10). His concern also reflects the later Torah teaching, *"do not harden your heart and shut your hand against your needy kinsman"* (Deut. 15:7).

Above all, Ruth's actions follow a pattern of love, compassion, kindness, and loyalty that personifies the very definition of *hesed*. The Book of Ruth seems to repeatedly emphasize the rather remarkable notion that, in the words of Eskenazi, "it is almost as if human actions and words bring God into the world. God-centered people prompt God to show up, as it were." In her commentary to Ruth, Eskenazi cites several others who notice the same idea. As the poet and scholar Alicia Ostriker writes, "God's kindness, invoked by human beings, is also by them. To put it another way, the kindness of human beings reveals the kindness of God." Biblical scholar Robert Hubbard Jr. explains: "God acts through human agents . . . when people act with *hesed*, God is acting in them."

An ancient text may go even a step further in crediting the actions of the three major characters in this book in prompting God to act. In the Pesikta de-Rav Kahana, a midrashic text of uncertain authorship from the fifth or sixth century, God exclaims, "Boaz comforts. Will I not comfort?" Later the text says, "Boaz did his [part], and Ruth did hers, and Naomi did hers; [then] the Holy One said: 'I too will do mine.'" Kahana was likely responding to the curious fact that although the Book of Ruth records many invocations of God, there is only one explicit reference to a divine action: After Boaz marries Ruth, *"The Lord let her conceive and she bore a son"* (4:13).

This is very close to the conclusion of the book. Just four verses later comes the shocker: *"They named him Obed; he was the father of Jesse, father of David"* (4:17). Ruth the Moabite emerges as the great-grandmother of King David!

It is a startling proposition, but upon reflection, an appropriate one. For the Book of Ruth is proclaiming the defining characteristic of the upstanding human being, whether Israelite or foreigner: *hesed*. A woman of valor, measured by loving-kindness, Ruth merits the honor of being foremother to a king—and, some would say, a messiah.

Walking with Ruth: The Path of Kindness

The path of kindness and compassion is central to Judaism. The word *hesed* occurs in the Bible nearly 250 times. Two other terms are also used to convey this path. The Hebrew term *rachamim,* often translated as "mercy" or "compassion," is employed nearly one hundred times. And the Hebrew term for love, *ahava,* while covering a range of meanings from the romantic to the platonic, sometimes points to the altruistic impulse of *hesed* as well.

Taken together, it is not surprising that the Rabbinic tradition is replete with statements and stories that emphasize compassion and kindness:

≈ *The prophet Micah's famous trio of characteristics of the ethical life urges us to "be just, be compassionate, and be humble." (Mic. 6:8)*

- *The Psalmist testifies repeatedly to hesed, nowhere more prominently than when he avows, "I will sing of the Lord's hesed forever . . . I declare Your hesed eternally." (Ps. 89:2–3)*
- *In Jewish tradition, God is frequently called "The Compassionate One" and "The Father of Compassion." The quality of compassion is listed among God's essential attributes in the Book of Exodus: "The Lord God, compassionate and gracious, slow to anger, and abundant in kindness and truth." (Exod. 34:6)*
- The Talmud explains *that the world rests on "study, prayer, and acts of kindness."*
- *In the Rabbinic literature, the children of Israel are called "children of compassion."*
- *A talmudic verse identifies compassion as the defining characteristic of human beings: "Whoever lacks compassion for his fellow man is no seed of Abraham."*
- *A prayer recited daily in the morning service includes the words, "Blessed is the One who has compassion on the earth; blessed is the One who has compassion on creation."*
- *A provocative discussion in a midrash about whether the world would be better off with or without the creation of human beings resolves in our favor by means of hesed. Even as the Rabbis are cognizant of monstrous evil perpetrated by human beings, they have also witnessed countless acts of goodness, which becomes the prevailing argument. "Rabbi Simon said, 'When the Holy One, blessed be He, came to create Adam, the ministering angels formed themselves into groups and parties, some of them saying, Let him be created, whilst others urged, Let him not be created.' The angel representing Hesed said, 'Let him be created, because he will practice acts of hesed.'"*

Throughout the generations, Jewish sages have eloquently expressed our obligation to emulate God's attributes and actions, most of all God's compassion. The talmudic sage Abba Saul says plainly, "Be like God; just as God is gracious and merciful, so you too should be gracious and merciful." Rabbi Simlai, from the same era, specifies acts of divine kindness in the Torah: "The beginning of Torah is in kind deeds, as it is written: *'And the Lord God made for Adam and his wife clothes of skin, and clothed them'*" (Gen. 3:20).

When God appears to Abraham by the terebinths of Mamre (Gen. 18:1), the sages note that this verse immediately follows Abraham's circumcision and construe it as evidence of *bikur holim*, the mitzvah of visiting the sick.

Even as he is healing, Abraham then performs his own act of kindness. Spotting three strangers approaching his tent, Abraham runs to greet them and offer the dusty and tired travelers food and drink. Both Abraham and his wife Sarah (who does the cooking and serving) perform the mitzvah of *hachnassat orchim*, welcoming the guest. One midrash says that the flaps of Abraham's tent were open on all four sides to allow Abraham to look for people to welcome. The sages also point out that the Torah text makes it appear as if Abraham was in the middle of a conversation with God when he breaks it off to welcome the strangers. "Hospitality to wayfarers is greater than welcoming the divine presence" the Talmud declares. (Little did Abraham and Sarah know that these three individuals are not ordinary men, but bearers of a special message from God that the couple would conceive a child!)

When Abraham's son Isaac grows up, his father sends his trusted servant Eliezer on a mission to find his son a wife. Eliezer needs a sign to know which woman in Abraham's hometown will be right for his master's son—and decides on a sign that conveys basic kindness to people and animals alike. Eliezer looks for a woman at the well who will offer water to him and his camels. When Rebecca does just that, and offers him food and lodging, Eliezer knows he has found the right match. Bowing low, he says, *"Blessed be the Lord, the God of my master Abraham, who has not withheld His steadfast kindness from my master"* (Gen. 24:26).

Moreover, the Torah ends with a deed of kindness. After Moses dies on the mountain looking into the Promised Land of Israel, God buries Moses, as it is written, *"And He buried Moses in the valley"* (Deut.

34:6). With Moses away from his people and alone, it is up to God to offer the esteemed prophet a proper burial.

In the course of time, wishing to perpetuate deeds of kindness, Jewish communities established various societies to visit the sick, aid the poor, and bury the dead. The burial societies became known as *Hesed shel emet* (True Kindness). Since no material reward can come from the deceased, the various acts connected with proper burial—washing and preparing the deceased, watching over the body, accompanying the casket to the grave, covering the grave, and reciting the proper words (prayers and a eulogy)—were all considered the highest acts of compassion. Serving on such a burial society was a great honor and much sought-after distinction.

Many of the societies that arose in the medieval Jewish community continue on today, from the burial society to those that provide for holiday celebrations and weddings for the needy. Many are connected to synagogues; others are independent or part of Jewish Family Services or Jewish Community Centers.

Ultimately, the path of kindness and compassion is born of empathy and responsibility.

As Rabbi Samson Raphael Hirsch wrote in *Horeb*, his classic nineteenth-century work of philosophy:

> *Compassion is the feeling of empathy which the pain of one being of itself awakens in another; and the higher and more human the beings are, the more keenly attuned are they to re-echo the note of suffering which, like a voice from heaven, penetrates the heart . . . the very nature of his heart must teach him that he is required above everything else to feel himself the brother of all beings, and to recognize the claim of all beings to his love and beneficence. Do not suppress this compassion, this sympathy, especially with the sufferings of your fellow. It is the warning voice of duty, which points out to you your brother in every sufferer.*

From a religious perspective, kindness is the highest imitation of God. From a humanistic perspective, it is the highest expression of our humanity, for the ability to empathetically choose to help another is what best defines our highest selves.

Long ago a young woman made that choice at a decisive moment in her life. Little did Ruth know that her words would be immortalized. Little did she know how far-reaching the consequences of her kindness would be.

And little do we know how our acts of compassion will touch another soul.

10

Elisha's Invitation

THE PATH OF HEALING

I Am Elisha

I will never forget the day my master Elijah came calling. I was plowing in my family's field when this man of God came to me and threw his mantle upon me. In that instant I knew my life had changed—I had been called to serve as my master served.

Dropping the yoke, I ran after Elijah. "Let me kiss my father and mother good-bye," I said, "and I will follow you." Elijah tried to dissuade me, a test of my resolve, and I would not yield. Taking the yoke of my twelve oxen, I slaughtered them, boiled their meat, and prepared a farewell feast for my family and village. And then I left to follow Elijah.

Four years passed. I could see my master's days were coming to an end. By the banks of the Jordan River Elijah took off his mantle, as he had done in the field, and cast it upon the waters. In the sight of our followers the waters parted and my master and I crossed over to dry land. Elijah asked me, "What can I do for you before I am taken from you?" I replied, "Let a double portion of your spirit pass on to me." He said, "You have asked a difficult thing. If you see me as I am being taken from you, this will be granted to you; if not, it will not."

A moment later a fiery chariot appeared and my master went up to heaven in a whirlwind. I saw it all with my own eyes. Elijah had dropped his mantle. I picked it up, and when I held it over the river, the waters again parted. I returned to our followers grateful to the Living God that my master's spirit had been bestowed upon me and I was humbly to be numbered among His faithful prophets.

Not long after that we were put to the test. Naaman, commanding general of the army of Aram, sought healing for his affliction from me. The king of Israel immediately thought it a ruse, a pretext for attack. No one can cure leprosy, he thought, and what foolishness for an enemy commander to be let loose on Israelite soil. Then, fearing that our country would soon be invaded for denying his request, the king of Israel rent his clothes. I sent the king a message: "Why have you rent your clothes? Let this man come to me and he will learn that there is a prophet in Israel."

The Lord God is powerful and merciful. If He desires the healing of this Naaman, it will be granted; if not, it will not.

Elisha's Invitation: From the Bible

Elisha and Naaman (2 Kings 5:1–19):

[1]Naaman, commander of the army of the king of Aram, was important to his lord and high in his favor, for through him the Lord had granted victory to Aram. But the man, though a great warrior, was a leper. [2]Once, when the Arameans were out raiding, they carried off a young girl from the land of Israel, and she became an attendant to Naaman's wife. [3]She said to her mistress, "I wish Master could come before the prophet in Samaria; he would cure him of his leprosy." [4][Naaman] went and told his lord just what the girl from the land of Israel had said. [5]And the king of Aram said, "Go to the king of Israel, and I will send along a letter."

He set out, taking with him ten talents of silver, six thousand shekels of gold, and ten changes of clothing. [6]He brought the letter to the king of Israel. It read: "Now, when this letter reaches you, know that I have sent my courtier Naaman to you, that you may cure him of his leprosy." [7]When the king of Israel read the letter, he rent his clothes and cried, "Am I God, to deal death or give life, that this fellow writes to me to cure a man of leprosy? Just see for yourselves that he is seeking a pretext against me!"

[8]When Elisha, the man of God, heard that the king of Israel had rent his clothes, he sent a message to the king: "Why have you rent your clothes? Let him come to me, and he will learn that there is a prophet in Israel."

[9]So Naaman came with his horses and chariots and halted at the door of Elisha's house. [10]Elisha sent a messenger to say to him, "Go and bathe seven times in the Jordan, and your flesh shall be restored and you shall be clean." [11]But Naaman was angered and walked away. "I thought," he said, "he would surely come out to me, and would stand and invoke the Lord his God by name, and would wave his hand toward the spot, and cure the affected part. [12]Are not the Amanah and the Pharpar, the rivers of Damascus, better than

all the waters of Israel? I could bathe in them and be clean!" And he stalked off in a rage.

[13]But his servants came forward and spoke to him. "Sir," they said, "if the prophet told you to do something difficult, would you not do it? How much more when he has only said to you, 'Bathe and be clean.'" [14]So he went down and immersed himself in the Jordan seven times, as the man of God had bidden; and his flesh became like a little boy's, and he was clean. [15]Returning with his entire retinue to the man of God, he stood before him and exclaimed, "Now I know that there is no God in the whole world except in Israel! So please accept a gift from your servant." [16]But he replied, "As the Lord lives, whom I serve, I will not accept anything." He pressed him to accept, but he refused. [17]And Naaman said, "Then at least let your servant be given two mule-loads of earth; for your servant will never again offer up burnt offering or sacrifice to any god, except the Lord. [18]But may the Lord pardon your servant for this: When my master enters the temple of Rimmon to bow low in worship there, and he is leaning on my arm so that I must bow low in the temple of Rimmon—when I bow low in the temple of Rimmon, may the Lord pardon your servant in this." [19]And he said to him, "Go in peace."

Elisha's Invitation: The Prophetic Moment

But [Elisha] replied, "As the Lord lives, whom I serve, I will not accept anything. . . . Go in peace." (2 Kings 5:16, 19)

The prophet Elisha is much less known than his famous predecessor Elijah, but the second book of Kings is full of his miracle-working wonders.

Among Elisha's most dramatic encounters is with the military commander of Aram, Israel's enemy to the north. The story of an enemy general given free passage into the heartland of Israel for medical treatment initially defies belief. Yet the prophets were often politically savvy, and perhaps not beyond self-promotion (which they would have said was for the purpose of glorifying God). In this vein, Elisha may have seen the opportunity to publicly effect a cure for Naaman's leprosy as a "propaganda coup" for God, for Israel, and even for himself. Even so, this story sounds a rare note of humanitarian compassion amidst conflict.

A captive Israelite girl, an attendant to Naaman's wife, first makes the *"great warrior who was a leper"* aware that a certain prophet in Samaria can cure leprosy. Desperate for a cure, Naaman petitions his own king for a letter of safe passage to the man of God. When the king of Israel reads the letter, he rends his clothes and cries out, *"Am I God, to deal death or give life, that this fellow writes to me to cure a man of leprosy. Just see for yourselves that he is seeking a pretext against me!"* (2 Kings 5:7). The text thus acknowledges the risky scenario of allowing a powerful adversary into Israel.

But Elisha intervenes. Having evidently amassed significant credibility, he persuades the king to let the warrior enter the land to be healed.

When at first Elisha directs Naaman to bathe in the Jordan seven times to be cured, the general is indignant. He expects something more elaborate, perhaps the prophet's invocation of God's name and the laying of hands. Naaman declares that the rivers of Aram are greater than those of the Jordan and stalks off in a rage. Fortunately his servants convince him to calm down and do as Elisha says. And when at last his flesh turns as pure as a baby's, Naaman is profoundly moved.

Now, Naaman acknowledges the supreme power of the Israelite God. He desires to bestow gifts on Elisha, but the prophet steadfastly refuses to accept anything, thereby reinforcing that this is God's healing, not his.

Before leaving, Naaman asks to take two mule-loads of precious Israelite soil back home with him. When Naaman must pray to the local gods, at least, he says, he will be prostrating on holy ground. Elisha replies with a simple expression (still used in modern Hebrew today) declared when someone sets off on a journey, "Go in peace."

This story can be read as a testimonial to the power of the Israelite's God and His prophet. But at the same time it is the story of a man in search of a cure for his terrible affliction and the compassionate response of a fellow man that can offer help, and does. Elisha must convince the king to see beyond the political. He must convince the general to see beyond the conventional. And after he has accomplished both, and gone on to cure Naaman of a disease many people believe is incurable, Elisha refuses any gifts in return. It is enough for a man, even an enemy, to be cured and to go home in peace.

This is the prophetic moment: when compassion trumps realpolitik. Elisha urges and ultimately convinces the king to overcome political calculation because the saving of a life takes precedence.

Even if we admit that Elisha's action may have been somewhat self-serving, this does not take away from the prophetic power of the moment. Perhaps the story is subtly suggesting that compassion may be a tool in foreign policy. The overture to Aram may improve relations between the warring nations. Naaman certainly returns home a changed man. Elisha's final words are most accurately rendered as "go to peace." Is it too much to think that the warrior can become a peacemaker?

Although it would be ideal to end the story right at this point (as is done when the story is read in the synagogue as a haftarah portion), that would not be fully faithful to the biblical text. In an oft-overlooked postscript, Elisha's servant Gehazi solicits money from Naaman as he is departing. Naaman obliges by giving him two talents of silver. Upon Gehazi's return, Elisha confronts him: *"Where have you been?"* Gehazi lies, *"Your servant has not gone anywhere,"* to which Elisha acidly retorts, *"Is this a time to take money in order to buy clothing and olive groves and vineyards, sheep and oxen, and male and female slaves?"* And then, in a most uncompassionate ending, Elisha pronounces, *"Surely, the leprosy of Naaman shall cling to you and to your descendants forever."* The Bible reports that as Gehazi left Elisha's presence, *"he was snow-white with leprosy"* (2 Kings 5:20–27).

More than any prophet since Moses, and like his mentor Elijah, Elisha is the rare miracle worker who can summon God's healing power. The Bible recounts another equally dramatic healing story often referred to as "The Shunammite's Son." A certain woman from Shunem is in the habit of offering Elisha a meal whenever he passes by the town. She senses that he is "a holy man of God." She also convinces her husband to build a small room for Elisha to lodge in whenever he needs. Elisha seeks to return the favor in some way. Eventually he predicts that the childless woman will give birth to a son. A year later the woman indeed gives birth—but her joy turns to sorrow when her young son is stricken with an illness and apparently dies. She sends for Elisha, and the prophet comes.

Elisha attempts to revive the boy by having his servant place his staff on him. When that fails, *"Elisha came into the house, and there was the boy, laid out dead on the couch. He went in, shut the door behind the two of them, and prayed to the Lord. Then he mounted the bed and placed himself over the child. He put his mouth on its mouth, his eyes on its eyes, and his hands on its hands, as he bent over. And the body of the child became warm . . . the boy sneezed seven times, and the boy opened his eyes"* (2 Kings 4:32–35). Readers will note that the action described resembles the mouth-to-mouth resuscitation commonly called CPR. But the point of the biblical story is not how Elisha effects the boy's healing, but the extent of the effort he is willing to make. Placing his staff on the boy—and via a third party—is not enough. Praying over the boy is not enough. Elisha must fully engage to help the boy breathe again.

Walking with Elisha: The Path of Healing

The ancient tale of humanitarian outreach amidst conflict has echoes in our generation. Hadassah Hospital in Jerusalem, for example, treats Palestinians even during times of uprising. Israel has opened its border and provided safe passage to Syrian refugees needing medical treatment in the midst of hostilities during that country's long civil war. In times of natural disasters Israel has dispatched rescue teams to afflicted countries around the world, friends or foes—including aiding Turkey, a Muslim country with which Israel has had complicated relations, after a massive earthquake; and helping Indonesia, another Muslim nation that has been critical of Israel, after the devastating tsunami there. The imperative to heal and save lives is so strong that ultra-Orthodox rescuers in all these places work around the clock and even violate the Sabbath if need be. As one of the rescuers, Mati Goldstein, said of his mission in Haiti after its devastating earthquake, "We did everything to save lives, despite Shabbat . . . we are here because the Torah orders us to save lives."

Such compassion rests on a value deeply embedded in Jewish tradition: *pikuach nefesh*, the imperative to save a life. It emerges, first, in the foundational Torah teaching that every human life, created in God's image, is precious and of infinite worth. The sages understand other biblical verses to amplify the theme. "*You shall keep My laws and My rules by the pursuit of which man shall live*" (Lev. 18:5) points to the purpose of the Torah's laws: to sustain life. "*You shall not stand idly [stand by the blood] of your neighbor*" (Lev. 19:6) is understood to express the necessity of acting to prevent bloodshed. "*See, I set before you this day life and prosperity, death and adversity. . . . I have put before you life and death, blessing and curse. Choose life*" (Deut. 30:15, 19) starkly emphasizes our moral responsibility.

The Talmud famously teaches, "Whoever saves one life, it is as if he saved an entire world." Here our sages are sensitive not just to the infinite value of each human life, but also to the radiating circles of influence a single life may have, both biologically and spiritually. An act of healing that saves a life is the most precious act of all—so much so that Jewish law enshrines the principle that "the saving of life supersedes the Sabbath." The Shulchan Arukh, a famous Jewish law code, puts it even more strongly: "It is a religious precept to desecrate the Sabbath for any person afflicted with an illness that may prove dangerous. He who is zealous [about this] is praiseworthy while he who asks questions sheds blood."

When human beings heal others, this is considered *imitatio dei*, the imitation of God. Both the Bible and the Talmud regard God as the source of healing. When Miriam is struck by leprosy, Moses cries out, *"O God, pray heal her!"* (Num. 12:13). Elisha is careful to convey that it is God, not he, who heals Naaman. The tenth benediction of the weekday *tefillah* reads: "Heal us, Adonai, and we shall be healed; save us, and we shall be saved. Grant full healing [*r'fuah sh'leima*] to our every illness, wound, and pain. Blessed are You, Adonai, who heals the sick."

The sages understood that visiting the sick can help in the healing process. They noted that the verse *"The Lord appeared to him [Abraham] by the terebinths of Mamre"* (Gen. 18:1) occurs just after Abraham's circumcision, and conclude that God was visiting Abraham to distract him from the pain of recovery. Likewise, the human mitzvah of *bikur holim* (visiting and aiding the sick) is important in Judaism. Medieval Jewish communities had special societies for this purpose. Today many congregations have "caring communities" that perform the same function.

In the synagogue, when the Torah is read, Jews also support family and friends in need of healing, body and soul, by offering a *Mi She Berakh*, a public prayer or blessing for someone who is ill. The traditional text begins, "May the One who blessed our ancestors . . . bless and heal those who are ill," and the names of loved ones are then recited. The prayer concludes, "May the Blessed Holy One be filled with compassion for their health to be restored and strength to be revived. May God swiftly send them a complete renewal of body and spirit." Some years ago the popular singer-songwriter Debbie Friedman wrote a version of this prayer and set it to music; her "Mi She Berakh" song has a cherished place in countless synagogues.

Elisha teaches us: We each possess the ability to save lives, however daunting, frightening, challenging, and/or incongruous the task may sometimes seem (e.g., saving the lives even of probable enemies). We may not have—and probably do not have—the magical healing capacities of Elijah and Elisha. Still, we can gather up our innate God-given (if we thus believe) abilities to heal and help others, each in our own ways. Some of us may have medical knowledge and/or other special skills. Almost all of us can visit the sick. We can contribute to life-saving organizations and centers of healing. Saving lives, healing souls, are means of continuing on the prophetic path: These are profound blessings from God, and sacred tasks for us.

11

Jeremiah's Scroll

THE PATH OF HOPE

I Am Jeremiah

I cannot say there has been an easy day in my life since the word of the Lord came to me. When God first spoke God said, "Before I created you in the womb, I selected you; before you were born, I consecrated you; I appointed you a prophet concerning the nations." I resisted; this was not the life I wanted. I replied: "Ah, Lord God! I don't know how to speak, for I am still a boy." God would have none of it. "Do not say, 'I am still a boy.' Go wherever I send you and speak whatever I command you."

My life has been miserable. I have been harassed and hounded. I have been arrested and thrown in prison. Israel has lost its way. The House of David is doomed. No leader follows in the footsteps of Josiah; his memory is forgotten. My countrymen foolishly believe that if they ally themselves with Egypt they can resist Babylonia. Hardest for them to hear is that God has chosen Nebuchadnezzar as God's instrument of punishment for our sins. Our betrayal of God's commands; our whoring after idols . . . we have been warned of the consequences, and now the decisive hour is upon us.

I am in hiding and likely to be arrested again by King Jehoiakim. So I have commissioned my closest disciple, Baruch ben Neriah, to write a scroll with all the words that the Lord has spoken to me. If I cannot preach the word, at least he can do so in my name. I will station him at the new gateway to the House of the Lord so that none will miss my message: Resisting Babylonia is futile. A time of exile is coming. None can escape the wrath of God.

But neither can one can escape the love of God. As a parent loves a child, so the Lord loves us. I ask you, does a parent who loves a child not disciple him for his own good? Does a parent not punish in order to teach? Are not chastisements of love for our own sake? My people must hear that our time of affliction, however grievous, will not last forever. It is not the end of the story. Darkness will be followed by light. Exile will be followed by return. Despair will be followed by hope.

This is the reason that God commanded me to do a most unusual thing: buy land in my hometown of Anathoth from my cousin Hanamel. At first I thought: "Why in the world should I do this if my country is to be destroyed? Why should I spend my last bit of savings on land that will be in ruin and useless, and with no chance of my ever living upon it? And will it not send the wrong message to my people?"

But God helped me to understand why I should do this. I shall proclaim it as an act of the living God who will not abandon God's people. I have given the deed of purchase to Baruch and told him to show it to the people along with the scroll he has written. I have told him to wave it in front of my people and tell them why I bought land on the eve of our destruction. I want young and old alike to know that we will not witness our return to our land. Neither will our children. But our children's children, they will witness the acts of our mighty and loving God.

All we must do is keep the faith, and never lose hope. God does not forget but God does forgive. The time of mourning is at hand but the time of rejoicing will come again.

My last instruction to Baruch was to put the deed of purchase in an earthen jar, so that it may last a long time. For it will be read again in the home of my fathers. Not now, not tomorrow, but in seventy years. Of that I have no doubt.

Jeremiah's Scroll: From the Bible

Jeremiah's purchase of land (Jer. 32:6–15, 32:24–25, 32:36–44):

> [6]*Jeremiah said: The word of the Lord came to me:* [7]*Hanamel, the son of your uncle Shallum, will come to you and say, "Buy my land in Anathoth, for you are next in succession to redeem it by purchase."* [8]*And just as the Lord had said, my cousin Hanamel came to me in the prison compound and said to me, "Please buy my land in Anathoth, in the territory of Benjamin; for the right of succession is yours, and you have the duty of redemption. Buy it." Then I knew that it was indeed the word of the Lord.*
>
> [9]*So I bought the land in Anathoth from my cousin Hanamel. I weighed out the money to him, seventeen shekels of silver.* [10]*I wrote a deed, sealed it, and had it witnessed; and I weighed out the silver on a balance.* [11]*I took the deed of purchase, the sealed text and the open one according to rule and law,* [12]*and gave the deed to Baruch son of Neriah son of Mahseiah in the presence of my kinsman Hanamel, of the witnesses who were named in the deed, and all the Judeans who were sitting in the prison compound.* [13]*In their presence I charged Baruch as follows:* [14]*Thus said the Lord of Hosts, the God of Israel: "Take these documents, this deed of purchase, the sealed text and the open one, and put them into an earthen jar, so that they may last a long time."* [15]*For thus said the Lord of Hosts, the God of Israel: "Houses, fields, and vineyards shall again be purchased in this land."*
>
> [24]*"Here are the siegemounds, raised against the city to storm it; and the city, because of sword and famine and pestilence, is at the mercy of the Chaldeans who are attacking it. What You threatened has come to pass—as You see.* [25]*Yet You, Lord God, said to me: Buy the land for money and call in witnesses—when the city is at the mercy of the Chaldeans!"*
>
> [36]*But now, assuredly, thus said the Lord, the God of Israel, concerning this city of which you say, "It is being delivered into the hands of the king of Babylon through the sword, through famine,*

and through pestilence": [37]See, I will gather them from all the lands to which I have banished them in My anger and wrath, and in great rage; and I will bring them back to this place and let them dwell secure. [38]They shall be My people, and I will be their God. [39]I will give them a single heart and a single nature to revere Me for all time, and it shall be well with them and their children after them. [40]And I will make an everlasting covenant with them that I will not turn away from them and that I will treat them graciously; and I will put into their hearts reverence for Me, so that they do not turn away from Me. [41]I will delight in treating them graciously, and I will plant them in this land faithfully, with all My heart and soul.

[42]For thus said the Lord: As I have brought this terrible disaster upon this people, so I am going to bring upon them the vast good fortune which I have promised for them. [43]And fields shall again be purchased in this land of which you say, "It is a desolation, without man or beast; it is delivered into the hands of the Chaldeans."

[44]Fields shall be purchased, and deeds written and sealed, and witnesses called in the land of Benjamin and in the environs of Jerusalem, and in the towns of Judah; the towns of the hill country, the towns of the Shephelah, and the towns of the Negeb. For I will restore their fortunes—declares the Lord.

Jeremiah's Scroll: The Prophetic Moment

Yet you, Lord God, said to me: Buy the land for money and call in the witnesses—when the city is at the mercy of the Chaldeans . . . fields shall be purchased, and deeds written and sealed. . . . I will restore their fortunes. (Jer. 32:25,44)

Jeremiah lived at an agonizing time in the history of ancient Israel. Since its inception, tiny Israel always seemed to be caught between the superpowers of the North and the South. The ten tribes of Northern Israel had disappeared from history when Assyria overran the country and dispersed them in 721 BCE. This national calamity is still very much in the minds of Jeremiah and his compatriots when, in 605 BCE, Babylonia, another empire from the North, arises and vanquishes its rival to the South, Egypt, in the epic battle of Carchemish.

For some time Jeremiah has been warning against making alliances with Egypt. He saw the Babylonian invasion not only as inevitable, but as the express will of God. Astonishingly he preaches, *"Assuredly, thus said the Lord of Hosts: Because you would not listen to My words, I am going to send for all the peoples of the north—declares the Lord—and for My servant Nebuchadnezzar of Babylon, and bring them against this land and its inhabitants"* (Jer. 25:8–9). Jeremiah predicts that servitude to Babylon will last seventy years—a message of doom, pronounced in the Temple courtyard, that, unsurprisingly, does not go over well with the political establishment:

> [1]*At the beginning of the reign of King Jehoiakim son of Josiah of Judah, this word came from the Lord:*
>
> [2]*"Thus said the Lord: Stand in the court of the House of the Lord, and speak to [the men of] all the towns of Judah, who are coming to worship in the House of the Lord, all the words which I command you to speak to them. Do not omit anything.* [3]*Perhaps they will listen and turn back, each from his evil way, that I may renounce the punishment I am planning to bring upon them for their wicked acts.*
>
> [4]*"Say to them: Thus said the Lord: If you do not obey Me, abiding by the Teaching that I have set before you,* [5]*heeding the words of My servants the prophets whom I have been sending to you persistently—but you have not heeded—*[6]*then I will make this House like Shiloh, and I will make this city a curse for all the nations of earth." (Jer. 26:1–6)*

The Bible notes that *"the priests and the prophets and the people"* rise up against Jeremiah's words, and when the palace officials arrive on the scene, they demand the death penalty for Jeremiah. Defending himself, the prophet manages to convince the officials and the people that his life should be spared. In fact, a group of elders speak up, pointing out that in the time of Hezekiah, the prophet Micah spoke out and was not harmed. The account of Jeremiah's tribulation is among the most dramatic of the prophets:

[7]The priests and prophets and all the people heard Jeremiah speaking these words in the House of the Lord. [8]And when Jeremiah finished speaking all that the Lord had commanded him to speak to all the people, the priests and the prophets and all the people seized him, shouting, "You shall die! [9]How dare you prophesy in the name of the Lord that this House shall become like Shiloh and this city be made desolate, without inhabitants?" And all the people crowded about Jeremiah in the House of the Lord.

[10]When the officials of Judah heard about this, they went up from the king's palace to the House of the Lord and held a session at the entrance of the New Gate of the House of the Lord. [11]The priests and prophets said to the officials and to all the people, "This man deserves the death penalty, for he has prophesied against this city, as you yourselves have heard."

[12]Jeremiah said to the officials and to all the people, "It was the Lord who sent me to prophesy against this House and this city all the words you heard. [13]Therefore mend your ways and your acts, and heed the Lord your God, that the Lord may renounce the punishment He has decreed for you. [14]As for me, I am in your hands: do to me what seems good and right to you. [15]But know that if you put me to death, you and this city and its inhabitants will be guilty of shedding the blood of an innocent man. For in truth the Lord has sent me to you, to speak all these words to you."

[16]Then the officials and all the people said to the priests and prophets, "This man does not deserve the death penalty, for he spoke to us in the name of the Lord our God."

[17]And some of the elders of the land arose and said to the entire assemblage of the people, [18]"Micah the Morashtite, who prophesied

in the days of King Hezekiah of Judah, said to all the people of Judah: 'Thus said the Lord of Hosts:

Zion shall be plowed as a field,
Jerusalem shall become heaps of ruins
And the Temple Mount a shrine in the woods.'

[19]*"Did King Hezekiah of Judah, and all Judah, put him to death? Did he not rather fear the Lord and implore the Lord, so that the Lord renounced the punishment He had decreed against them? We are about to do great injury to ourselves!" (Jer. 26:7–19)*

Jeremiah persists in his agitation. He rails against what today we would call both domestic policy (inequality and injustice) and foreign policy (unholy alliances).

Eventually he is forced into hiding and later arrested and imprisoned. During this time the prophet dictates his pronouncements so that his disciple Baruch can read them from a scroll even if he is silenced. He also takes another dramatic step to insure that the other half of his message—that God will not forsake Israel forever—will not be ignored.

Jeremiah hails from a village outside Jerusalem named Anathoth, which is likely already under enemy control. When Jeremiah receives word from a cousin that as kin he has an opportunity to acquire land there, he decides to do so, though [in the words of one prominent commentator] "it must have seemed like sheer madness." To buy land controlled by the Babylonians that Jeremiah himself was preaching would capture Jerusalem, destroy the country, and exile its population, seems to make no sense. Yet Jeremiah goes through the procedure of securing and preserving the deed, and insuring that the public knows about it. He grasps that he has been given a way to dramatize that the exile of his people will not last forever—that God's turn away is not a sign of forsaken love for all time.

Recall Heschel's definition of the prophet as combining "a very deep love, a very powerful dissent, a painful rebuke, with unwavering hope." To Jeremiah and the classical prophets, no one could be shielded from the harsh reality of God's judgment, but neither would anyone be denied the consolation of God's ultimate love, nor the hope that comes from that knowledge.

Jeremiah continues to have run-ins with the authorities; apparently he is in and out of jail multiple times. King Jehoiakim orders the burning of the original scroll Jeremiah dictated to his scribe Baruch, and so the duo write another scroll while in hiding (Jer. 36:26–32). When King Zedekiah takes the reigns, Jeremiah regains his freedom and remains in Jerusalem throughout the Babylonian siege. He chooses to cast his lot with his people even as he castigates and consoles them. Curiously, he does not accompany the exiles to Babylon, but ends up (perhaps involuntarily) with a remnant that flees to Egypt.

During his lifetime, opinions of Jeremiah were surely divided. In later generations, though, both Jews and Christians viewed him as a powerful, deeply critical, and yet compassionate prophet. To this day we use the term *jeremiad* to mean "a lamentation; mournful complaint," or further, "a cautionary or angry harangue." Indeed, sometimes when he preached, Jeremiah was angry, but at other times he delivered words of comfort that are second to none among the prophets in their eloquence:

> *Eternal love I conceived for you then; therefore I continue my grace to you. [4]I will build you firmly again. O Maiden Israel! Again you shall take up your timbrels and go forth to the rhythm of the dancers. [5]Again you shall plant vineyards on the hills of Samaria. Men shall plant and live to enjoy them. [6]For the day is coming when watchmen shall proclaim on the heights of Ephraim: "Come, let us go up to Zion, to the Lord our God!" (Jer. 31:3–6)*

> *In a vast throng they shall return here. [9]They shall come with weeping, and with compassion I will guide them. I will lead them to streams of water, by a level road where they will not stumble. For I am ever a Father to Israel; Ephraim is my firstborn. (Jer. 31:8–9)*

> *A cry is heard in Ramah—wailing, bitter weeping—Rachel weeping for her children. She refuses to be comforted for her children, who are gone.* [16]*Thus said the Lord: Restrain your voice from weeping, your eyes from shedding tears. For there is a reward for your labor—declares the Lord. They shall return from the enemy's land.* [17]*And there is hope for your future. (Jer. 31:15–17)*

Jeremiah dies in obscurity in Egypt, but his ideas endure. His famous prophesy—*"When Babylon's seventy years are over, I will take note of you, and I will fulfill to you My promise of favor—to bring you back to this place"* (Jer. 29:10)—deeply influences the Judean exiles, and their prophets Ezekiel and Second Isaiah. Remarkably, the book of Ezra, which chronicles the Jews' return from exile, opens with a nod to the prophet: *"In the first year of King Cyrus of Persia, when the word of the Lord spoken by Jeremiah was fulfilled"* (Ezra 1:1). So too does the history recap that closes the Hebrew Bible, which utilizes almost identical language: *"And in the first year of King Cyrus of Persia, when the word of the Lord spoken to Jeremiah was fulfilled, the Lord roused the spirit of King Cyrus of Persia to issue a proclamation.... Anyone of you of all His people, the Lord His God be with him and let him go up"* (1 Chron. 36:22–23).

An interesting passage in the *Mekhilta*, an ancient midrashic text, stipulates that there are three types of prophets: those who insist on the honor due the father (God), those who insist on the honor due the son (the people), and those who insist on both. The text presents Elijah, who was zealous to preach God's word, as an example of the first; Jonah, the reluctant prophet who tried to flee his mission and worried about his and Israel's reputation, as an example of the second—and Jeremiah, who has both God and the people always in his sights, approvingly as an example of the third ("insisting upon the honor due the father and the honor due the son").

Jeremiah's prophetic moment is a statement of faith in God and in the future of his people.

Walking with Jeremiah: The Path of Hope

"Unwavering hope" is as much a part of Jeremiah's message as *"painful rebuke."* At one point Jeremiah uses the unique expression *"hope of Israel"* to refer to God (Jer. 17:13). He would have approved of Zechariah's reference to the people as *"prisoners of hope"* (Zech. 9:12). As he did when he purchased his ancestral land, Jeremiah repeatedly speaks about the coming restoration of Israel's fortunes. In fact, one of his best-known declarations is repeated at Jewish weddings to this day; *"Again there shall be heard . . . in the towns of Judah and the streets of Jerusalem . . . the sound of mirth and gladness, the voice of groom and bride . . . for I will restore the fortunes of the land as of old—said the Lord"* (Jer. 31:10–11).

The prophetic message of hope he instills is echoed to a degree by almost all of the prophets, most notably Isaiah:

> *Comfort, oh comfort My people, says your God. Speak tenderly to Jerusalem, and declare to her that her term of service is over; that her iniquity is expiated. For she has received at the hand of the Lord double for all her sins. (Isa. 40:1–3)*

> *But you, Israel, My servant, Jacob, whom I have chosen, seed of Abraham My friend—You whom I drew from the end of the earth and called from its far corners . . . Fear not, for I am with you, be not frightened for I am your God; I strengthen you and I help you. (Isa. 41:8–10)*

The prophetic message of hope is not simply a "generic" optimism based on faith in God. There are multiple and specific elements to the prophets' confidence that the future will be better, even if it does begin with the unshakable conviction that God will take the initiative, as Amos, for example, declares, *"I will restore My people Israel"* (Amos 9:14), and Jeremiah affirms, *"Sing aloud in praise, and say: The Lord has saved your people, the remnant of Israel"* (Jer. 31:7). As Jeremiah Unterman notes, "The most common denominator that is presented as an essential element in the age of redemption is the return of the exiles to their land—without which, of course, no restoration could occur. So Isaiah: '*He will hold up a signal to the nations and assemble the banished of Israel, and gather the dispersed of Judah from the four corners of the earth*' (Isa. 11:12) and Ezekiel '*I will take you from among the nations and gather you from all the countries, and I will bring you back to your land*' (Ezek. 36:24)."

Ezekiel, a prophet of the Babylonian exile whose visions and oratory can often be difficult to follow, waxes most eloquently in his message of restoration and hope: "*Thus said the Lord God: When I have cleansed you of all your iniquities, I will people your settlements, and the ruined places shall be rebuilt; and the desolate land after lying waste in the sight of every passerby, shall again be tilled. And men shall say, 'That land, once desolate, has become like the Garden of Eden; and the cities, once ruined, desolate and ravaged, are now populated and fortified'*" (Ezek. 36:33–36).

Ezekiel's famous "vision of the dry bones" is a classic prophetic statement of hope, symbolizing the restoration of the people and the land of Israel:

> [1]*The hand of the Lord came upon me. He took me out by the spirit of the Lord and set me down in the valley. It was full of bones.* [2]*He led me all around them; there were very many of them spread over the valley, and they were very dry.* [3]*He said to me, "O mortal, can these bones live again?" I replied, "O Lord God, only You know."* [4]*And He said to me, "Prophesy over these bones and say to them: O dry bones, hear the word of the Lord!* [5]*Thus said the Lord God to these bones: I will cause breath to enter you and you shall live again.* [6]*I will lay sinews upon you, and cover you with flesh, and form skin over you. And I will put breath into you, and you shall live again. And you shall know that I am the Lord!"*
>
> [7]*I prophesied as I had been commanded. And while I was prophesying, suddenly there was a sound of rattling, and the bones came together, bone to matching bone.* [8]*I looked, and there were sinews on them, and flesh had grown, and skin had formed over them; but there was no breath in them.* [9]*Then He said to me, "Prophesy to the breath,*

prophesy, O mortal! Say to the breath: Thus said the Lord God: Come, O breath, from the four winds, and breathe into these slain, that they may live again." [10]*I prophesied as He commanded me. The breath entered them, and they came to life and stood up on their feet, a vast multitude.*

[11]*And He said to me, "O mortal, these bones are the whole House of Israel. They say, 'Our bones are dried up, our hope is gone; we are doomed.'* [12]*Prophesy, therefore, and say to them: Thus said the Lord God: I am going to open your graves and lift you out of the graves, O My people, and bring you to the land of Israel.* [13]*You shall know, O My people, that I am the Lord, when I have opened your graves and lifted you out of your graves.* [14]*I will put My breath into you and you shall live again, and I will set you upon your own soil. Then you shall know that I the Lord have spoken and have acted"—declares the Lord. (Ezek. 37:1–14)*

Once back in their land, the people will again prosper economically and politically. They will be freed from both physical deprivation and emotional insecurity. Amos declares, "*I will plant them upon their soil, nevermore to be uprooted from the soil I have given them*" (Amos 9:15), and Hosea affirms, "*In that day . . . I will banish bow, sword, and war from the land. Thus, I will let them lie down in safety*" (Hosea 2:20). Micah (echoed by Isaiah) perhaps puts it most memorably when he says, "*And they shall beat their swords into plowshares and their spears into pruning hooks. Nation shall not take up sword against nation; they shall never again know war. . . . But every man shall sit under his vine and fig tree, and none shall make them afraid*" (Mic. 4:3–4).

To many of the prophets, restoration meant that the Davidic monarchy would be restored, and the new kings would be models of justice. They also looked for the restitution of the Temple, priesthood, and sacrifices in Jerusalem, as well as the national pilgrimages for the festivals that took place there. In dramatic flair, Ezekiel follows up his vision of the dry bones with another vivid "prophecy of the two sticks":

[15]The word of the Lord came to me: [16]And you, O mortal, take a stick and write on it, "Of Judah and the Israelites associated with him"; and take another stick and write on it, "Of Joseph—the stick of Ephraim—and all the House of Israel associated with him." [17]Bring them close to each other, so that they become one stick, joined together in your hand. [18]And when any of your people ask you, "Won't you tell us what these actions of yours mean?" [19]answer them, "Thus said the Lord God: I am going to take the stick of Joseph—which is in the hand of Ephraim—and of the tribes of Israel associated with him, and I will place the stick of Judah upon it and make them into one stick; they shall be joined in My hand." [20]You shall hold up before their eyes the sticks which you have inscribed, [21]and you shall declare to them: Thus said the Lord God: I am going to take the Israelite people from among the nations they have gone to, and gather them from every quarter, and bring them to their own land. [22]I will make them a single nation in the land, on the hills of Israel, and one king shall be king of them all. Never again shall they be two nations, and never again shall they be divided into two kingdoms. [23]Nor shall they ever again defile themselves by their fetishes and their abhorrent things, and by their other transgressions. I will save them in all their settlements where they sinned, and I will cleanse them. Then they shall be My people, and I will be their God.

[24]My servant David shall be king over them; there shall be one shepherd for all of them. They shall follow My rules and faithfully obey My laws. [25]Thus they shall remain in the land which I gave to My servant Jacob and in which your fathers dwelt; they and their children and their children's children shall dwell there forever, with My servant David as their prince for all time. [26]I will make a covenant of friendship with them—it shall be an everlasting covenant with them—I will establish them and multiply them, and I will place My Sanctuary among them forever. [27]My Presence shall rest over them; I will be their God and they shall be My people. [28]And when My Sanctuary abides among them forever, the nations shall know that I the Lord do sanctify Israel. (Ezek. 37:15–28)

Jeremiah goes even further. With this majestic passage, he envisions a restitution of the national spirit:

> *See, a time is coming—declares the Lord—when I will make a new covenant with the House of Israel and the House of Judah. It will not be like the covenant I made with their fathers, when I took them by the hand to lead them out of the land of Egypt, a covenant which they broke. . . . But such is the covenant I will make with the House of Israel after those days—declares the Lord: I will put My Teaching into their innermost being and inscribe it upon their hearts. Then I will be their God, and they shall be My people. No longer will they need to teach one other and say to one another, "Heed the Lord"; for all of them, from the least of them to the greatest, shall heed Me—declares the Lord. For I will forgive their iniquities and remember their sins no more. (Jer. 31:31–34).*

These words of comfort and hope from the age of classical prophecy took deep hold in the Jewish psyche. The Psalmist speaks for many when he declares, "*As for me, I will hope always, and add to the many praises of You*" (Ps. 71:14). So too does the talmudic sage who uttered, "As long as there is life, there is hope." It may be this quality, more than any other, that enabled the Jewish people to survive the near constant travails of its three-thousand-year history. The great historian Heinrich Graetz put it best: "Such a people, which discounts its present and has the eye fixed steadily on its future, which lives, as it were, on hope, is on that very account eternal, like hope." Earlier, Spinoza, the master of unvarnished truth, admitted: "There is no hope unmingled with fear, and no fear unmingled with hope." The gift of the Jews has always been the ability, time and again, to overcome fear with the belief that the future will be better.

The French Jewish writer Edmond Fleg, who had distanced himself from his heritage only to rediscover his Judaism late in life, wrote a moving essay entitled "Why I Am a Jew" (1927). One line reads,

"I am a Jew because in every age when the cry of despair is heard, the Jew hopes." Some two decades later, when the modern State of Israel was born, its leaders chose as the national anthem "Hatikvah" ("The Hope"), which itself is based on Naphtali Imber's poem of the same name, which states: "We have not yet lost our hope; the hope of two thousand years."

In essence, the Israeli nation anthem is the anthem of the Jewish people. Like the ancient prophet Jeremiah, the Jewish people faced calamity and weathered adversity confident in the knowledge that their mission and destiny would endure. One might call this "purpose-driven hope."

12

Jonah's Lesson

THE PATH OF COMPASSION

I Am Jonah

When God called me to go to the heart of darkness I thought it was a bad dream. Just to make sure, I took a boat in the opposite direction. Who in their right mind would want to go to Nineveh, the capital of Assyria, from whence came the destroyers of Israel? I fled instead to Tarshish.

Only God had other plans.

I went from a bad dream to a nightmare. A huge storm threatened to capsize our boat. Since I was a passenger, not a sailor, there was nothing I could do but go all the way to the hold and sleep through the worst of it. I was sound asleep when the captain roused me. "How can you be sleeping so soundly? Up, call upon your god! Perhaps He will be kind enough to us and we will not perish."

I was fleeing from God's call. I did not think God would deal kindly with me or this crew.

They cast lots to determine on whose account this misfortune had come upon us—and it fell on me. Then I told them my sad story. When they asked me what they might do to turn back God's wrath, I knew there was only one answer: "Heave me overboard, and the seas will calm down."

These sailors, pagan though they were, refused to do so. They rowed harder against the mighty gale—but it was to no avail.

When there was no hope left, I repeated my words. And then they cried out to my God, begging forgiveness, and threw me into the raging waters.

When I regained consciousness, I was clinging to a piece of wood in a calm sea. My lips murmured a prayer of thanks for being alive. All was well, I drifted to shore . . . and then the voice called again!

Now, I knew: There was no escaping it. If I was destined to die among the infidels who had all but destroyed my people, what could I do? I wearily trudged on to that dreaded place, to proclaim judgment on the people of Nineveh for their wickedness. I felt like old Samson pulling down the Temple of the Philistines. I would go down in flames with the enemy—that had to be God's plan.

I preached God's word in the public square—and was dumbfounded. The people began nodding and agreeing! Word traveled to the palace, and the king himself rose from his throne, took off his robe, put on sackcloth, and sat in ashes! Then the people, by the thousands, great and small alike, rent their clothes and fasted and cried out to God! Imagine it: their bloodstained hands in folded supplication. On and on it went, this sickening spectacle of wickedness beseeching for solace.

In the broad light of day my nightmare persisted. I had feared all along that God might relent. That is why I'd wanted nothing to do with this crazy mission. Now God told me to proclaim that Nineveh would live. I said to God that I would rather die.

The Lord replied, "Are you so deeply grieved?"

As I sat in a hut overlooking the city awaiting my fate, a vine grew over my head as if by magic: blessed shade from the blazing sun. Then it withered, and an east wind brought a blast of heat so intense I knew I would pass out in minutes. "Take me now, God," I begged, "for I am finished."

The Lord replied, "Are you so deeply grieved . . . about the plant?"

"Yes," I said. "That is all that I had, and now it is gone, so take me."

The Lord replied, "You cared so deeply about a plant, here and gone. And should I not care about this great city? Should I not care about its one hundred and twenty thousand souls; its men, women, and children; its animals?

I did not reply.

The Torah teaches that our God is compassionate and gracious, slow to anger, abounding in kindness, renouncing punishment. The world is not that way . . . but God is . . . and I can deny it no longer.

Jonah's Lesson: From the Bible

God's lesson of compassion to Jonah (Jon. 3:5–4:11):

> [5]*The people of Nineveh believed God. They proclaimed a fast, and great and small alike put on sackcloth.* [6]*When the news reached the king of Nineveh, he rose from his throne, took off his robe, put on sack-cloth, and sat in ashes.* [7]*And he had the word cried through Nineveh: "By decree of the king and his nobles: No man or beast—of flock or herd—shall taste anything! They shall not graze, and they shall not drink water!* [8]*They shall be covered with sackcloth—man and beast—and shall cry mightily to God. Let everyone turn back from his evil ways and from the injustice of which he is guilty.* [9]*Who knows but that God may turn and relent? He may turn back from His wrath, so that we do not perish."*
>
> [10]*God saw what they did, how they were turning back from their evil ways. And God renounced the punishment He had planned to bring upon them, and did not carry it out.*
>
> [4:1]*This displeased Jonah greatly, and he was grieved.* [2]*He prayed to the Lord, saying, "O Lord! Isn't this just what I said when I was still in my own country? That is why I fled beforehand to Tarshish. For I know that You are a compassionate and gracious God, slow to anger, abounding in kindness, renouncing punishment.* [3]*Please, Lord, take my life, for I would rather die than live."* [4]*The Lord replied, "Are you that deeply grieved?"*
>
> [5]*Now Jonah had left the city and found a place east of the city. He made a booth there and sat under it in the shade, until he should see what happened to the city.* [6]*The Lord God provided a ricinus plant, which grew up over Jonah, to provide shade for his head and save him from discomfort. Jonah was very happy about the plant.* [7]*But the next day at dawn God provided a worm, which attacked the plant so that it withered.* [8]*And when the sun rose, God provided a sultry east wind; the sun beat down on Jonah's head, and he became faint. He begged for death, saying, "I would rather die than live."* [9]*Then God said to*

Jonah, "Are you so deeply grieved about the plant?" "Yes," he replied, "so deeply that I want to die."

[10]*Then the Lord said: "You cared about the plant, which you did not work for and which you did not grow, which appeared overnight and perished overnight.* [11]*And should not I care about Nineveh, that great city, in which there are more than a hundred and twenty thousand persons who do not yet know their right hand from their left, and many beasts as well!"*

Jonah's Lesson: The Prophetic Moment

"And should I not care about Nineveh, that great city?" (Jon. 4:11)

Jonah is largely an enigma to us. The book of Jonah, only four brief chapters, relates just one episode in his life—we learn nothing of Jonah before or after.

We do know he is a reluctant prophet. The opening lines of the book establish that when Jonah hears God's call, he tries to run away from his responsibility. *"The word of the Lord came to Jonah son of Amittai: Go at once to Nineveh, that great city, and proclaim judgment upon it; for their wickedness had come before Me. Jonah, however, started out to flee to Tarshish from the Lord's service"* (Jon. 1:1–3).

Jonah takes a boat in the opposite direction. Yet as the tale that unfolds comes to teach us, one cannot evade God's call.

God sends a great storm. In his defensive and perhaps depressed state, Jonah seeks refuge from the chaos by retreating deep into the ship and falling asleep. The captain finds him and asks Jonah to pray to his god—which Jonah evidently also evades, because the sailors then cast lots *"to know on whose account this misfortune has come upon us."*

The lot falls on Jonah, who then explains he is a God-fearing Hebrew. The men quickly figure that Jonah may be God-evading as well: *"What have you done! . . . the men learned he was fleeing from the presence of the Lord"* (1:7, 10).

Jonah realizes that God will only be placated if he offers himself as a sacrifice. He instructs the men to throw him overboard, *"for I know this terrible storm came upon you on my account"* (1:12).

At this point in the narrative, the biblical author seems to be commenting on the innate goodness that resides in human beings. Even though the sailors are pagan, they are loathe to harm Jonah. They redouble their efforts to regain dry land. It is only when there is no other choice—either Jonah will be thrown overboard or they all will—and Jonah urges them once again to toss him in the sea—that they reluctantly heed his words. *"Then they cried out to the Lord: Oh, please, Lord, do not let us perish on account of this man's life. Do not hold us guilty of killing an innocent person! For you, O Lord, by your will, have brought this about"* (1:14). As Uriel Simon writes in his commentary to the Jonah, "The contrast between the idolatrous sailors and the prophet of the Lord reaches its zenith; not only do they call upon the Lord his God when [Jonah] himself refuses to pray, but in utter contrast to his stubborn rejection of his mission, they accept the burden of being the instrument of God's will."

The lesson—it is futile to evade God's call—may be one reason the Rabbis chose this story to be read on the afternoon of Yom Kippur. And a second, profound, Yom Kippur lesson emerges in the saving of the great but sinful city of Nineveh.

Here is some background to understand Jonah's aversion to Nineveh: In the eighth century BCE, Nineveh was already among the most ancient and populous cities in Mesopotamia—possibly then the largest city in the world. It was also the capital of the mighty Assyrian Empire, notorious for its cruel and ruthless treatment of the vanquished. In 721 BCE, Assyria overran the Northern Kingdom of Israel—so effectively exiling and dispersing the ten Northern tribes that they disappeared from history. The Assyrians nearly destroyed the Southern Kingdom of Judah as well.

The book of Jonah may have been written long after these events (a scholarly consensus is emerging for a considerably later date: either during the Babylonian exile or even after the Jews returned to Israel under the Persians). Nevertheless, the memory of the Assyrian invasion and the fate of the ten lost tribes would have been deeply ingrained in the ancient audience of the book of Jonah. To these generations, to say "Nineveh" would have been akin to us saying "Nazi Germany."

Jonah himself likely lived before the Assyrian catastrophe. Based on the mention of a *"Jonah son of Amittai"* in 2 Kings 14:25, scholars believe that Jonah was active during the reign of Jereboam II (785–749 BCE). Even though this predates the invasion, Jonah would have had reason to fear and loathe the threatening empire: Assyria was reputed as ruthless and had already vanquished lesser states and harassed Israel. Furthermore, as Rabbi Steven Bob points out in his book *Jonah and the Meaning of Our Lives,* later commentators thought that Jonah's prophetic powers enabled him to see the destructive role Assyria would play. The text says twice that Jonah is fleeing *"from the service of the Lord."* Why would Jonah be apprehensive about this mission? Are the fear of Nineveh and the fear of God connected? Does Jonah harbor a suspicion that if he warns Nineveh as God commands, the people might repent, God might forgive them and not destroy the city—and then the enemy will live to see another evil day? Does Jonah sense that the Assyrians will turn again to their wickedness and destroy his people?

As Jonah fears, Nineveh's repentance is quick and apparently sincere. One might think that Jonah would be happy to see such repentance. Yet, Jonah is so aggrieved that he asks to die. Instead, God decides to teach Jonah a lesson. God must find a way to convey to the prophet why mercy should extend to the wicked who have repented.

God points out how attached Jonah has become to a vine that provides welcome (maybe even life-saving) shade. Jonah cares deeply about the plant, even though he had no hand in growing it. Then, in a prophetic moment of compassion—from God, not Jonah—God queries Jonah as to why he should object to God's caring for an entire great city of people who have repented.

Jonah's reply is not given at the end of the book; it ends with God's word to the prophet. Did Jonah get the point? Did he learn the lesson of compassion? The answer is kept from us. So we are forced to conclude that the true teacher of compassion in this story is God. Jonah is largely a teacher by negative example. He was a reluctant prophet. He first chose to evade his call to Nineveh. He was afraid of witnessing the repentance of the people, and when he saw it, he did not rejoice but sulked and even despaired.

But let's not be wholly critical of Jonah. For one thing, he embodies the weaknesses that often plague us. At the same time, we can admire some of his story. When Jonah sees the sailors in danger, he is willing to sacrifice his life. When he survives a near drowning, he does pick up and make the prophetic journey to the most challenging of places. He does preach the word and act as a catalyst of transformation.

We should judge Jonah . . . with compassion!

The primary point of the story of Jonah is clear from its conclusion: God is merciful; we should be too. This lesson is powerful at any time, and all the more so on the Day of Atonement. Even the wicked can repent, and be forgiven. "All [the commentators] agree that God is telling Jonah that the Ninevites need to be taken seriously as human beings," writes Rabbi Bob. "They have intrinsic value because they *are* people."

Walking with Jonah: The Path of Compassion

Kindness and compassion (*rachamim, hesed*) are central teachings of Judaism and defining characteristics of our highest humanity. The stories of both Jonah and Ruth (see chapter 9) encourage us to practice the highest expressions of *"Love your neighbor as yourself."* Who, after all, could be more foreign than the Ninevite or the Moabite?

It's especially interesting how the Bible and Talmud build the case for human compassion based on its divine counterpart. Compassion is perhaps the distinguishing characteristic of God, with deep roots in Scripture and Rabbinic thought. The well-known verse in Exodus that describes God's attributes begins, *"The Lord, the Lord, a God compassionate and gracious, slow to anger, abounding in kindness and faithfulness*" (Exod. 34:6). The Ten Commandments describes God as "*showing kindness to the thousandth generation*" (Exod. 20:6, Deut. 5:10). The prophet Jeremiah refers to this very same expression in his prayer to God: "*Ah, Lord God! You made heaven and earth. . . . Nothing is too wondrous for You! You show kindness to the thousandth generation*" (Jer. 32:17–18). To this day, the memorial chant in Judaism begins, *El malei rachamim* (O God, full of compassion).

Perhaps the most remarkable teaching in this regard is the talmudic passage that speculates about what God's prayer might be: "What does God pray? R. Zutra said in the name of Rab: May it be My will that My Mercy may suppress My anger, and that My compassion may prevail over My [other] attributes, so that I may deal with My children through the attribute of compassion and, on their behalf, stop short of the limit of strict justice." Leaving aside the startling (and philosophically problematic) notion that God has human-like emotions, and apparently struggles with anger management issues (which a close reading of the Torah makes less surprising than we might initially think), the bold teaching highlights the constant internal struggle of human beings. Kindness and compassion mitigate our darker side even as they elevate us.

Rabbinic Judaism developed a notion that even our administration of justice should be tempered with mercy. The sages find a suggestion of that idea in the very first portion of Genesis, where they note that two names for the deity, "*Lord God,*" are used side-by-side (Gen. 2:4 and elsewhere): "Lord" (YHVH—*Adonai*) is associated with the quality of mercy, and "God" (*Elohim*) with the quality of justice. Rabbinic midrash explains that God as *Elohim* originally created the world (Gen. 1), but God as *Adonai* continued the process (Gen. 2), because God saw that without the added quality of mercy, creation could not sustain itself. Rashi makes this very point in his comment to the first verse of Genesis: "It does not state [in that verse] that *Adonai* created, because at first God intended to create it [the world] to be placed under the attribute of strict justice, but He realized that the world could not thus endure and therefore gave precedence to Divine mercy, allying it with Divine Justice. It is to this that what is written in [Genesis 2:4] alludes, 'In the day that the Lord God made heaven and earth.'" In both our systems of law and personal lives, the role of forgiveness and leniency born of mercy cannot be neglected. As Shakespeare memorably wrote in *The Merchant of Venice*, "[Mercy] is an attribute to God himself, and earthly power doth then show likest God's when mercy seasons justice."

The Bible tells us we are to imitate God (the Latin expression is *imitatio dei*). We are commanded to *"walk in God's ways"* (Deut. 28:9, 13:5). The Talmud explicitly says, "Be like God; just as God is merciful and gracious, so you likewise should be merciful and gracious." The Talmud also details God's specific acts of compassion, among them clothing the naked (Adam and Eve), visiting the sick (Abraham), comforting the mourner (Isaac), and burying the dead (Moses)—and in each instance, the text says "so you too" should do the same.

"Have we not all one Father? Did not one God create us?" asks the prophet Malachi (2:10), attempting to elicit empathy by pointing to our common humanity. "Jews are compassionate children of compassionate parents, and one who shows no mercy for fellow creatures is assuredly not of the seed of Abraham, our father," declares the Talmud. *"If your enemy is hungry, give him bread to eat,"* says Proverbs (25:21). Rabbi Samson Raphael Hirsch, the father of Modern Orthodox Judaism, counseled, "Do not suppress this compassion, this sympathy especially with the sufferings of your fellowman. . . . See in it the admonition of God that you are to have no joy so long as a brother suffers by your side."

The Bible also speaks of compassion's power to affect others. In the Joseph story, one sibling is missing when the brothers come to Egypt in search of food: Benjamin, the youngest (and Joseph's only full brother), whom their father Jacob has held back. Joseph insists that he be brought down. When the brothers return with him, and at long last Joseph sees Benjamin again, he is *"overcome with feeling"* (Gen. 43:30), so much so that he has to leave the room and weep. This expression is even stronger in the Hebrew, *nichmeru rachamav*, which can be translated as "his compassion was stirred" or even "his innards were burning up" (based on the fact that *rechem* also refers to "womb" or "innards"). Joseph is so stirred by this brotherly emotion that when another brother, Judah, steps forward to admit the siblings' past sin and take responsibility for the present, Joseph is finally able to reveal who he is and to forgive the grave injustice done to him (see chapter 8).

An expression of compassion so intense that it feels like it is burning one's body is employed again in the famous story of two women before King Solomon who both claim to have given birth to the same baby. When the king proposes to solve the dispute by cutting the baby in half, the real mother cries out *"because she was overcome with compassion for her son"* (1 Kings 3:26).

Interestingly, the prophet Hosea uses a similar expression of stirring when he relates that God will not lose faith with Israel. God, he explains, has had a change of heart toward God's people because *"All My tenderness is stirred. I will not act on My wrath"* (Hosea 12:8–9). God allows compassion to overcome anger. In following this example, Hosea encourages us to be similarly stirred to the point where our better instincts will prevail.

Leo Rosten, author of the classic *The Joys of Yiddish*, notes that the Yiddish term *rachmones* (the Ashkenazic pronunciation of the Hebrew *rachamim*, one of the Bible's words for kindness) becomes key to another Jewish sensibility: *Yiddishkeit* (the way a Jew behaves). "This quintessential word [*rachmones*] lies at the heart of Jewish thought and feeling," he writes. "All of Judaism's philosophy, ethics, ethos, learning, education, hierarchy of values, are saturated with a sense of, and heightened sensitivity to *rachmones*."

Jonah sought justice (maybe even revenge) against evildoers—as we often do. But God calls Jonah to announce to the people that they have another chance. God pushes Jonah past his comfort level, until he can view the situation differently. Here God is a model of both character (the spirit of forgiveness) and action (compassionately saving the great city and its people). The lesson is simple, but whether

Jonah, and we, truly "get it" is another matter, since the story ends without noting Jonah's response. Nonetheless, we are left hoping that Jonah goes home a changed man.

Abraham Lincoln pointed to the same human impulse of compassion over anger or vengeance. In his second inaugural address, as the Civil War was just ending, he uttered his now famous phrase, "With malice toward none; with charity toward all." He knew that the path of compassion accords with the "better angels of our nature." Though by no means easy, it is our highest calling.

PART 3

To Walk Humbly

13

Miriam's Celebration

THE PATH OF JOY

I Am Miriam

When I was just a girl, my mother gave birth to a boy at a dangerous time, when Pharaoh was killing our babies. She hid my brother for three months, and when she could hide him no longer, she put him in a wicker basket among the reeds on the bank of the Nile. She told me to stay concealed among the reeds and watch what would become of him.

The daughter of Pharaoh herself came down to bathe, and spied the basket. When she opened it, she saw my brother crying. I heard her say to her slave girl that it was a Hebrew baby, and I held my breath to see what she would do next. I saw her smile and coo at my baby brother, and knew she had taken pity on him.

I stepped forward and without introducing myself blurted out, "Shall I go and get you a Hebrew nurse to suckle the child for you?" Pharaoh's daughter looked at me strangely and answered, "Yes."

This is how I came to save my brother, though I never told him and I doubt he knew it.

When I saw him again Moses was already a grown man. I knew he had fled Egypt for a long time and then returned burning with zeal—a man on a mission. And what an astonishing message he had—that the Lord our God had remembered us; that we are to cast off the yoke of our slavery; that we are to return to the Promised Land of our fathers!

Moses was much closer to my other brother Aaron than to me, for they worked together day by day to free our people. But when we reached the moment of deliverance from slavery to freedom, when we had crossed over to the other side of the sea, it was the women and I who led the celebration. How we sang and danced! "Sing to the Lord, for He has triumphed gloriously."

Then came the years of desert wandering: endless and full of toil. The women of Israel would turn to me for counsel and sustenance, for their faith was flagging. My task was to never let us forget that glorious moment of liberation, or that staggering moment of Revelation that followed at the mountain.

My lowest point came when Aaron and I lost patience with our brother and criticized him over his marriage. Whether that criticism was valid or not . . . I will not say. I was severely punished. Moses prayed for my life, and maybe because he forgave me, God forgave me. Then the three of us continued to lead our people forward.

Miriam's Celebration: From the Bible

Miriam's celebration of the liberation from Egypt (Exod. 15:20–21):

[20]*Then Miriam the prophetess, Aaron's sister, took a timbrel in her hand, and all the women went out after her in dance with timbrels.* [21]*And Miriam chanted for them: Sing to the Lord, for He has triumphed gloriously; Horse and driver He has hurled into the sea.*

Miriam's punishment after criticizing Moses (Num. 12:1–15):

When they were in Hazeroth, [1]*Miriam and Aaron spoke against Moses because of the Cushite woman he had married: "He married a Cushite woman!"*

[2]*They said, "Has the Lord spoken only through Moses? Has He not spoken through us as well?" The Lord heard it.* [3]*Now Moses was a very humble man, more so than any other man on earth.* [4]*Suddenly the Lord called to Moses, Aaron, and Miriam, "Come out, you three, to the Tent of Meeting." So the three of them went out.* [5]*The Lord came down in a pillar of cloud, stopped at the entrance of the Tent, and called out, "Aaron and Miriam!" The two of them came forward;* [6]*and He said, "Hear these My words: When a prophet of the Lord arises among you, I make Myself known to him in a vision, I speak with him in a dream.* [7]*Not so with My servant Moses; he is trusted throughout My household.* [8]*With him I speak mouth to mouth, plainly and not in riddles, and he beholds the likeness of the Lord. How then did you not shrink from speaking against My servant Moses!"* [9]*Still incensed with them, the Lord departed.*

[10]*As the cloud withdrew from the Tent, there was Miriam stricken with snow-white scales! When Aaron turned toward Miriam, he saw that she was stricken with scales.* [11]*And Aaron said to Moses, "O my lord, account not to us the sin which we committed in our folly.* [12]*Let her not be as one dead, who emerges from his mother's womb with half his flesh eaten away."* [13]*So Moses cried out to the Lord, saying, "O God, pray heal her!"*

[14]But the Lord said to Moses, "If her father spat in her face, would she not bear her shame for seven days? Let her be shut out of camp for seven days, and then let her be readmitted." [15]So Miriam was shut out of camp seven days; and the people did not march on until Miriam was readmitted.

Miriam's Celebration: The Prophetic Moment

"Then Miriam the prophetess, Aaron's sister, took a timbrel in her hand, and all the women went out after her in dance." (Exod. 15:20)

Living in the shadow of her famous brothers, Miriam receives scant attention in the Torah. Yet three episodes of her life are significant because of the epic events to which they are connected: the birth of Moses, the Exodus, and the journey to the Promised Land. The first of these establishes Miriam's tie to her brother. The second represents Miriam's shining moment. The third, a painful and provocative episode, may be understood as her moment of failure, or alternatively (and subversively), as her moment of courage.

When Moses' mother puts her baby in the Nile the Torah adds, *"And his sister stationed herself at a distance, to learn what would befall him"* (Exod. 2:4). A few verses later we are told *"Then his sister said to Pharaoh's daughter, Shall I go and get you a Hebrew nurse to suckle the child for you?"* (2:6). Miriam is not even named (and neither is her mother). *"The girl,"* which is how the Torah describes her (2:9), calls her mother. This is all we hear of Miriam until the Israelites cross the sea in the Exodus from Egypt.

The moment of crossing from slavery to freedom is the most exhilarating in the Torah. The great "Song at the Sea," thought to be among the oldest writing in the Bible (Exod. 15:1–18), gives poetic voice to the experience. Although the Torah says it was sung by *"Moses and the Israelites"* (15:1), from the subsequent verse, *"And Miriam chanted for them"* (15:21), one gets the impression it is Miriam who gets the people off their feet singing and dancing. She is the one who seems to embody the extraordinary moment of celebration. She dances, she plays, and she sings. Her own song, in just one verse, is a visceral cry of triumph. *"Sing to the Lord, for He has triumphed gloriously; horse and driver has had hurled into the sea"* (15:21).

Some Bible scholars now argue that the entire "Song at the Sea" should be called "The Song of Miriam." As the important feminist work *The Torah: A Women's Commentary* states, "Beginning in the mid-20th century, a considerable body of literary, historical, sociological, and musicological evidence has been amassed to suggest that the Song should be attributed to Miriam." The commentary notes that one ancient manuscript tradition titles the song in Miriam's name, and the song belongs to a victory song genre typically composed and performed by women.

The fact that Miriam is called "the prophetess" is stunning—both unexpected and unexplained. Also stunning is that she is the first individual in the Torah, after Abraham, to be called a prophet. Only later is her brother given that designation. The sages gamely tried to fill in the biblical gap by suggesting that Miriam predicted Moses' birth—and even that it was she as a young girl who convinced her parents to stay together and conceive another child. But the Rabbis' attempts are not convincing. Perhaps it is best to honor the Torah's enigmatic hint that Miriam has a special status all her own. This seems to be recognized centuries later, when the prophet Micah, recalling the Exodus, emphasizes that God says, "I sent you Moses, Aaron, and Miriam" (6:4).

As Miriam is remembered for her decisive moment of joy and celebration, how are we to understand the final disturbing story about her? It is unclear why Miriam and Aaron criticize their brother over his Cushite wife. Is it that she is not an Israelite? Is it her appearance, perhaps her dark skin (Cush is probably present-day Ethiopia or Sudan)? Or does their criticism mask a deeper discontent: the siblings' desire to share in the leadership?

From the plain sense of the Torah text, the criticism of Moses is unjustified. Miriam is severely punished by a skin affliction, likely leprosy, and while Aaron appears equally culpable, he is inexplicably spared. Here, too, alternative interpretations challenge our conventional understanding of the story. An ancient midrash had the audacity to suggest that Miriam reprimands Moses for essentially abandoning his wife by abstaining from sexual intercourse. In another unusual reading, Miriam sees and chastises Moses for verbally mistreating his wife. Either way, these notions posit that Miriam's punishment masks a legitimate point, and that she was brave to raise it.

The pioneering feminist bible scholar Phyllis Trible believes the real issue at stake appears in the second verse of this story: Miriam and Aaron seem to challenge Moses' prophetic authority when they ask *"Has the Lord spoken only through Moses? Has He not spoken through us as well?"* (Num. 12:2). Though the Torah clearly records God's angry response, Trible argues that if Miriam is a prophet, she has the right to raise the point. "She understands leadership to embrace diverse voices, female and male," she writes, adding, "but the price for speaking out is severe."

Fortunately, both of Miriam's brothers come to her defense, or at least plead for mercy that she not die from her punishment. Aaron's plea seems heartfelt; Moses' prayer is brief but pithy. The Torah clearly states that the people do not move forward until Miriam is healed and rejoins them. Perhaps this waiting is recognition of her status not only as Moses' sister, but as a leader in her own right.

In our own day, women have enhanced the biblical portrait of Miriam in part by speaking of "Miriam's Well," a unique well that sustained the Israelites in the desert. The idea is rooted in ancient midrash. As explained by scholar Tamar Meir, the Rabbis noticed that the description of Miriam's death is immediately followed by the episode of the waters of Meribah: *"Miriam died there. . . . The community was without water"* (Num. 20:1–2). From this juxtaposition they concluded that Miriam's death resulted in the dearth of water, and accredited to her a well that accompanied and provided the wandering Israelites with drinking water in the wilderness. It was a wondrous well, they said, that flowed from itself, like a rock full of holes, created on the eve of the Sabbath at twilight. A mural in the Dura Europus synagogue (third century CE) portrays the well—streams of water issuing forth to each of the tents of the twelve tribes of Israel.

Today, some Jewish families also add a "Miriam's Cup" to the Passover table, to recognize Miriam's unique role in the Exodus. At the same time, this affords an opportunity to reflect on other women's special contributions to the liberation saga, from the midwives (see chapter 2) to Pharaoh's daughter and Moses' wife, Zipporah.

Perhaps Miriam's wisdom and joy are best expressed nowadays in "Miriam's Song," by the late beloved composer of Jewish folk music Debbie Friedman: "Sing a song to the One whom we've exalted," Friedman wrote. "Miriam and the women danced and danced the whole night long."

Walking with Miriam: The Path of Joy

Miriam, timbrel in her hand, leading the Israelites in celebration at the shore of the sea, exemplifies the joy of faith. She is the exemplar of the Torah's call to *"love the Lord your God"* with heart, soul, and might (Deut. 6:5) and the embodiment of the Psalmist's jubilant cry, *"This is the day that the Lord has made—let us exult and rejoice in it"* (118:24). Miriam gives expression to a primal function of religion—the response of the soul to the wonder of the world.

The Torah actually commands joy, instructing the Israelites to *"rejoice before the Lord your God"* at many auspicious occasions (Deut. 12:12). Almost every Jewish holiday has a joyful component. The three great pilgrimage festivals of Sukkot, Pesach, and Shavuot, all harvest festivals in origin, were the times of greatest rejoicing. At the ingathering of Sukkot we are instructed to *"rejoice before the Lord your God seven days"* (Lev. 23:40). The Talmud's description of the festivities that ended this week in the Second Temple period, called "the water-drawing celebration," almost reads like a Mardi Gras festival. Although this wild celebration disappeared with the destruction of the Temple, some of its exuberance was transferred to the added holiday of "Simchat Torah" (Celebration of the Torah), with its parading and dancing with the Torah scrolls. Purim is an overtly jubilant time, and the joy at Hanukkah is also palpable.

The Psalmist most vitally expresses the feeling of joy: *"Serve the Lord in gladness"* (100:2). Time and again he declares: *"I will glorify God with my song"* (28:7); *"Your presence is perfect joy"* (16:11); *"You put joy in my heart"* (4:8); *"I will sacrifice . . . with shouts of joy, singing and chanting a hymn to the Lord"* (27:6).

The Rabbis availed themselves of a series of psalms (113–118) to enhance the joyousness of the festival prayers. They called these psalms *Hallel* (praise), and to this day *Hallel* psalms are sung with great relish in the synagogue. They also taught in the Talmud: "In the world to come we will be asked: Why were there times when you could have rejoiced and did not?"

Even the prophets, despite their often harsh rhetoric, speak of joy. Isaiah, for example, proclaims: *"O Shout for joy, you who dwell in Zion"* (12:6); and *"Then the humble shall have increasing joy through the Lord"* (29:9).

One of Isaiah's expressions, *"You shall go out in joy"* (55:12), became like a mantra to an eighteenth-century movement that sought to recapture joy as a central expression of Judaism. Rabbi Israel Baal Shem Tov, who founded the Hasidic movement and exemplified its spirit, reportedly was once asked "Why is that you and your followers burst into song and dance at the slightest provocation?" After responding with a story about a musician whose great talent stirs the townspeople to get up and dance, and a deaf man who happens by and thinks they are all mad, the Baal Shem Tov replied: "Chasidim are moved by the melody that issues forth from every creature in God's creation. If this makes them appear mad to those with less sensitive ears, should they therefore cease to dance?"

Furthermore, the Baal Shem Tov taught that "the ability to be joyous, by discerning the good and joyous within every experience" was to Hasidim "a biblical command." He quoted the Talmudic adage, "All your actions should be for the sake of heaven," and linked it to the Psalmist and Isaiah's words, *"to serve God with joy,"* to argue that this command applied at all times and situations. As Rabbi Menachem Mendel of Lubavitch expressed the legacy of Hasidism's founder, "The Baal Shem Tov wiped away tears from the Jewish people. He worked hard to ensure that every Jew would be happy simply because he is a Jew."

The path of joy does not overlook the reality of suffering and pain in the world. Indeed the world of the Hasidic masters was replete with it. They knew quite well that *"Weeping may tarry for the night, but joy comes in the morning"* (Ps. 30:6). They were mindful of the ancient Rabbinic teaching, "In this world, there is no perfect joy, unmixed with anxiety; no perfect pleasure, unmixed with envy." But the Hasidic masters refused to see the proverbial cup half empty. Instead, they dwelt on the *"my cup runneth over"* of the Psalmist. They understood that finding joy, and with it, clinging to hope, can lift our spirits and change our lives.

While the Torah does not elaborate on why Miriam was called a prophetess, we can speculate that her joyfulness and wisdom drew people to her. The trek through the desert was full of travail, and Miriam's smiling countenance gave people comfort and hope. Just like the people who *"did not march on until Miriam was readmitted"* (Num. 12:15), we all need those who embrace what the French call joie de vivre—the "joy of life"—to remind us that, even amidst the dark, there is light.

14

Caleb's Spirit

THE PATH OF FAITH

I Am Caleb

After all the years of wandering . . . the Promised Land was finally in sight! Moses chose twelve of us, one from each of the tribes, to scout out the good land. From the tribe of Judah he chose me.

We went up and scouted from north to south. We indeed found a land of milk and honey. We found suitable grazing for our flocks and rich soil for our crops. We found fruit, clusters of grapes so large we had to carry them on poles borne by two men. We found luscious pomegranates, delectable figs, and succulent olives.

And we also found fierce people in fortified cities: Amalekites, Hittites, Jebusites, Amorites, and Canaanites.

When we delivered our report, though, everyone seemed to hear only that last part about the fearsome inhabitants. They began murmuring.

Hushing them, I said, "Let us by all means go up, and we shall gain possession of the land, for we shall surely overcome."

To my shock and dismay, the other scouts, all of them except Joshua, objected. "We cannot attack," they moaned. "The people are stronger than we are. They are giants; we are grasshoppers. They will eat us alive."

All hell broke loose. My fellow Israelites railed against Moses and Aaron. I could not believe what they were saying. "If only we had died in the land of Egypt," they cried. "Better to die there than see our wives and children carried off," they sobbed. "Let us go back to Egypt," they wailed.

Joshua and I stood up. We rent our clothes. We pleaded with the mob to back off. We said, "The Land is good. The Lord is with us. He will bring us into the land of milk and honey. He will give it to us. Have no fear. Have some faith. The Lord is with us."

The mob reached for stones to pelt us. As I stood trembling before them, I felt God's spirit upon me and my shaking legs stood firm. Over and over I exhorted my people to keep the faith.

Finally Moses arose, and with him the glory of God. Moses began to speak, and the people began to listen.

Caleb's Spirit: From the Bible

Caleb stands firm in his faith (Num.: 13:25–14:24):

[25]At the end of forty days they returned from scouting the land. [26]They went straight to Moses and Aaron and the whole Israelite community at Kadesh in the wilderness of Paran, and they made their report to them and to the whole community, as they showed them the fruit of the land. [27]This is what they told him: "We came to the land you sent us to; it does indeed flow with milk and honey, and this is its fruit. [28]However, the people who inhabit the country are powerful, and the cities are fortified and very large; moreover, we saw the Anakites there. [29]Amalekites dwell in the Negeb region; Hittites, Jebusites, and Amorites inhabit the hill country; and Canaanites dwell by the Sea and along the Jordan."

[30]Caleb hushed the people before Moses and said, "Let us by all means go up, and we shall gain possession of it, for we shall surely overcome it."

[31]But the men who had gone up with him said, "We cannot attack that people, for it is stronger than we." [32]Thus they spread calumnies among the Israelites about the land they had scouted, saying, "The country that we traversed and scouted is one that devours its settlers. All the people that we saw in it are men of great size; [33]we saw the Nephilim there—the Anakites are part of the Nephilim—and we looked like grasshoppers to ourselves, and so we must have looked to them."

[14:1]The whole community broke into loud cries, and the people wept that night. [2]All the Israelites railed against Moses and Aaron. "If only we had died in the land of Egypt," the whole community shouted at them, "or if only we might die in this wilderness! [3]Why is the Lord taking us to that land to fall by the sword? Our wives and children will be carried off! It would be better for us to go back to Egypt!" [4]And they said to one another, "Let us head back for Egypt."

[5]Then Moses and Aaron fell on their faces before all the assembled congregation of the Israelites. [6]And Joshua son of Nun and Caleb son of Jephunneh, of those who had scouted the land, rent their clothes [7]and exhorted the whole Israelite community: "The land that we tra-

versed and scouted is an exceedingly good land. [8]If the Lord is pleased with us, He will bring us into that land, a land that flows with milk and honey, and give it to us; [9]only you must not rebel against the Lord. Have no fear then of the people of the country, for they are our prey: their protection has departed from them, but the Lord is with us. Have no fear of them!" [10]As the whole community threatened to pelt them with stones, the Presence of the Lord appeared in the Tent of Meeting to all the Israelites.

[20]And the Lord said, "I pardon, as you have asked. [21]Nevertheless, as I live and as the Lord's Presence fills the whole world, [22]none of the men who have seen My Presence and the signs that I have performed in Egypt and in the wilderness, and who have tried Me these many times and have disobeyed Me, [23]shall see the land that I promised on oath to their fathers; none of those who spurn Me shall see it. [24]But My servant Caleb, because he was imbued with a different spirit and remained loyal to Me—him will I bring into the land that he entered, and his offspring shall hold it as a possession.

Caleb's Spirit: The Prophetic Moment

"But My servant Caleb, because he was imbued with a different spirit and remained loyal to Me—him will I bring into the land." (Num. 14:24)

At a critical juncture in Israelite history, Caleb has the fortitude to stand against his fellow spies. He must take a stand because his fellows have given an excessively pessimistic report of their foray into the Promised Land. Caleb knows that this report, a distortion of the truth as he sees it, will gravely weaken community morale. He tries to hush the people even before the spies have finished, only to see them turn more unequivocally against the mission. Caleb's fears are realized: Pandemonium and outright rebellion against Moses and Aaron ensue.

When the other spies' account first emerges, Caleb alone attempts to calm the people. He does not contradict the content of their report so much as their conclusion. Caleb sees the same thing as his fellows—but his perspective is different because of his faith. Caleb does not view the Israelites as grasshoppers who will be crushed by giants—he is confident the mission can succeed. His reply is captured in the emphatic form of the Hebrew expressions *aloh na'aleh, "let us by all means go up"* and *yachol nuchal, "we shall surely overcome"* (Num. 13:30).

When his initial effort fails, Caleb is compelled to rebut his fellows and again exhort the community. He specifically appeals to faith: *"If the Lord is pleased with us, He will bring us into that land." "Have no fear,"* he continues, *". . . the Lord is with us"* (Num. 14:8–9).

Caleb's courage and loyalty is praised, and his reward is substantial—only he and Joshua (who soon allies with Caleb) of the Exodus generation will enter the Promised Land.

For his brave stand against the "establishment" Caleb is described as *"My servant"* and imbued with a *"different spirit"* (Num. 14:24). The Hebrew *ruach acheret* is sometimes translated as *"another spirit"* (in the "old" JPS TANAKH) or *"added spirit."* This rendering seems to follow Rashi, who makes the intriguing comment that Caleb had to let his heart (which knew the truth) overrule his head (which wanted to follow the lead of the other spies). The more recent translation of *"different spirit"* (in the new JPS TANAKH) is more in accordance with Ibn Ezra, who emphasizes Caleb's contrarianism against the majority. In any case, it is a special measure of faith that enables Caleb to both maintain hope in the mission and resist those who would succumb to despair.

The Hebrew word *ruach* is intriguing. Like many ancient Hebrew words, it is grounded in a concrete meaning but takes on more abstract definitions as well. *Ruach* means both "spirit" and "wind." The context determines the meaning. For example, in the book of Exodus the Israelites suffer from *kotzer ruach*, a *"crushed spirit,"* because of their enslavement (Exod. 6:9).

Sometimes, though, the biblical context is indeterminate. Consider the first use of *ruach* in the Bible, already in the second verse, *"the earth being unformed and void, with darkness over the surface of the deep and ruach of God sweeping over the water"* (Gen. 1:2). Is Genesis referring to *"the spirit of God"* or *"a wind from God"*? The new JPS TANAKH translation chooses the latter, but offers a footnote mentioning the former.

Biblical scholar Jeremiah Unterman, however, directs our attention to an evocative and rarely noticed aspect of the first use of *ruach*: The verb that describes the wind, or spirit, in the creation narrative, *m'rachefet,* is rarely used. While it could signify wind blowing or sweeping, the only other use of the term in the Bible is in connection with an eagle hovering, or fluttering, over its young: *"Like an eagle who rouses his nestlings, gliding down to his young, so did He spread His wing and take him, bear him along on His pinions"* (Deut. 32:11). "Apparently," Unterman observes, "the intention in Genesis is to bring to mind a mother bird (the Hebrew verb here is in the feminine), that is, God's spirit is hovering over the stuff of creation like a mother bird over her young. Creation, as it were, is being born, and the goodness of that birth is best understood as ethical."

Most interesting is when the Bible speaks of *ruach Elohim,* God's spirit, imparted in human beings. Prior to Caleb, Joseph is described (by Pharaoh no less!) as *"a man in whom is the spirit of God,"* which enables him to be *"so discerning and wise"* (Gen. 41:38). In the book of Exodus, Bezalel, the architect and craftsman of the Tabernacle, is twice described as *"endowed with the divine spirit,"* which gives him *"skill, ability, and knowledge . . . to give directions [teach]"* (Exod. 31:3, 35:31–34). Ezekiel speaks of God putting a *"new spirit"* in the people that will lead them away from idolatry (Ezek.11:19, 18:31, 36:26). Hosea refers to an anonymous prophet as *"a man of the spirit"* (Hosea 9:7). Samuel repeatedly describes the young Saul with the words *"the spirit of God gripped him."* Saul is also repeatedly described as speaking in the ecstatic tones of the prophets of that time (perhaps similar to what is called "speaking in tongues" among evangelicals today) (1 Sam. 10:10, 11:6, 19:20,23). Later, the young David is described with the same expression (1 Sam. 16:15), while we are told, *"the spirit of the Lord departed from Saul, and an evil spirit from the Lord began to terrify him"* (1 Sam. 16:16,23).

The word "inspiration" derives from "spirit." In the Torah, God's spirit can artistically inspire (Bezalel), intellectually inspire (Joseph), prophetically inspire (Saul, David, and the prophets), and morally inspire (Caleb). In each case, the individual is transformed into a leader, and elevated even higher when his self-awareness of his special gift inspires faith. Bezalel is able to motivate the entire community to draw together to build the Tabernacle. Joseph is able to devise a plan to save Egypt, while forgiving his brothers. Saul and David are able to overcome their youthful inexperience and gain the confidence to lead a nation. The prophets are able to overcome their trepidations and critique their countrymen. And Caleb, stalwart in his optimism in the face of deep pessimism, is able to keep hope and faith in the Israelites' mission alive until God intercedes.

Walking with Caleb: The Path of Faith

The great Modern Orthodox theologian Joseph Soloveitchik authored the book *The Lonely Man of Faith*. Indeed, faith can be a daunting proposition. Caleb's prophetic moment teaches that those who seek to journey to a better place sometimes have to stand against the majority to get there.

Ironically, Abraham is considered both the epitome of faith and a pioneer of protest (the latter for standing his ground with God over the destruction of Sodom and Gomorrah; see chapter 1). Overall, the Bible portrays him as a man of utter obedience. With nary a word of comment or objection, he submits to God's commands: whether in response to the call to uproot himself and his family, to journey to the unknown *"land that I will show you,"* to establish a covenant, to circumcise himself and all the males in his household, even to sacrifice his beloved son Isaac. Note: The same initial command, *lech lecha*, "go forth," in Genesis 12 occurs again in Genesis 22, when God summons Abraham (and Isaac) to go to *"one of the heights that I will point out to you."* Abraham does not know where he is going, but the fact that he is going with God is enough. That is faith.

Some contemporary commentators see Abraham's example as extreme—blind faith at best, fanaticism at worst. The line between admirable and excessive faith can be a fine one. But the Torah states approvingly of Abraham: *"Now I know that you fear God. . . . Because you have done this and have not withheld your son, your favored one, I will bestow My blessing upon you"* (Gen. 22:12,16–17). Elsewhere in Genesis the Torah states succinctly and definitively, *"And because he put his trust in the Lord, God reckoned it to his merit"* (Gen. 15:6). The root for *"put his trust," he'emin*, forms the classic Hebrew term for faith, *emunah*. The same root is again applied to Abraham in the book of Nehemiah, in the Levites' lovely recollection of the relationship between God and Abraham: *"Finding his heart true [ne'eman] to You, You made a covenant with him"* (Neh. 9:8).

This same expression of faith also appears in the beautiful words of the prophet Hosea, who looks forward to the day when God will declare, *"I will espouse you forever; I will espouse you with righteousness and justice, and with goodness and mercy. And I will espouse you with faithfulness [emunah]. Then you shall be devoted to the Lord"* (Hosea 2:21–22). The Psalmist also acknowledges this faith: *"Give ear to my plea, as you are faithful"* (Ps. 143:1). He desires to model that divine faithfulness, declaring: *"I have chosen the way of faithfulness; I have set your rules before me"* (Ps. 119:30).

Hosea and the Psalmist speak of a pure faith that is enviable but difficult. While Abraham and Caleb are models of faith, what was really happening internally during their moments of great challenge? The Torah is silent regarding Abraham's inner thoughts. Did he not have some trepidation as he bound Isaac on the altar? So, too, we know nothing of Caleb's inner state. Was he in turmoil as the people threatened to riot? Did he have any doubts along the lines of his fellow spies—or perhaps qualms about being the sole voice to advocate for entering the land? After all, it can be difficult to be the "Lonely Man of Faith." If so, how did Caleb combat his self-doubt?

The questions that come with faith apply to us as well. How do we deal with doubt? Are we strong enough to take on the challenges in our lives that are necessary but difficult? Can we withstand the skepticism of others, or their outright antagonism?

The Torah, as epitomized in the Ten Commandments, calls us to affirm the presence of God (*"I the Lord am your God"*), the redeeming involvement of God (*"who brought you out of the land of Egypt, the house of bondage"*), and the exclusivity of God (*"you shall not make for yourself a sculptured image or any likeness"*) (Exod. 20:1–4). Such faith is intended to lead to the reverence and love of God that perhaps settled any doubts in Caleb's mind.

On another level, faith is a form of courage: the refusal to succumb to our fears. The prophet Haggai seemed to have Caleb in mind when he said, *"So I promised you when you came out of Egypt, and My spirit is still in your midst. Fear not!"* (Hag. 2:5). So too the prophet Zechariah memorably said, *"Not by might, nor by power, but by my spirit—said the Lord of Hosts"* (Zech. 4:6). Surely it takes a special faith to swim against the tide; to challenge pessimism; to confront injustice; and to bring ourselves and our community one step closer to the land of promise.

Caleb summons the courage to stand out by first being willing to stand up against his peers. But to take that stand requires the ability to see the world differently. Rabbi Shai Held comments: "Ultimately, the question posed by the text is whether what we imagine possible is limited to what we see before us, or whether we can discern possibilities not immediately apparent to the eye." "Faith sees beyond fate," observes the contemporary writer Noah benShea. Rabbi Leo Baeck, the brave leader of German Jewry on the eve of the Holocaust, wrote, "In Judaism faith is . . . the capacity of the soul to perceive the abiding . . . in the transitory, the invisible in the visible." This special insight is perhaps the greatest gift faith can give us.

Caleb and his fellow scouts visited the same place and saw the same things. For the others, seeing "giants" meant that they themselves were like "grasshoppers." Seeing fortified cities meant no entry. Seeing no way forward meant turning back. Caleb took a different view. He did not deny the challenges ahead, but neither did he forget how the Israelites had overcome one daunting obstacle after another—

from the Exodus itself to the travails of accessing water, food, and leadership in the desert. What is more, Caleb knew that God's protection and help would sustain the Israelites in the Promised Land. Unlike his compatriots, he was able to see his people with a future—dwelling securely in the fertile land. He said, "We can surely do this. We can ascend the heights."

Edward Kennedy captured this spirit when he remembered his brother Bobby: "Some see the world as it is and ask—why?; others see the world as it might be, and ask—why not?"

15

Hannah's Prayer

THE PATH OF PRAYER

I Am Hannah

Did Sarah doubt Abraham's love? She was taunted by Hagar and bereft of child. Then the Lord remembered her, and the covenant was sustained through her son Isaac.

Did Rachel doubt Jacob's love? She was taunted by Leah and bereft of child. Then the Lord remembered her, and the covenant was sustained through her son Joseph.

Did I, Hannah, ever doubt my husband Elkanah's love? I was taunted by Peninnah and bereft of child. Then the Lord remembered me, and the covenant was sustained through my son Samuel.

Every year we would go up to the shrine in Shiloh to offer sacrifices. Peninnah did not even have to say anything: The sight of that woman and all her children offering their portions would send me weeping. Elkanah said to me, "Hannah, why are you crying and why aren't you eating? Why are you so sad? Am I not more devoted to you than ten sons?" This made me want to cry even more.

I could not stop weeping that day I turned in prayer to the Lord. I beseeched the Lord to grant me a child. I vowed that if my prayer was answered that child would be dedicated to the Lord. No razor would touch his head; no task would be given to him other than to serve at Shiloh. I prayed and prayed, and old Eli, the priest, sitting at the doorpost of the Temple, saw my lips moving but heard no voice. He thought me drunk. He said to me, "How long will you make a drunken spectacle of yourself? Sober up!"

"Oh, no my lord," I replied. "I have drunk no wine, but have poured out my heart to the Lord."

Eli looked at me, and his expression grew kind. "Do not take your maidservant for a worthless woman," I continued. "I have only been speaking all this time out of my great anguish and distress."

Eli nodded. I knew this old man had problems of his own, for his sons did not follow in his ways. "Go in peace, my child," he said to me, "and may the God of Israel grant you what you have asked of Him."

When my son Samuel was born, I kept him by my side until he was weaned. Then I fulfilled the vow I had made; on the next trip to Shiloh, there he remained. I said to Eli, "For as long as he lives he is lent to the Lord."

In the years that followed, I was blessed with more sons and daughters. Yet I never forgot my Samuel. At every pilgrimage I made a little robe for him. I kissed my boy as he put it on, and I cried some more.

Hannah's Prayer: From the Bible

Hannah's prayer to the Lord over her barrenness (1 Sam. 1:1–19):

> [1]*There was a man from Ramathaim of the Zuphites, in the hill country of Ephraim, whose name was Elkanah son of Jeroham son of Elihu son of Tohu son of Zuph, an Ephraimite.* [2]*He had two wives, one named Hannah and the other Peninnah; Peninnah had children, but Hannah was childless.* [3]*This man used to go up from his town every year to worship and to offer sacrifice to the Lord of Hosts at Shiloh.—Hophni and Phinehas, the two sons of Eli, were priests of the Lord there.*
>
> [4]*One such day, Elkanah offered a sacrifice. He used to give portions to his wife Peninnah and to all her sons and daughters;* [5]*but to Hannah he would give one portion only—though Hannah was his favorite—for the Lord had closed her womb.* [6]*Moreover, her rival, to make her miserable, would taunt her that the Lord had closed her womb.* [7]*This happened year after year: Every time she went up to the House of the Lord, the other would taunt her, so that she wept and would not eat.* [8]*Her husband Elkanah said to her, "Hannah, why are you crying and why aren't you eating? Why are you so sad? Am I not more devoted to you than ten sons?"*
>
> [9]*After they had eaten and drunk at Shiloh, Hannah rose.—The priest Eli was sitting on the seat near the doorpost of the temple of the Lord.—*[10]*In her wretchedness, she prayed to the Lord, weeping all the while.* [11]*And she made this vow: "O Lord of Hosts, if You will look upon the suffering of Your maidservant and will remember me and not forget Your maidservant, and if You will grant Your maidservant a male child, I will dedicate him to the Lord for all the days of his life; and no razor shall ever touch his head."*
>
> [12]*As she kept on praying before the Lord, Eli watched her mouth.* [13]*Now Hannah was praying in her heart; only her lips moved, but her voice could not be heard. So Eli thought she was drunk.* [14]*Eli said to her, "How long will you make a drunken spectacle of yourself? Sober up!"* [15]*And Hannah replied, "Oh no, my lord! I am a very unhappy woman.*

I have drunk no wine or other strong drink, but I have been pouring out my heart to the Lord. [16]*Do not take your maidservant for a worthless woman; I have only been speaking all this time out of my great anguish and distress."* [17]*"Then go in peace," said Eli, "and may the God of Israel grant you what you have asked of Him."* [18]*She answered, "You are most kind to your handmaid." So the woman left, and she ate, and was no longer downcast.* [19]*Early next morning they bowed low before the Lord, and they went back home to Ramah.*

Hannah's Prayer: The Prophetic Moment

"She kept on praying." (1 Sam. 1:12)

One might think that the Bible is full of people praying, but this is hardly the case. One of the few acts of overt spiritual expression comes from Hannah.

Hannah's story begins the first book of Samuel. One brief chapter conveys the despondency of a barren woman, the empathy of a solicitous husband, and the confusion of an aged priest.

Hannah is one of Elkanah's two wives. His other spouse, Peninnah, is blessed with multiple children, but Hannah is barren. And so, while Hannah may be Elkanah's favorite, she is profoundly unhappy. She deeply wants to have a child, and her rival ups the ante by taunting her about her childlessness. The taunting is worst when the family makes an annual pilgrimage to the cultic center at Shiloh. It reduces Hannah to tears, and she is so distressed she is unable to eat. Elkanah, possibly trying to comfort her, asks, *"Am I not more devoted to you than ten sons?"* (His words can be understood as intending to pacify her or as meaning to reprimand.)

The Bible next informs us: *"In her wretchedness, she prayed to the Lord, weeping all the while."* The temple priest, Eli, seeing her lips moving but no intelligible words coming from her mouth, mistakes her for a drunk, when instead *"Hannah was praying in her heart . . . but her voice could not be heard."* When Hannah clears up the misunderstanding and receives Eli's blessings, she is immediately uplifted, although her basic situation has not changed. Perhaps she feels that, with the priest's blessing, her fortune will change, or the simple act of kindness his words represent is enough.

In any case, Hannah does conceive a long-hoped-for child a short time later. The name she gives him, Samuel, means "God has heard," or, as the text explains it, *"asked of God."*

As the first chapter of Samuel ends, Hannah is fulfilling her vow to give the boy over to God's service. He is left in Eli's care. In the second chapter a poignant verse describes how Hannah makes a little robe for her son and brings it for him at her yearly visits. We also read several paragraphs of a psalm-like prayer that Hannah is purported to have prayed: an elaborate literary poem that feels like a later addition to the text, as it is not in the spirit of the simple, emotional words Hannah might have prayed. Nevertheless, it underscores Hannah's spiritual nature.

Eli's initial misunderstanding and rebuff of Hannah may also be a subtle acknowledgment of how institutional religion may sometimes distrust individual spirituality. Intense devotion and piety can be perplexing and even threatening to an establishment set in its ways.

Yet, to Eli's credit, he then proceeds to listen to Hannah and to realize her distress and earnestness. Her faithfulness, apparent at the annual pilgrimage, stands in marked contrast to the spiritual and moral bankruptcy that evidently characterizes his sons. They will fail their father and Israel, while Hannah's son, Samuel, will be the savior of the people.

For Hannah, the prophetic moment begins in a brief instant of intense emotion: a passionate yet humble appeal to God. The epitome of prayer is the plea of the broken heart. Hannah pours out her soul. We are witness to a moment of unvarnished piety. Yet Hannah follows her prayer with action. She makes a vow that if she gives birth to a son she will dedicate him to God for life. She mentions that no razor will touch his head—indicative of the special rules observed by the *Nazirim*, a group of priests in ancient Israel (Samson is another *Nazir*). Hannah keeps her vow by giving up her son Samuel to the priesthood.

To this day Jews read Hannah's story as a supplemental reading (haftarah) on Rosh Hashanah morning. The themes of creation and the renewal of life as symbolized in the birth of a son to a previously barren woman are certainly apt at the Jewish New Year (that is traditionally considered the birthday of the world). But so too is the story of Hannah herself. The petitionary purpose of the High Holy Days is no better exemplified than in the example of this humble wife and mother who seeks to overcome her heartbreak through the power of prayer.

Her son attained prophetic immortality; more quietly so did Hannah.

Walking with Hannah: The Path of Prayer

The sincerity and humility of Hannah's moment of prayer shines through her story. Hannah refers to herself as a simple *"maidservant"* when addressing Eli. Without pretension, she pleads that she not be seen as a *"worthless woman."* She speaks of *"pouring out her heart"* out of *"great anguish and distress."*

The Rabbinic sages saw in Hannah a model of piety—indeed, her name comes from the Hebrew word *hen*, which means "grace." They cite four qualities of sincere prayer they learn from her example: that it should be from the heart, offered in a low voice, with lips visibly moving, and in a sober state. For these men, it is a woman who models what true spiritual intent (*kavanah*) is about.

Perhaps this is why Hannah is actually counted among the prophets in another tractate of the Talmud (where she is one of seven female prophets, the others being Sarah, Miriam, Deborah, Avigail, Huldah, and Esther). While the predictive nature of her prayer in the second chapter is the ostensible explanation for her prophetic designation, her devotion and sincerity are the qualities that truly distinguish her.

The Psalmist is considered the biblical author who best exemplifies devotional prayer. (While the majority of the psalms are traditionally ascribed to King David, the scholarly consensus posits a collection of authors from a variety of periods whose names are lost to history.) Like Hannah, the Psalmist cries out: *"Out of the depths have I called You"* (Ps. 130:1). The Psalmist also declares, *"The Lord is close to the broken-hearted; those crushed in spirit God delivers"* (Ps. 34:19); *"God heals their broken hearts, and binds up their wounds"* (Ps. 147:3).

Of all the 150 Psalms, the twenty-third, beginning *"The Lord is my shepherd,"* is perhaps best known and loved. Famed American clergyman Henry Ward Beecher described it as "the nightingale of the Psalms. It is small, of a homely feather, singing shyly out of obscurity; but oh! it has filled the air of the whole world with melodious joy, greater than the heart can conceive." The pastoral imagery of walking in God's providential care imparts great comfort and faith, and seems to bring us back to the security of the covenantal relationship that underlies the entire prophetic path.

Moses de Leon, the likely author of the Zohar, the greatest work of Jewish mysticism, captures both Hannah's and the Psalmist's devotion when he writes, "The heart's cry to God is the highest form of prayer. Tears smash through the gates and doors of heaven." Kauffman Kohler, a late-nineteenth-century theologian, expressed it this way: "Prayer is the expression of man's longing and yearning for God in times of dire need and of overflowing joy."

Prayer became increasingly important in Judaism after the destruction of the Second Temple. Historical reality necessitated a transformation: The sacrifice (*avodah*) of the Temple cult was replaced with the sacrifice-of-the-heart (*avodah sh'belev*). The sages never gave up the hope that the Temple, with its sacrifices, would be restored, but the establishment of communal prayer that also featured reading the Torah heralded the Rabbinic revolution. The Mishnah introduced thrice-daily prayer that mirrored the morning (*Shacharit*), afternoon (*Mincha*), and evening (*Ma'ariv*) Temple sacrifices. The Talmud openly acknowledges, "What is the service (sacrifice) of the heart? It is prayer."

The introduction of communal liturgy sharpened the inherent tension between fixed, prescribed prayer (*keva*) and spontaneous, personal prayer (*kavanah*). This tension is common to all religious traditions—and, like other faiths, Judaism has a place for both. Certain key prayers (such as the *Amidah* and *Kaddish*) require a minyan of ten Jewish adults, per Jewish law designed to emphasize community. Private devotion has its place both outside the synagogue and, as indicated by this talmudic passage, within the service itself: "The pious men of ancient times used to spend an hour meditating before praying, and then pray, so that they could direct their heart towards their faith."

Like the Matriarchs, Sarah, Rebecca, and Rachel, childless Hannah understands her situation as a test of faith. She believes that the power to conceive and bear a child ultimately rests with God. As a Talmudic dictum teaches: "Three keys the Holy One blessed be He has retained in His own hand and not entrusted to the hand of any messenger, namely, the key of Rain; the key of Childbirth; and the key of the Revival of the Dead." Hannah believes in the power of prayer to move the Divine. When God answers her prayer, there is no question in her mind that she must keep the vow that was integral to her appeal.

A central passage of the High Holy Day liturgy evokes the transformational power of prayer to move not only the one who prays but the One who listens. Unique to these days is a section of prayer that emphasizes Rosh Hashanah and Yom Kippur as times of judgment. A key verse, perhaps the most essential one of the holidays, proclaims, "But repentance, prayer and charity temper the severe decree." Whether or not we accept the theological implications of swaying the divine will, this is a prominent statement for the power of prayer.

"As a tree torn from the soil; as a river separated from its source," reads the prayer book *Gates of Prayer*, "the human soul wanes when detached from what is greater than itself." In her time of need, Hannah seeks to connect to God. Having experienced her prayers answered, Hannah responds with further words of praise and thanksgiving. Our sages saw this as a model of spiritual sincerity and piety.

Abraham Joshua Heschel wrote: "Prayer invites God's presence to suffuse our spirit; God's will to prevail in our lives. Prayer may not bring water to parched fields, nor mend a broken bridge, not rebuild a ruined city. But prayer can water an arid soul, mend a broken heart, and rebuild a weakened will." Hannah's prayer seems to do all three—her pain is assuaged, her despair eased, and her resolve strengthened.

The path of prayer responds to our most basic emotional and spiritual needs: the mind yearning for understanding, the heart yearning for healing, and the soul yearning for transcendence.

16

Elijah's Voice

THE PATH OF HUMILITY

I Am Elijah

The life of a prophet is never easy; nor is it supposed to be.

No sooner did I declare the drought during the reign of the sinful King Ahab than I was forced into hiding.

No sooner did I emerge from hiding than I was compelled to confront the king. Catching sight of me, he said, "Is that you, you troubler of Israel?" "It is not I who have brought trouble on Israel," I retorted, "but you and your father's house, by forsaking the commandments of the Lord and going after the idols."

Ahab agreed to a challenge on Mount Carmel—his 450 false Baal prophets against me. I alone was left among the prophets. I reprimanded all the people who gathered, "How long will you keep hopping between two boughs? If the Lord is God, follow God; and if Baal, follow him!" The people stood in stony silence; they have always been stiff-necked and of fickle faith. Only after my fire devoured the sacrifices did they cry out to God.

No sooner did I prevail then Jezebel, the king's wife (and even more wicked then he, if that is possible), sought my life, and I had to flee once again. True, I had ordered all her false prophets put to the sword, just as she had murdered so many of my brothers. I was moved by zeal for the Lord, and I alone was left among the prophets.

As before, God saved me and brought me deep into the wilderness to his holy mountain. God called out to me and I explained my zeal. God brought wind and quake and fire and then called out to me, ever so softly, in the silence that ensued. I answered my Lord in the same way: I was moved by zeal; I alone am left.

God told me to go back, to anoint the new kings of Aram and Israel. I will do that. I know I will have to confront Ahab and Jezebel again. But God also said something else to me: to anoint my successor, Elisha. Is it time? Have I failed my Lord? Twice my Lord asked me why I was here. Twice I told God. But did I miss something in that still, small voice?

Elijah's Voice: From the Bible

Elijah confronts Ahab and the people (1 Kings 18:16–22,36–40):

[16]Obadiah went to find Ahab, and informed him; and Ahab went to meet Elijah. [17]When Ahab caught sight of Elijah, Ahab said to him, "Is that you, you troubler of Israel?" [18]He retorted, "It is not I who have brought trouble on Israel, but you and your father's House, by forsaking the commandments of the Lord and going after the Baalim. [19]Now summon all Israel to join me at Mount Carmel, together with the four hundred and fifty prophets of Baal and the four hundred prophets of Asherah, who eat at Jezebel's table."

[20]Ahab sent orders to all the Israelites and gathered the prophets at Mount Carmel. [21]Elijah approached all the people and said, "How long will you keep hopping between two opinions? If the Lord is God, follow Him; and if Baal, follow him!" But the people answered him not a word. [22]Then Elijah said to the people, "I am the only prophet of the Lord left, while the prophets of Baal are four hundred and fifty men."

[36]When it was time to present the meal offering, the prophet Elijah came forward and said, "O Lord, God of Abraham, Isaac, and Israel! Let it be known today that You are God in Israel and that I am Your servant, and that I have done all these things at Your bidding. [37]Answer me, O Lord, answer me, that this people may know that You, O Lord, are God; for You have turned their hearts backward."

[38]Then fire from the Lord descended and consumed the burnt offering, the wood, the stones, and the earth; and it licked up the water that was in the trench. [39]When they saw this, all the people flung themselves on their faces and cried out: "The Lord alone is God, The Lord alone is God!"

[40]Then Elijah said to them, "Seize the prophets of Baal, let not a single one of them get away." They seized them, and Elijah took them down to the Wadi Kishon and slaughtered them there.

Elijah confronts God (1 Kings 19:8–16):

[8]He arose and ate and drank; and with the strength from that meal he walked forty days and forty nights as far as the mountain of God at Horeb. [9]There he went into a cave, and there he spent the night.

Then the word of the Lord came to him. He said to him, "Why are you here, Elijah?" [10]He replied, "I am moved by zeal for the Lord, the God of Hosts, for the Israelites have forsaken Your covenant, torn down Your altars, and put Your prophets to the sword. I alone am left, and they are out to take my life." [11]"Come out," He called, "and stand on the mountain before the Lord."

And lo, the Lord passed by. There was a great and mighty wind, splitting mountains and shattering rocks by the power of the Lord; but the Lord was not in the wind. After the wind—an earthquake; but the Lord was not in the earthquake. [12]After the earthquake—fire; but the Lord was not in the fire. And after the fire—a soft murmuring sound. [13]When Elijah heard it, he wrapped his mantle about his face and went out and stood at the entrance of the cave. Then a voice addressed him: "Why are you here, Elijah?" [14]He answered, "I am moved by zeal for the Lord, the God of Hosts; for the Israelites have forsaken Your covenant, torn down Your altars, and have put Your prophets to the sword. I alone am left, and they are out to take my life."

[15]The Lord said to him, "Go back by the way you came, [and] on to the wilderness of Damascus. When you get there, anoint Hazael as king of Aram. [16]Also anoint Jehu son of Nimshi as king of Israel, and anoint Elisha son of Shaphat of Abel-meholah to succeed you as prophet."

Elijah's Voice: The Prophetic Moment

"And after the fire—a still, small voice." (1 Kings 19:11–13)

Elijah the prophet is everywhere in Jewish tradition. When a male child is born he is entered into the covenant during the ceremony of circumcision known as *brit milah* or bris, on a special seat called Elijah's chair. After eating, the grace after meals (*Birkat ha-Mazon*) that is recited invokes Elijah's name. Jews sing a song yearning for Elijah's return during the *Havdalah* ceremony at the end of the Sabbath. At the Passover seder we open the door for Elijah and set aside a special Elijah's cup of wine. In countless Jewish folktales Elijah returns, often in the disguise of a beggar, to bring support and sustenance to the downtrodden. In other stories Elijah heralds the Messiah. Malachi, one of the later prophets, declares, *"Lo, I will send the prophet Elijah to you before the coming of the awesome, fearful day of the Lord"* (Mal. 3:23), and, in his book's conclusion, adds that Elijah shall *"reconcile parents with their children and children with their parents"* (3:24). The ongoing appeal of this enigmatic figure, who upon his death *"went up to heaven in a whirlwind"* (2 Kings 2:11), is curious and remarkable.

In some ways Elijah is looked upon as a second Moses. While not quite the explicit lawgiver like his illustrious predecessor, Elijah nonetheless is said in the Talmud to settle seemingly unsolvable legal (*halachic*) disputes. The sages employ the term *teku* ("let it stand [unresolved]") at the end of such arguments, but the tradition reads that as *tyku*, an acronym for *tishbi y'taretz kushyot u'va'ayot* ("[Elijah] the Tishbite will solve difficulties and problems"). The presumption is that Elijah's unique prophetic gift, like Moses', will clarify the law . . . even (many sages hasten to add) if we have to wait for the Messiah to arrive to get the answer!

The parallels to Moses begin in the biblical text. Moses is on Mount Sinai for forty days; Elijah journeys to Horeb in forty days. Sinai explodes with thunder, lightning, and fire. Elijah experiences wind, quakes, and fire. The Lord *"passed before him [Moses]"* in a cleft of a rock. The Lord *"passed by"* Elijah in the same way. Rabbinic tradition claims that both Moses and Elijah visited the same cave on Mount Sinai. The sages note that both Moses and Elijah are called *"man of God."* One source boldly concludes: "Moses and Elijah are equivalent to the other."

The Bible introduces Elijah in the throes of his prophetic clashes with King Ahab, who ruled Israel's Northern Kingdom from approximately 870 to 850 BCE. Elijah is a classic prophet in the mode of Samuel and Nathan, who speak truth to power. Ahab calls him the *"troubler of Israel,"* and Elijah throws the accusation back in the king's face. His last confrontation with King Ahab is the most vivid. The monarch, in cahoots with his wife Jezebel, has ordered a man named Navot executed on trumped-up charges solely because he is unwilling to relinquish his vineyard, which adjoins the king's lands. Elijah thunders at the king, *"Thus said the Lord: Would you murder and take possession?"* (1 King 21:19). He predicts utter devastation for the house of Ahab. In a description that echoes the Nathan-David confrontation, Ahab rends his clothes, quickly dons sackcloth, and apparently attempts to repent. Elijah then conveys to Ahab that because the king has humbled himself, he will not experience disaster in his lifetime, but his line will indeed be gravely punished.

As a prophet, Elijah is both a seeker of justice and a seeker of humility—the latter because of one of the most heralded yet mysterious moments in Scripture. Like Jonah's lesson, the experience may be understood as a possible rebuke to the prophet. If this interpretation is correct, then the prophetic moment teaches by negative example. Could it be that the great Elijah, ever zealous for the Lord, is too zealous? Jonah needed to learn compassion. Elijah needs to learn humility.

Fleeing for his life from Jezebel, Elijah is at the point of despair. *"Enough,"* he cries, *"Now, O Lord, take my life, for I am no better than my fathers"* (1 Kings 19:4). While one may view this as a crisis of faith, Elijah seems to have a close relationship with God. More likely, Elijah may be experiencing a crisis of pride. He is feeling emotionally wounded; his great zealousness has not reaped the expected dividends. An angel guides Elijah even deeper into the wilderness. Spending the night in a cave, Elijah hears God call to him, *"Why are you here, Elijah?"* (19:9). Elijah's reply is like a refrain to his life's song, already stated on Mount Carmel: *"I am moved by zeal for the Lord, the God of Hosts, for the Israelites have forsaken Your covenant, torn down Your altars, and put your prophets to the sword. I alone am left, and they are out to take my life"* (19:10).

God then asks Elijah to step out of the cave and stand before the Lord. The Bible explicitly states that *"the Lord passed by"* and (regarding the fearsome storm) that *"the Lord was not in the wind," "the Lord was not in the earthquake,"* and *"the Lord was not in the fire"* (19:11–12). Elijah only hears God again after the *"soft murmuring sound"* (19:12; new JPS TANAKH) that the King James Bible indelibly translates as the *"still, small voice."* God again asks Elijah why he is here, and the prophet responds just as he did before. The Lord then tells Elijah to go back the way he came, to anoint the new kings of Aram and Israel—and also to appoint a successor, named Elisha.

What is the meaning of the biblical account that God is not in the wind, the quake, or the fire, but in the softest sound of a voice? Is God's revelation to Elijah meant to comfort or rebuke? God calls to Jonah at the end of that book apparently to admonish the prophet about his lack of compassion for the repentant city of Nineveh. God speaks out of the whirlwind to Job at the end of that book seemingly to reprimand his long-suffering servant for the hubris of thinking he understands the divine plan. Here, God does not speak from the whirlwind, but rather from the calm before and after the storm. Is it to allay the weary prophet that he will not die at Jezebel's hand—that he has not been abandoned? Is his question to Elijah meant to help the prophet renew his faith and determination before he returns from his wilderness escape to the dangerous and messy real world? Or is God subtly conveying to Elijah that his stormy countenance and fiery zeal is overwrought, and it is time to pass the mantle to a less confrontational successor? Is the humbling of Elijah an act of aid or abandonment?

The midrash takes the humbling of Elijah a step further. It records the moment as a dialogue:

ELIJAH: "The Israelites have broken Your covenant."
GOD: "Is it then *your* Covenant?
ELIJAH: "They have torn down Your altars."
GOD: But were they *your* altars?
ELIJAH: "They have put Your prophets to the sword."
GOD: "But you are alive."
ELIJAH: "I alone am left."
GOD: "Instead of hurling accusations against Israel, should you not have pleaded their cause?"

Rabbi Jonathan Sacks comments: "The zealot takes the part of God. But God expects His prophets to be defenders, not accusers." Biblical scholar Reuven Kimelman notes, "Seeking a 'people's defender' like Moses, God instead [gets] a prosecuting attorney." As a result, "He is thus sent back to anoint a prophetic successor. . . . He is to tender his resignation." Another biblical scholar, Mordecai Kogan, agrees: "Elijah has, in effect, been relieved of his mission."

Yet a third biblical scholar, Richard Nelson, sees it exactly the other way. The now humbled Elijah has been given a "new commission," he insists, and "God simply will not permit Elijah to give up his office." A fourth biblical scholar, Walter Brueggemann, seconds that, heralding Elijah's "new mandate" and "the restoration of a man of faith."

Rabbi Shai Held poses the question, "Where (and why) does Elijah go wrong?" As he notes, "The line between righteousness and self-righteousness is exceedingly fine, and Elijah's zealotry leads him to cross it. The story does not condemn zealotry outright, but it does worry about the ways it can blind us—and lead us to see others in a spectacularly ungenerous light. A prophet can love God with abiding passion, but if he comes to hate God's people, God will look elsewhere for faithful servants." Similarly, Rabbi Sacks comments, "A prophet hears not one imperative but two: guidance and compassion, a love of truth and a binding solidarity with those for whom that truth had become eclipsed. To preserve tradition and at the same time to defend those that others condemn is the difficult, necessary task of religious leadership."

Elisha's subsequent anointment does not signify the end of Elijah's prophetic career, though it signals the end is in sight. The scathing second encounter with Ahab and Jezebel is still before him. While this is the only remaining episode described in the Bible before Elisha's anointment, it is significant. Elijah summons the courage to again confront Ahab and Jezebel, though he justifiably fears for his life. The Bible says simply, *"Then the word of the Lord came to Elijah the Tishbite: 'Go down and confront King Ahab'"* (1 Kings 21:17). The story continues, *"Ahab said to Elijah, 'So you have found me, my enemy?' 'Yes, I have found you,' he replied"* (1 Kings 17:20). While the prophecy Elijah pronounces on the House of Ahab is devastating, it is telling that Ahab averts the disaster in his lifetime, because *"he has humbled himself"* (1 Kings 21:29) by fasting, wearing sackcloth, and repenting. Perhaps God is reinforcing the lesson of humility by in effect saying to Elijah, "Look at the power of humility to help even that scoundrel Ahab."

In this respect there is a parallel to the story of Jonah, where the king and people of Nineveh avert destruction by taking similar actions. And, just as the Bible leaves us wondering if Jonah really understands the lesson in compassion, we are similarly left unsure if Elijah is truly humbled.

The supernatural story of his death seems to indicate that Elijah is dearly cherished by God. Perhaps the *"still, small voice"* moment was meant both to comfort and rebuke the prophet, and Elijah's renewed courage indicates to God (and to us) that the imperfect prophet nevertheless closes his career with a job well done.

Walking with Elijah: The Path of Humility

A modern interpretation of the Elijah story might offer that the Divine Presence is not found in the storms of life so much as the quiet and reflective times that follow. Such a proposition is heartening in that God's presence, while seemingly missing in tumultuous times, is never truly absent. We are not abandoned; the voice will return. Yet, like Elijah, we must listen very hard to the soft call, to the God who speaks in whispers.

Another lesson might be that zealotry may win the battle—after all, Elijah's zeal enables him to challenge and prevail over the 450 false prophets of Ba'al—but not the war. While his missions are understandably difficult and his accomplishments impressive, Elijah appears to despair of the people in fits of self-righteousness. At Mount Carmel he berates them for vacillating between idolatry and faith, even after they apologize. His recurring complaint—that he is the only true believer left—can be seen as elitist and judgmental. God, speaking in a soft voice, commands Elijah to *"go back."* God does not want Elijah to disengage from either the mission or the people. Elijah is to go back *"the way you came"* to the messy world with all its problems.

Elijah, like so many of the prophets, is dedicated to waging a war against idolatry as forbidden by the second (*"You shall have no other gods before me"*) and third (*"You shall not make for yourself a sculptured image, or any likeness"*) of the Ten Commandments (Exod. 20:3,4). Why do we find these incessant diatribes against idolatry in the Bible? The idea that the prophets were solely concerned with the making and worshipping of pagan figurines is simplistic. Consider a broader definition of idolatry as the worship of anything but God. If we do not venerate God, what are we most likely to worship? Our selves! Noted critic Norman Podhoretz makes this point in his book *The Prophets*: "My thesis, in short, is that to the classical prophets idolatry amounts to self-deification, the delusion that we humans could become '. . . as gods.'" Elijah's complaint that he is the only true believer—concomitant with the whiff of self-righteousness—is ironically antithetical to the very campaign against idolatry he is conducting! The focus should be ostensibly and exclusively on God, but in his self-absorption, Elijah is shifting the spotlight. God is saying, as it were, "It's not about you, Elijah!"

Elijah's story is read in the synagogue as the supplemental haftarah reading for the portion Pinḥas in the book of Numbers. Pinchas, a grandson of Aaron, is described as a zealot, a word (translated more gently as "passion" by the new JPS TANAKH) used three times in three verses. Pinchas kills an Israelite man who was showing off his Midianite woman to his companions, and, according to the plain reading of the text, God rewards him for doing so: *"Say, therefore, I grant him My pact of friendship . . . because he took impassioned action for his God, thus making expiation for the Israelites"* (Num. 25:12–13). Some commentators understand the choice of the Elijah story as a counterweight to the Pinchas story: Whereas Pinchas is rewarded for zealotry, Elijah is chastened. This school of interpretation adds to Elijah's humbling by not only citing the previously mentioned midrash ("Instead of hurling accusations against Israel, should you not have pleaded their cause?") but referencing another: that Elijah is compelled to attend every circumcision as a way of constantly reminding him of the people's faithfulness. As Rabbi Shoshana Boyd Gelfand puts it, "Elijah is the character who has spent eternity learning how to curb his zealotry and to embrace nuance."

The *Mekhilta*, an ancient midrashic text (quoted in the discussion of Jeremiah; see chapter 11), stipulates that there are three types of prophets: those who insist on the honor due the father (God), those who insist on the honor due the son (the people), and those who insist on both. Elijah, as much as he is esteemed by the sages, is nevertheless given as an example of the first type, for his zealousness to preach God's word. Elijah may be a true prophet, but he is not the ideal prophet. Jonah is given as an example of the second type—the reluctant prophet who tried to flee his mission and worried about his and Israel's reputation. He too is not the ideal. Jeremiah is most approvingly characterized as "insisting upon the honor due the father and the honor due the son." Both God and the people are always in his sights.

Jeremiah, in turn, reflects the greatest of the prophets—Moses—who steps into the breach between God and man, advocating one to the other as the times necessitate. Yet even Moses needs to learn a lesson or two in humility before he emerges fully as the unique leader of the Israelites.

Early on, Moses' father-in-law, Jethro, points out to his son-in-law that he has taken the entire burden of leadership upon himself. *"Why do you act alone?"* asks Jethro, pointing out that people have been waiting all day long to see Moses. Explaining that he is the mediator of the divine law—*"It is because the people come to me to inquire of God . . . I make known the laws and teachings of God"* (Exod. 18:15–16)—Moses appears to deem himself indispensable. *"The thing you are doing is not right; you will surely wear yourself out, and these people as well,"* replies the wizened elder (Exod. 18:13,17). Moses then shows humility: *"He heeded his father-in-law and did just as he [Jethro] had said. Moses chose capable men"* (Exod. 18:24–25).

Later on in the desert come two challenges to his authority that again demonstrate Moses' humility. First, two elders, Eldad and Medad, begin prophesying. While Joshua is alarmed and asks them to be restrained, Moses calmly and graciously replies, *"Would that all the Lord's people were prophets, that the Lord put His spirit upon them"* (Num. 12:29). Then the challenge comes, unbelievably and most hurtfully, from his very own brother and sister, who criticize his choice of a wife [apparently a second woman, who is "Cushite," likely meaning dark skinned] and add, *"Has the Lord spoken only through Moses? Has He not spoken through us as well?"* (Num. 12: 2). The Torah then adds this extraordinary editorial comment: *"Now Moses was a very humble man, more so than any other man on earth"* (Num. 12:3). Moses does not lash out at his siblings. Rather, after his sister is struck by a leprosy-like affliction, he prays for Miriam's healing.

"This is a novum in history," Rabbi Jonathan Sacks points out. "The idea that a leader's highest virtue is humility must have seemed absurd, almost self-contradictory, in the ancient world. Leaders were proud, magnificent, distinguished by their dress, appearance, and regal manner. They built temples in their own honor. They had triumphant inscriptions engraved for posterity. Their role was not to serve but to be served. Everyone else was expected to be humble, not they. Humility and majesty could not coexist. In Judaism, this entire configuration was overturned. Leaders were to serve, not to be served. Moses' highest accolade was to be called *eved Hashem*, God's servant."

Rabbi Sacks also believes that suffering may lead to humility, by "making us realize that what matters is not self-regard but rather the part we play in a scheme altogether larger than we are." It may have taken multiple crises in Moses' life to impart this humility, but it came. It may have also taken God's final rebuke of Elijah to temper the self-righteous zealot, but he too appears to have "gotten it."

Some modern interpreters understand the elusive *"still, small voice"* as the voice within: the voice of conscience. From a psychological perspective, this is the inner voice of reason that curbs our baser instincts. From a religious standpoint, this is the inner voice of revelation that enables us to discern God's direction.

Whether it originates strictly in the human realm, or is inspired by a power beyond us, conscience plays a crucial role in ethical decision making. To "follow one's conscience" or to "hear the call of conscience" is to see the moral path when others may not, and to accept the consequences. Freud explained that to hear the superego, we must restrain the ego. Elijah (if we give him the benefit of the doubt), like Moses, was finally able to rein in a powerful sense of self to make room for the other. Those who can humble themselves in the service of something greater will truly lead. C. S. Lewis said that "humility is not thinking less of yourself; it is thinking of yourself less."

"Those who have humility are open to things greater than themselves while those who lack it are not," Rabbi Sacks concludes. "That is why those who lack [humility] make you feel small while those who have it make you feel enlarged. Their humility inspires greatness in others."

17

Isaiah's Vision

THE PATH OF PEACE

I Am Isaiah

God gave me the years to live through the reign of four kings of Judah: Uzziah, Jotham, Ahaz, and Hezekiah.

The year King Uzziah died, while I was still a young man, I heard the Lord's call. God came to me in a dream. The Lord was on God's throne; the angels were attending to God, calling out to one another, "Holy, holy, holy is the Lord of Hosts! The whole earth is full of His glory!"

One of the angels flew over to me with a live coal, taken from the very altar before God. He touched it to my lips. He said my guilt had departed; my sins were purged away. Then I heard the voice of my Lord saying, "Whom shall I send? Who will go for us?" I replied, "Here I am; send me." Then and there I knew that my life was to deliver the word of the living God to the people of Israel.

The year the kings of Aram and Israel threatened Ahaz, the Lord called me to the Siloam pool—that is, the Upper Pool, by the road called Fuller's Field. The Lord told me to bring along my son, the one I had named Shear-Yashuv, "Remnant-Shall-Return."

As the king was inspecting the waterworks, I called out to him to keep the faith. I told him the present invasion would not come to pass—though I also warned him that a yet greater calamity would come from his erstwhile ally, Assyria. "Why," I asked, "have you spurned the gently flowing waters of Siloam? Now the flood waters of the Euphrates will sweep through the land like a flash flood in the Negev."

By my life, in this very spot where I stood, another man would stand before King Hezekiah three decades hence, and I would witness the tragedy. This man, the Assyrian envoy, was called the Rabshakeh, and he made the king of Judah tremble like a tree in the wind. Once again I told a king of Judah that in the short term this invasion would not come to pass, but in the long term the people of Israel would be punished for their sins. Lo and behold, the Lord sent a plague upon the Assyrian camp before they could destroy the Holy City. Yet I know judgment will come. Hezekiah built a marvelous tunnel to safeguard the precious waters of Gihon—but the only true defense for the children of Israel is their return to righteous living.

All my long life, my people and my country have known only violence and bloodshed. I tremble knowing there is more to come, the likes of which we have not seen.

Yet woe is the one who thinks the children of the covenant are forsaken. A time of peace will come, a time of harmony among men. Even the beasts of the field shall know the tranquility of the Lord. After the flood . . . the sun . . . and the rainbow.

Isaiah's Vision: From the Bible

Isaiah's Vision of Peace: Nations in Harmony (Isa. 2:2–4):

> [2]*In the days to come,*
> *The Mount of the Lord's House*
> *Shall stand firm above the mountains*
> *And tower above the hills;*
> *And all the nations*
> *Shall gaze on it with joy.*
> [3]*And the many peoples shall go and say:*
> *"Come,*
> *Let us go up to the Mount of the Lord,*
> *To the House of the God of Jacob;*
> *That He may instruct us in His ways,*
> *And that we may walk in His paths."*
> *For instruction shall come forth from Zion,*
> *The word of the Lord from Jerusalem.*
> [4]*Thus He will judge among the nations*
> *And arbitrate for the many peoples,*
> *And they shall beat their swords into plowshares*
> *And their spears into pruning hooks:*
> *Nation shall not take up*
> *Sword against nation;*
> *They shall never again know war.*

Isaiah's Vision of Peace: Nature in Harmony (Isa. 11:6–9):

> [6]*The wolf shall dwell with the lamb,*
> *The leopard lie down with the kid;*
> *The calf, the beast of prey, and the fatling together,*
> *With a little boy to herd them.*
> [7]*The cow and the bear shall graze,*
> *Their young shall lie down together;*

And the lion, like the ox, shall eat straw.
[8]*A babe shall play*
Over a viper's hole,
And an infant pass his hand
Over an adder's den.
[9]*In all of My sacred mount*
Nothing evil or vile shall be done;
For the land shall be filled with devotion to the Lord.

Isaiah's Vision of Peace: People in Harmony (Isa. 60:18–22, 65:21–25):

[18]*The cry "Violence"*
Shall no more be heard in your land,
Nor "Wrack and ruin!"
Within your borders.
And you shall name your walls "Victory"
And your gates "Renown."
[19]*No longer shall you need the sun*
For light by day,
Nor the shining of the moon
For radiance [by night];
For the Lord shall be your light everlasting,
Your God shall be your glory.
[20]*Your sun shall set no more,*
Your moon no more withdraw;
For the Lord shall be a light to you forever,
And your days of mourning shall be ended.
[21]*And your people, all of them righteous,*
Shall possess the land for all time;
They are the shoot that I planted,
My handiwork in which I glory.
[22]*The smallest shall become a clan;*
The least, a mighty nation.
I the Lord will speed it in due time.

[65:21]They shall build houses and dwell in them,
They shall plant vineyards and enjoy their fruit.
[22]They shall not build for others to dwell in,
Or plant for others to enjoy.
For the days of My people shall be
As long as the days of a tree,
My chosen ones shall outlive
The work of their hands.
[23]They shall not toil to no purpose;
They shall not bear children for terror,
But they shall be a people blessed by the Lord,
And their offspring shall remain with them.
[24]Before they pray, I will answer;
While they are still speaking, I will respond.
[25]The wolf and the lamb shall graze together,
And the lion shall eat straw like the ox,
And the serpent's food shall be earth.
In all My sacred mount
Nothing evil or vile shall be done
—said the Lord.

Isaiah's Vision: The Prophetic Moment

"And they shall beat their swords into plowshares, and their spears into pruning hooks." (Isa. 2:4)

Isaiah is the most oft-quoted of all the prophets (the venerable words above, for example, are inscribed on the United Nations building in New York). His language is peerless in its beauty and power. His vision of peace ranks supreme in its evocative character.

What is all the more remarkable, Isaiah lived through a time of dire national crisis. He experienced the calamity of seeing half his country vanquished and the other half subjugated. That a man could witness so much war and still dream of peace is the crown of his esteemed legacy.

However, the vast majority of modern scholars believe the book of Isaiah was written by two or maybe three individuals who used the same name. First Isaiah, who lived in the Southern Kingdom of Judah during the eighth century BCE, is said to have authored chapters 1–39. Second Isaiah, who likely lived during the Babylonian exile of the sixth century BCE, is said to have authored chapters 40–66. Those who posit a Third Isaiah living in exile, though, point to his authorship of chapters 56–66.

Nonetheless, even if different men wrote in varying periods, each Isaiah offers a powerful critique of social justice at a time of corruption and a compelling vision of peace at a time of destruction.

Like Elijah, Isaiah can be heralded as a seeker of justice. First Isaiah, who lived through the reign of four kings of Judah, pleads for the people to stay strong internally to withstand the threats they face externally. He exhorts them: "*Your hands are stained with crime. Wash yourselves clean. Put your evil doings away from my sight. Devote yourselves to justice; aid the wronged. Uphold the rights of the orphan; defend the cause of the widow*" (1:15–17).

Second Isaiah also rails against the people's moral degeneracy. His call for justice reaches its pinnacle in a celebrated chapter, read in synagogues on Yom Kippur morning, in which we are urged to "*raise your voice like a ram's horn!*" Isaiah then takes dead aim at the ritual of fasting:

> *Why, when we fasted, did you not see? When we starved our bodies, did you pay no heed? Because on your fast day you see to your business and oppress all your laborers! Because you fast in strife and contention, and you strike with a wicked fist! Your fasting today is not such as to make your voice heard on high. Is such the fast I desire, a day for men to starve their bodies? Is it bowing the head like a bulrush and lying in sackcloth and ashes? Do you call that a fast, a day when the Lord is favorable? (58:3–5)*

The prophet follows immediately with a grand call for justice:

> *No, this is the fast I desire: to unlock the fetters of wickedness, and untie the cords of the yoke; to let the oppressed go free; to break off every yoke. It is to share your bread with the hungry, and to take the wretched poor into your home; when you see the naked, to clothe him, and not to ignore your own kin.* (58:6–7)

The chapter concludes with a majestic description of how Israel's glory will then be restored:

> *Then shall your light burst through like the dawn, and your healing spring up quickly . . . you shall be like a watered garden; like a spring whose waters do not fail.* (58:8,11)

Importantly, Isaiah also frames the mission statement of the Jewish people: as *"a covenant-people, a light of nations"* (42:6, 49:6). In just one phrase, *"covenant-people and light of nations,"* the prophet recaptures the charge that hearkens all the way back to Abraham, when God promises to *"make of you a great nation . . . you shall be a blessing . . . all the families of the earth shall bless themselves by you"* (Gen. 12:2–3).

The heart of the covenant is the ethical monotheism that demands righteous behavior. After all, God too references Abraham's unique calling (see chapter 1): *"Shall I hide from Abraham what I am about to do, since Abraham is to become a great and populous nation, and all the nations of the earth are to bless themselves by him?"* (Gen. 18:16). And, as if to leave no doubt in the mind of the reader (or listener), the Torah adds, *"For I have singled him out, that he may instruct his children and his posterity to keep the way of the Lord by doing what is just and right"* (Gen. 18:19). Isaiah, likewise, seeks to remind his beleaguered people that the mission statement of the Jewish people has not expired. Indeed, it is the only way to move forward—the only path of light in a dark world, the only hope in an age of travail.

Throughout Isaiah's career, he pleads with kings not to lose their faith. Early on, King Ahaz (ca. 735–715 BCE), frightened of a Northern Israelite/Syrian alliance against him, considers enlisting Assyria, the rising power from the east, to protect him. A vehemently opposed Isaiah views alliance with Assyria as a repudiation of trust in God—and may also have a (tragically true) premonition that Assyria will eventually turn against all of Israel. And so, accompanied by his little son (named *Shear-yashuv,* "saving remnant," to dramatize faith in God's power), Isaiah confronts King Ahaz at the Upper Pool. (This reservoir of water from Jerusalem's Gihon spring, also known as Siloam, was its sole water source; the king was likely inspecting the site, concerned about Jerusalem's vulnerable water supply.) Isaiah pleads with Ahaz: don't lose faith and don't make unwise alliances. He predicts that the two enemy kings (*"those two smoking stubs of firebrands"*) will soon be dead, and the Northern Kingdom of Israel *"shattered as a people"*; indeed, Assyria laid waste to Syria in 732 BCE and Samaria in 721 BCE. Alluding to the waters in front of and beyond them, Isaiah mournfully rues that that the nation *"has spurned the gently flowing waters of Siloam"* (8:6)—and as a result, the people will face the mighty waters of the Euphrates, and be swept away by the *"flash flood"* that is Assyria.

Isaiah also reports that by this very same Jerusalem spring, in the exact spot where he confronted Ahaz, the king's successor, Hezekiah, encounters the Assyrian envoy Rabshakeh. Assyria warns Hezekiah not to make a pact with Egypt, and Isaiah, as he did some thirty years before, counsels Hezekiah to stay clear of all alliances. And, just as Ahaz spurned Isaiah's advice and became a vassal to Assyria to ward off his more immediate threat, so Hezekiah joins with his neighbor to the south to counter the threat from the east. Assyria then attacks and quite nearly succeeds in destroying Judah. In the midst of the awful siege of Jerusalem, Isaiah urges Hezekiah to hold firm; he declares the siege will lift. Miraculously it does; a plague strikes the Assyrian camp, and soon after King Sennacherib is dethroned.

An interesting archeological aside: King Hezekiah too worried about Jerusalem's modest and exposed water supply, and launched an ambitious project to fortify the conduit. In a remarkable engineering feat, a 1,700-foot-long tunnel was cut though solid rock from the Gihon spring to the Siloam pool. Workers started digging from both sides and met in the middle. The Bible records the endeavor: *"he made the pool and the conduit and brought the water into the city"* (2 Kings 20:20). And, astoundingly, an inscription cut into the tunnel to memorialize the event—in the paleo-Hebrew of the eighth century BCE—has survived.

Archeologists discovered Hezekiah's tunnel in 1838, but it was only in 1880—after nearly half a century had passed—that a boy wading through spotted the inscription. Eleven years later, the priceless inscription was vandalized—cut from the wall and broken into several fragments in the process. The British recovered it and turned it over to the Ottoman Turk authorities; today it resides at the Istanbul Archeology Museum. The tunnel itself is open to visitors, who can experience the *"gently flowing waters"* Isaiah described.

Another archeological discovery testifies to the troubled times Isaiah lived through. A clay prism containing the Annals of Sennacherib—in which the Assyrian king boasts that he has shut up Hezekiah in Jerusalem "like a caged bird"—was discovered in Nineveh in 1830. (It is now housed in the British Museum; two other copies, discovered in later years, are in the Oriental Institute of Chicago and the Israel Museum.) For his part, Isaiah likens the destruction to that of Sodom and Gomorrah (Isa. 1:10), with Zion left *"like a booth in a vineyard; like a hut in a field"* (Isa. 1:8).

Several generations later, in 587 BCE, Israel's worst fears are realized: the devastation of Zion is complete. The Southern Kingdom of Judah has gone the way of the Northern Kingdom of Israel. The Babylonians, like the Assyrians before them, force the leaders of the community, and much of the populace, into exile. Unlike the earlier exile, when the Assyrians dispersed the captive Israelites throughout their empire, the Babylonians permitted the Judean community to settle together *"by the waters of Babylon"* (Ps. 137:1). Second Isaiah may have been an eyewitness to the destruction of Jerusalem and Judea or, at the very least, privy to the community's living memory.

In the shadow of endless war and calamity, Isaiah's prophetic visions shine brightly forth. Both First and Second Isaiah consoled their followers and dreamed of a better place.

Walking with Isaiah: The Path of Peace

A remarkable aspect of Isaiah's vision is its inclusive scope. Isaiah dreams not only of nations in concord but of nature in harmony. While we most often think of peace as the absence of conflict among countries, peace is manifest at all levels of human existence. The Hebrew word for peace, *shalom*, itself has a broad range of meanings that encompass wholeness, well-being, harmony, and reconciliation. Jewish tradition speaks of *shalom nefesh*, the inner peace of the soul, and *shalom bayit*, the peace of the home (family).

It is axiomatic that unless peace prevails on the inside (of individuals, families, communities, or nations), there is no peace on the outside. Judaism thus puts a premium on the marital harmony that is *shalom bayit*. "One who creates peace at home builds peace in all Israel," said the talmudic sage Simeon ben Gamliel. Encouraging husbands and wives to make extra effort to insure domestic tranquility and well-being, the Talmud colorfully advises, "If your wife is short, bend down to hear her whisper." It adds, "Of a man who loves his wife as himself and honors her more than himself . . . Scripture says: 'and you shall know that your tent is in peace.'"

Spouses are encouraged to fulfill each other's physical and emotional needs to maintain matrimonial harmony. Maimonides points to a husband's three obligations to his wife as specified by the Torah: her food, her clothes, and her conjugal rights. He explains, "Her food signifies her maintenance; her clothes—what the term implies; her conjugal rights, sexual intercourse with her." For her part, the medieval sage Jonah Gerondi writes in his well-regarded *Letter of Repentance*, "A woman must see to it there is peace between herself and her husband, and that she is loving and kind to her husband." Another medieval sage, Nahmanides, writes in his equally renowned *Holy Letter*: "A husband should speak with his wife the appropriate words, some of erotic passion, and some words of fear of the Lord. . . . A man should never force himself upon his wife and never overpower her. . . . One should never argue with his wife, and certainly never strike her. . . . To conclude, when you are ready for sexual union, see that your wife's intentions combine with yours. Do not hurry to arouse her until she is receptive. Be calm . . . as you enter the path of love and will."

By virtue of a close reading of Genesis, the Rabbis even highlight God's role in insuring *shalom bayit.* When Abraham and Sarah first discover that Sarah will conceive a child, she laughs at the idea, saying to herself, *"Now that I am withered, am I to have enjoyment with my husband so old?"* (Gen. 18:12). Yet, one verse later, God says to Abraham, *"Why did Sarah laugh, saying, 'Shall I in truth bear a child, old as I am?'"* (Gen. 18:13). Note how God rephrases Sarah's remark to refer to her old age rather than Abraham's. We might even say that God has engaged in a "white lie"! The Talmud opines, "Great is the cause of peace, seeing that for the sake of peace even the Holy One, blessed be He, deviated from the truth and modified a statement."

The Bible itself promulgates the idea (and ideal) of peace even while recognizing the reality—and, sometimes, the necessity—of war. The Justice Code of Deuteronomy states: *"When you approach a town to attack it, you shall offer it terms of peace"* (Deut. 20:10). *"Seek peace, and pursue it,"* urges the Psalmist (Ps. 34:15). A midrash comments that peace is the only commandment one is told to actively pursue. The Talmud echoes this notion of active pursuit when it urges, "Be of the disciples of Aaron; one who loves peace and pursues it." Jeremiah too uses the language of shalom when he exhorts his fellow exiles to *"Seek the welfare (shalom) of the city . . . for in its prosperity you shall prosper"* (Jer. 29:7).

The Bible recounts how the great King David was denied the privilege of building the House of the Lord (the Temple) in Jerusalem, despite his keen desire to do so, because of his violent career. David says to his son Solomon (whose name derives from shalom):

> *"My son, I wanted to build a House for the name of the Lord my God. But the word of the Lord came to me saying, 'You have shed much blood and fought great battles; you shall not build a House for My name for you have shed much blood on the earth in My sight. But you will have a son who will be a man at rest, for I will give him rest from all his enemies on all sides. Solomon will be his name and I shall confer peace and quiet on Israel in his time.'"* (1 Chron. 22:7–9)

Although Jewish experiences in the Land of Israel and the diaspora were far from peaceful, that did not stop the sages from filling the siddur (prayer book) with entreaties for peace. We welcome the Sabbath (after saying "Shabbat Shalom") with the classic *Shalom Alechem,* praying, "Peace be to you, O ministering angels . . . Enter in Peace . . . Bless me with peace . . . Depart in peace." The *Hashkivenu* prayer begins, "Grant, O God, that we lie down in peace," and concludes, "Guard our going and coming, to life and peace, evermore. Blessed are You . . . whose *sukkat shalom,* shelter of peace, is spread over us, over all Your people Israel, and over Jerusalem." Both the morning and the evening versions of the *Amidah,* a central series of prayers that link us with our ancestors, conclude with a prayer of peace. In the morning, *Sim Shalom* (Grant Peace) begins with the plea to "Grant peace, goodness and blessing" and ends by thanking God "who blesses Your people Israel with peace." In the evening, *Shalom Rav* (Great Peace) similarly opens with the words, "Grant great peace to Israel" and ends in the same way as the morning version. The final words of the *Kaddish,* the Jewish memorial prayer said in honor of the departed, appeal to God: "May the One who makes peace in the high heavens make peace for us."

The yearning for peace in Jewish liturgy has inspired numerous poems and songs of peace in Israel. In his poem "Shir Yerushalayim," Yehuda Amichai, Israel's most famous poet, directly borrows these words from Isaiah, "beat[ing] their swords into plowshares," recommending the practice in order to "make musical instruments out of them." The song *Lo Yissa Goy* bases some of its lyrics on Isaiah: *"Nation shall not lift up sword against nation; neither shall they learn war anymore."* An Israeli band called Sheva, made up of both Jews and Arabs, had a hit with their song *Od Yavo* (It will come), which includes the word *salaam*, Arabic for peace and derived from the same Semitic root as shalom. Israelis will never forget that Prime Minister Yitzhak Rabin had just finished singing *Shir L'Shalom* (Song of peace) when he was assassinated in 1995. The words to the song were in his chest pocket when he fell.

The path to peace in modern Israel has been as troubled as it was in ancient Israel, and Isaiah's vision remains just as elusive. Since Israel's founding, the nation has fought five major wars (War of Independence–1948, Sinai War–1956, Six-Day War–1967, Yom Kippur War–1973, Lebanon War–1982) and an equal number of lesser wars and uprisings. Yet, one shining moment of peace has not been forgotten. In November 1977 Egyptian president Anwar el-Sadat shocked the world by announcing: "I am ready to go to the end of the world to get a settlement. I am even ready to go to Israel, to the Knesset, and to speak to all the members of the Israeli parliament there and negotiate with them over a peace settlement." Sadat predicted that the Israelis would be stunned by his offer, and they were. But to his and to all of Israel's credit, the newly elected prime minister, Menachem Begin, known for his right-wing and hardline political views, welcomed the man who only four years earlier had launched the bloodiest war in Israel's history.

I was living in Jerusalem that year, and I will never forget the euphoria of the moment. When the peace process floundered, President Jimmy Carter brought Begin and Sadat to Camp David. After thirteen tension-filled days, on September 17, 1978, an agreement was announced. Soon after, the three leaders were awarded the Nobel Peace Prize. On March 26, 1979, the peace treaty known as the Camp David Accords was signed. Despite Sadat's assassination in 1981 and other upheavals, peace has prevailed with Egypt for the last forty years.

Israeli prime minister Yitzhak Rabin and Jordan's King Hussein signed a similar treaty in 1994. It too has survived the test of time, including Rabin's subsequent assassination.

Rabin and Shimon Peres, along with Yasir Arafat of the Palestinian Liberation Organization, signed a peace agreement the same year, for which they were all awarded the 1994 Nobel Peace Prize. That agreement, however, has not fared as well; peace between the Israelis and the Palestinians is still far away.

Prime Minister Begin eloquently summed up the path of peace in his address at the signing of the Camp David Accords on the White House lawn:

> *The ancient Jewish people gave the world the vision of eternal peace, of universal disarmament, of abolishing the teaching and learning of war. Despite the tragedies and disappointments of the past, we must never forsake that vision, that human dream, that unshakable faith. Peace is the beauty of life. It is sunshine. It is the smile of a child, the love of a mother, the joy of a father, the togetherness of a family. It is the advancement of man, the victory of a just cause, the triumph of truth. Peace is all of these and more, and more. Now is the time for all of us to show civil courage in order to proclaim to our peoples, and to others: no more war, no more bloodshed, no more bereavement—peace unto you. Shalom, Salaam—forever.*

18

Ezra's Torah

THE PATH OF WISDOM

I Am Ezra

Blessed is the Lord God of our fathers, who put it into the mind of the king to glorify the House of the Lord in Jerusalem, and who inclined the king and his counselors and his military officers to be favorably disposed toward me. For my part, thanks to the care of the Lord for me, I summoned up courage and assembled leading men for the journey home.

You see, I was born in Babylon during the exile of my people. Yet I am ever their loyal son. My fathers and their fathers all served the Lord, for we are descendants of Aaron, brother of Moses, the high priest himself. We are keepers of the Law of Moses. I was taught to read and write the Holy Tongue. I was trained in the interpretation of the Law. I was schooled in the scribal arts. For these reasons King Artaxerxes appointed me head of the delegation that returned to the Holy Land and to the Holy City and to the Holy House Nehemiah was rebuilding.

Laden with our gold, silver, and bronze for the House of the Lord, we survived the perilous journey. We ascended the heights to Jerusalem. We offered thanks to our God for our release from captivity and for the wonder of treading again on our sacred soil.

But my tears of joy soon turned to tears of anguish. My people had forgotten who they were. They had forsaken the Torah. They had neglected the commandments. They had given their sons to foreign daughters. They had come back to the land only to break the covenant once again. I was overcome with grief.

I spoke to the people of their transgressions; I implored them to return.

Slowly, they saw the light and repented. As the walls of the Holy City rose again, so too did the people. When the seventh month arrived, the people left their towns and villages and gathered in a great convocation in Jerusalem. I brought out a scroll of the Teaching of Moses for everyone to see: Standing upon a wooden tower, I opened the scroll in the sight of all the people. I blessed the Lord, the great God, and all the people answered, "Amen, Amen." Then I read from the scroll from dawn to midday. The Levites with me translated the Teaching, word for word, and explained its meaning. The people understood. And they wept.

The people returned on the twenty-fourth day of the month, fasting, in sackcloth, and with earth upon them. They confessed their sins and the iniquities of their fathers. We again read from the Law, and the people pledged themselves to the covenant. The Levites lifted up a great prayer to God, and this is how it ended: "And now, our God, great, mighty, and awesome God, who stays faithful to His covenant, do not treat lightly all the suffering that has overtaken us—our kings, our officers, our priests, our prophets, our fathers, and all Your people—from the time of the Assyrian kings to this day. Surely You are in the right with respect to all that came upon us, for You have acted faithfully and we have been wicked. We did not listen to Your commandments or to the warnings that You gave us. Today we are slaves, and the land that You gave to our fathers to enjoy its fruit and bounty—here we are slaves on it. On account of our sins it yields its abundant crops to kings whom You have set over us. They rule over our bodies and our beasts and do as they please, and we are in great distress."

So the people pledged themselves that day to follow the Teaching of God, given through Moses the servant of God. The Levites specified the very commandments the people must observe, and it was put in writing and signed and sealed. And then I knew that my people would rise again, that they would long endure, for we are indeed a kingdom of priests and a holy nation.

Ezra's Torah: From the Bible

Ezra brings the Torah to the people (Neh. 8:1–12):

When the seventh month arrived—the Israelites being [settled] in their towns—[1]the entire people assembled as one man in the square before the Water Gate, and they asked Ezra the scribe to bring the scroll of the Teaching of Moses with which the Lord had charged Israel. [2]On the first day of the seventh month, Ezra the priest brought the Teaching before the congregation, men and women and all who could listen with understanding. [3]He read from it, facing the square before the Water Gate, from the first light until midday, to the men and the women and those who could understand; the ears of all the people were given to the scroll of the Teaching.

[4]Ezra the scribe stood upon a wooden tower made for the purpose, and beside him stood Mattithiah, Shema, Anaiah, Uriah, Hilkiah, and Maaseiah at his right, and at his left Pedaiah, Mishael, Malchijah, Hashum, Hashbaddanah, Zechariah, Meshullam. [5]Ezra opened the scroll in the sight of all the people, for he was above all the people; as he opened it, all the people stood up. [6]Ezra blessed the Lord, the great God, and all the people answered, "Amen, Amen," with hands upraised. Then they bowed their heads and prostrated themselves before the Lord with their faces to the ground. [7]Jeshua, Bani, Sherebiah, Jamin, Akkub, Shabbethai, Hodiah, Maaseiah, Kelita, Azariah, Jozabad, Hanan, Pelaiah, and the Levites explained the Teaching to the people, while the people stood in their places. [8]They read from the scroll of the Teaching of God, translating it and giving the sense; so they understood the reading.

[9]Nehemiah the Tirshatha, Ezra the priest and scribe, and the Levites who were explaining to the people said to all the people, "This day is holy to the Lord your God: you must not mourn or weep," for all the people were weeping as they listened to the words of the Teaching. [10]He further said to them, "Go, eat choice foods and drink sweet drinks and send portions to whoever has nothing prepared, for the day is holy to

our Lord. Do not be sad, for your rejoicing in the Lord is the source of your strength." [11]*The Levites were quieting the people, saying, "Hush, for the day is holy; do not be sad."* [12]*Then all the people went to eat and drink and send portions and make great merriment, for they understood the things they were told.*

Ezra's Torah: The Prophetic Moment

"Ezra the priest brought the Teaching before the congregation." (Neh. 8:2)

The Jews' return from the Babylonian exile to Israel, under the Persian king Cyrus's decree in the mid-sixth century BCE, offered a shattered people the chance to rebuild their country. If Nehemiah, governor of Judea, was their political leader, Ezra was their spiritual leader.

Ezra is described as a priest, but, more intriguingly, also as a scribe. A son of the Babylonian exile, he is of distinguished family lineage that traces all the way back to the High Priest Aaron. At the same time, he is one of the elite schooled in the reading and writing of Scripture, *"a scribe expert in the Teaching of Moses"* (Ezra 7:6). A few verses later, the Bible again says that Ezra is a priest-scribe and *"a scholar in matters concerning the commandments of the Lord"* (7:11). These dual credentials give him religious authority, as noticed by the Persian king, and establish him as a leader of the repatriated Israelite community in Babylon—and then in Jerusalem upon his return there.

Importantly, the Bible also describes Ezra as someone who *"had dedicated himself to study the Teaching of the Lord so as to observe it, and to teach laws and rules to Israel"* (7:10). Ezra is not just a priest and a scribe; he is a teacher. And the Torah is not just a document to be read and venerated; it is to be studied. Indeed, one chapter later the Bible describes how Ezra gathered the community leaders (heads of clans, priests, and Levites) *"to study [doresh] the words of the Teaching"* (Neh. 8:13). As Hebrew University legal scholar Moshe Halbertal points out, "A new verb is used to describe Ezra's way of studying: *doresh be-torat Moshe* [interpret Moses' teaching]. The verb *lidrosh* means to search, to inquire. The application of this verb to the study of Torah implies a notion of the text as something that requires probing, not only reciting or reading. . . . The Torah moves from being the basic contract—the text which is the core of obligation—to being the center of curriculum, a text that is studied and contemplated."

What Ezra sees and hears upon his arrival in 458 BCE makes him disconsolate: *"I rent my garment and robe, I tore hair out of my head and beard, and I sat desolate"* (Ezra 9:3). Of the host of transgressions Ezra bemoans, what seems to disturb him most is rampant intermarriage between Israelites and the surrounding peoples: *"After all that has happened to us because of our evil deeds and deep guilt . . . shall we once again violate your commandments by intermarrying with these peoples who follow such abhorrent practices?"* (9:13–14). To Ezra it is clear the Israelites have forgotten the commandments of the Torah. He is convinced that the stakes are mightily high: *"But now, for a short while, there has been a reprieve from the Lord our God, who had granted us a surviving remnant and given us a stake in His holy place. . . . Will You not rage against us till we are destroyed without remnant or survivor?"* (9:8,14).

Significantly, Ezra brings to Jerusalem a *"scroll of the Teaching of God"* (Neh. 8:8). What that scroll actually contained, how much of what we today call the Five Books of Moses, remains a source of vigorous debate. Some scholars argue that during the Babylonian exile the Torah as we know it was largely redacted if not canonized. Others contend that at this juncture it was a much more limited collection of mostly legal texts, amounting to excerpts of what is today part of the book of Exodus.

Regardless, Ezra confers great authority upon the scroll. He reads the scroll in the public square before the people. Its contents are presumably entirely in Hebrew, but by this time in history, the spoken language of the people is Aramaic, so the people are in need of translation. The attending Levites, who now are in charge of cultic sacrifice and worship and serve as custodians of sacred texts, not only translate the Teaching but explain it, *"giving the sense, so [the people] understood the reading"* (Neh. 8:8).

It becomes clear that the people are unfamiliar with the content of the Torah. The Bible notes that key festivals such as Passover and Sukkot have been neglected. The prohibition against intermarriage certainly has not been observed.

This is just the beginning. From a list of laws outlined in the book of Nehemiah, chapter 10, it's apparent that observance of the Sabbath, the sabbatical year, the shekel offering, the first-fruit offerings, the tithes, and the sacrifices are similarly absent or in disarray.

As biblical scholar Michael Satlow points out in his book *How the Bible Became Holy*: "Today we take for granted the religious authority of texts. Religion, as it is commonly understood, comes out of a book. [But] prior to Ezra, nobody (except, perhaps, priests) would have thought to turn to a book or text in order to learn proper religious behavior. Questions might be addressed to a parent, priest, or village elder, but they too would appeal to communal memory rather than an authoritative text. The Torah introduces not just a set of new rules but also a new source of religious authority that is rooted in texts." The book's concluding sentence testifies to the significance of this leap from oral to written authority: "This is perhaps the Bible's greatest legacy: the radically implausible notion that one can build a community, a religion, a culture, and even a country around a text."

Satlow also contends that the people's acceptance of the written rules Ezra reads to them from a Torah scroll is the first instance of a people accepting communal rules from a written text—and, as such, is the basis for all those who pledge allegiance to a constitution. Certainly not all constitutions are viewed as sacred Scripture emanating from God. But Ezra's popular conferral of a written set of rules as having binding authority (what Satlow calls "normative" authority) on a community's political and religious behavior is a unique and enduring contribution.

The public reading of Torah would of course become a central part of Judaism. While it is not clear that it did become a regular practice soon after Ezra, he is credited with initiating the practice. In the eyes of later tradition, then, Ezra's reading from the scroll is truly a pivotal, prophetic moment. Ezra's act, and the people's response, constitute a communal pledge to the written set of rules in Torah.

For this reason, sages and historians alike often view Ezra as occupying the same exalted status as Abraham and Moses: as a founding father of Judaism. The Talmud states: "Ezra was worthy of having the Torah presented through him, had not Moses preceded him." The passage continues by describing how Ezra compares to Moses in every way. "Of Moses it is written, *And Moses went up to God,* and of Ezra it is written, *He Ezra, went up from Babylon.* Concerning Moses, it is stated: *And the Lord commanded me at that time to teach you statutes and judgments,* and concerning Ezra, it is stated: *For Ezra had prepared his heart to expound the law . . . and to teach Israel statutes and judgments.*"

Then the Talmud takes an intriguing turn by claiming that "even though the Torah was not given through Ezra, the script was changed by him." Earlier passages in the Talmud explain that the Torah was presented to Israel in "Ivri" (ancient or paleo-Hebrew) and then, in the days of Ezra, in "Ashuri" (square Hebrew) and in Aramaic translation. So Ezra is credited not only with bringing the Torah to the masses but doing so in a way they could understand. *"Then all the people went to eat and drink and send portions and make great merriment, for they understood the things they were told"* (Neh. 8:12).

The "Torah revolution" of Ezra is thus daring in two ways: elevating the written Torah to sacred Scripture and bringing it to the people. Some historians and philosophers (including Spinoza) even credit Ezra rather than Moses with the writing of the Torah, or at least collecting the Five Books into one scroll, although there is no hard evidence to support this contention.

Like many revolutions, however, the seeds of change were planted earlier. Moses himself is described as taking *Sefer ha-Brit,* the book (or some sort of tablet or record) of the covenant, and reading it aloud to the people (Exod. 24:7). The people respond with an oft-quoted verse of Torah, *na'aseh vinishma*, which has variously been translated as "*we will do and we will listen*," "*we will faithfully do*," "*we will do and obey*," and "*we will do what we have heard.*" In effect, the people consent—they will be governed by the covenant stipulations.

When Moses is nearing his end, and the people are readying to enter the Promised Land without him, he gathers all the people for another great covenant reaffirmation. Moses proclaims: "*You stand this day, all of you, before the Lord your God—your tribal heads, your elders and your officials, all the men of Israel, your children, your wives, even the stranger within your camp, from the woodchopper to waterdrawer—to enter into the covenant of the Lord your God*" (Deut. 29:9). As if prescient of the covenant renewal ceremonies that will become part of the nation's future religious life, Moses adds, "*I make this covenant, with its sanctions, not with you alone, but with those who are standing here with us this day before the Lord our God and with those who are not with us here this day*" (Deut. 29:13–14). Moments later, Moses reaffirms the democratic nature of "*this book of the Teaching*" by emphasizing that this instruction "*is not in the heavens*" but "*very close to you, in your mouth and in your heart*" (Deut. 30:10–14).

The term *Sefer ha-Brit* is used just one other time in the Bible, in a striking episode of covenant reaffirmation. In 622 BCE, during the eighteenth year of King Josiah's reign, the High Priest Hilkiah discovers a "scroll of the Teaching [Torah]" in the Temple (2 Kings 22:8). A scribe named Shapan reads the scroll to King Josiah, who reacts in the same emotional way Ezra did when he realized the people were not in compliance with the covenant. Josiah seeks verification from his scribes, priests, minister—and, unexpectedly, from a female prophetess named Huldah—that he has understood the scroll correctly. When Huldah affirms the gravity of the situation—that disobedience will bring swift tragedy—Josiah summons all the people to a public reading of the scroll remarkably similar to that of Ezra's. "*And he read to them the entire text of the covenant scroll [Sefer ha-Brit] which had been found in the House of the Lord. . . . And all the people entered into the covenant*" (2 Kings 23:2–3).

After the convocation, King Josiah instituted various reforms to cleanse Israel of pagan practices. He eliminated Ba'al worship at sacred high places and *"did away with the necromancers and the mediums, the idols and the fetishes—all the detestable things that were to be seen in the land of Judah and Jerusalem"* (2 Kings 23:24). The reforms, however, seem not to have outlasted Josiah's battlefield death in 609 BCE. According to the Bible, his successors consistently *"did what was displeasing to the Lord"* (2 Kings 23:32, 23:37, 24:19, etc.). Still, the memory of Josiah's reforms may have inspired Ezra.

Ezra's Torah revolution can thus be seen as the culmination—or, better, the codification—of the prophetic message that flowed through the classic prophets and all the way back to Moses at Sinai. For the prophets, it was always all about the covenant, and the consequences of disobedience to it. Now there was a book that faithfully recorded the stipulations (and the crucial early history) of that covenant. And now there was a way to bring the message of that book to the masses.

Walking with Ezra: The Path of Wisdom

The Torah revolution of Ezra reaffirms the central notion of covenant that courses through the Hebrew Bible. It initiates, or at least accelerates, the codification of Scripture as a written record of that covenant. It commences the process of translation and interpretation of Scripture that lies at the heart of Rabbinic Judaism. Finally, it validates the daring proposition that the wisdom of Judaism belongs not to a privileged elite, but to the masses, to *K'lal Yisrael,* the entire community of Israel.

Yet could Ezra's Torah revolution survive the destruction of the country, when national assembly was no longer possible? Could it endure beyond the Land of Israel in the emerging Jewish diaspora? History provides us with a fascinating clue that predates yet foreshadows the rise of Rabbinic Judaism and its innovations that kept Judaism alive. The city of Alexandria in Egypt rose to become one of the great cities of antiquity. There, around the year 250 BCE, the growing

Jewish community added a unique, vital, and controversial chapter to the history of Judaism, by translating the Torah into Greek. Known as the Septuagint, this translation, which eventually grew to encompass all the Hebrew Bible, enabled a Hellenized minority to retain its sacred library in a sea of Greek influence. What is more, the Jews of Alexandria began gathering in "prayer halls" (that some scholars argue are the true forerunners of the synagogue) for the reading and study of the Pentateuch (first five books of the Bible). According to the first-century CE Jewish philosopher Philo of Alexandria: "The Jews every seventh day occupy themselves with the philosophy of their fathers, dedicating that time to the acquiring of knowledge and the study of the truths of nature." Both Jews in the mainstream and two small groups, the Essenes and the Therapeutae, he says, read and study "the holy writings."

History is full of ironies. It is possible that the composition of the Torah as we know it was accomplished in the Babylonia diaspora, and that the regular reading of it on the Sabbath and festivals originated in the Egyptian diaspora. Ezra himself was born in the Diaspora; he was the first of many great sages of Babylon who would propel Judaism forward in new forms in their own right and by influencing the homeland.

Not all the innovations of the Diaspora were welcome in Israel, however. The sages there were divided about the Greek translation; some called it a great accomplishment and others an abomination. In another irony, the Septuagint survived only in Christian circles. Our only extant manuscripts come from Christian monasteries in the early centuries of the Common Era. The sages of Israel rejected some holy writings of the Alexandria Jewish community; these so-called *sefarim hitzoni'im* (outside books) were likewise preserved by the early Christians.

Yet the very existence of arguments about what books constitute the Bible and in what language it should be read testify to the centrality of Torah as the new millennium dawned. The Jews had now become the "People of the Book" (a term coined much later, in yet another irony, by Muhammad).

Rabbinic Judaism would go on to elevate the study of Torah to a position of central importance. The sages did so in two ways. First, they posited that they, the Rabbis, were in a direct line of transmission of revelation from Moses to themselves. The famous tractate of the Talmud called Pirkei Avot (Ethics of the Fathers) opens with this bold claim: "Moses received the Torah from Sinai and gave it over to Joshua. Joshua gave it over to the Elders, the Elders to the Prophets, and the Prophets gave it over to the Men of the Great Assembly."

Further, the sages argued, even more boldly and ingenuously, that their oral interpretation (*Torah she-be-al peh*) of the Written Law (*Torah she-bi-khetav*) constituted a second Torah that was also revealed at Sinai. This audacious move not only affirmed the Rabbis as the successors to Moses and the prophets, but elevated study to the exalted position that sacrifice once held. When the Temple was destroyed, Judaism could persevere.

More than anyone else, it was the great Rabbi Yochanan ben Zakkai, an eyewitness to the cataclysm, who articulated this view. He understood that Judaism's focus had to shift from the great Temple (*Beit ha-Mikdash*) to the small temple (*mikdash hame'at*). The home was now an altar of holiness, and *shulchano shel adam m'kaper alav*—"a man's table atones for him." A cherished talmudic story tells of ben Zakkai's escape from war-torn Jerusalem (in a coffin) to meet the Roman general Vespasian. Sensing the seismic shift about to take place, ben Zakkai pleads only that a new center of Torah study be established when Rome's conquest is complete. "Give me Yavneh and its sages," he requests, knowing that the key to Jewish survival is keeping Torah learning alive.

The Rabbinic literature is replete with statements affirming the new standing of Torah study as the "Holy of Holies." A celebrated passage in the Mishnah lists a variety of important commandments and then concludes, "*Talmud torah k'neged kulam,*" the study of Torah equals (or exceeds) them all. "Turn [the Torah] again and again, for everything is in it," says the sage Ben Bag Bag, "contemplate it, grow gray and old over it, and swerve not from it, for there is no greater good." "Where two meet in Torah," says Rabbi Hanina, "God's presence (*Shekinah*) abides." "If you have learned much Torah, do not arrogate to yourself much credit," ben Zakkai cautions, "because you were created for that purpose." The Rabbis even had the temerity to avow: "From the time the Temple was destroyed, prophecy was taken away from the prophets and given to the sages . . . a sage even greater than a prophet!"

During the Rabbinic period it became the responsibility of every Jewish male to become literate in the basic laws of the Torah and Talmud, and to educate one's sons likewise. Maimonides would codify this duty in his great compilation of Jewish law, the *Mishneh Torah*: "Every Jew, rich or poor, or even a beggar, healthy or not, young or old, is obligated to study Torah." The great academic achievement of Jews during the modern era may be an outgrowth of this extraordinary emphasis on education and literacy.

Even before the Rabbinic period's emphasis on learning, the addition of a third part of the Hebrew Bible called Kethuvim (Writings), comprising what is often called the "Wisdom Literature," testifies to the import Judaism placed on seeking wisdom. *"For wisdom is better than rubies; no goods can equal her"* (Prov. 8:11), extols the book of Proverbs. *"Apply your mind to discipline, and your ears to wise sayings"* (23:12). One of the book's best-known passages, *"It is a tree of life to them that hold fast to it"* (3:18), is recited each time Jews return the Torah to the ark after its public recitation.

In another irony, the Wisdom Literature of this third part of the Hebrew Bible appears to have been influenced by the Hellenistic wisdom schools of the Greeks (who ruled Israel beginning in 333 BCE with the conquests of Alexander the Great). Nonetheless, the path of wisdom is deeply embedded in Deuteronomy. Moses speaks of the closeness of Torah (Deut. 30:14) to every person. A few chapters later, Torah is acclaimed as *"the heritage of the congregation of Jacob"* (Deut. 33:4). And, in words that became part of the central *Shema* prayer that is recited daily, we are told to *"take to heart these instructions which I charge you this day. Impress them upon your children. Recite them when you stay at home and when you are away, when you lie down and when you get up*" (Deut. 6:6–7).

In modern times, writers and thinkers continue to extol the centrality of Torah. Author Heinrich Heine remarks, "The Bible is the portable homeland of the Jews." "Torah is a Jew's sense of self, the beginning of it, and the foundation stone of it," writes novelist Chaim Potok. "[The Torah] tells who we are, where we came from, and what we are supposed to be," explains author Letty Pogrebin. "Torah is, effectively, our genetic code. Whether we embrace Torah and live it, reframe it and live informed by its values, we always react to it—and that is a defining element of our experience on this planet," says Jewish Publication Society past president David Lerman.

One of the great teachers of our day, Louis Finkelstein, puts it this way: "When I pray, I speak to God. When I study, God speaks to me."

A Prophetic Glossary

Expressions of Justice

1. *Mahloket*: argument	(The Path of Protest)
2. *Ometz Lev*: courage	(The Path of Civil Disobedience)
3. *Herut:* freedom	(The Path of Freedom)
4. *Mishpat Ehad:* "one law"	(The Path of Equality)
5. *Tochecha:* rebuke	(The Path of Rebuke)
6. *Tzedek:* justice	(The Path of Righteousness)

Expressions of Compassion

7. *Teshuvah*: repentance	(The Path of Repentance)
8. *Selicha*: forgiveness	(The Path of Forgiveness)
9. *Hesed:* loving kindness	(The Path of Kindness)
10. *Pikuach Nefesh:* saving a life	(The Path of Healing)
11. *Tikvah:* hope	(The Path of Hope)
12. *Rachamim*: mercy	(The Path of Compassion)

Expressions of Faith

13. *Simcha:* joy	(The Path of Joy)
14. *Ruach:* spirit; *Emunah:* faith	(The Path of Faith)
15. *Tefillah:* prayer	(The Path of Prayer)
16. *Anava:* humility	(The Path of Humility)
17. *Shalom:* peace	(The Path of Peace)
18. *Torah:* instruction	(The Path of Wisdom)

Study Guide
Living the Bible

Chapter 1. Exploring Protest

THE CALL TO ABRAHAM

Read the following biblical passages regarding the call and covenant to Abraham: Genesis 12:1–9, 13:14–18, 15:1–17, 17:1–27.

1. *"I will make of you a great nation, and I will bless you; I will make your name great, and you shall be a blessing."* (Gen. 12:2)

   What does it mean to be a blessing, as an individual and as a people?

2. *"For I have singled him out, that he may instruct his children and his posterity to keep the way of the Lord by doing what is just and right, in order that the Lord may bring about for Abraham what He has promised him."* (Gen. 18:19)

   In what sense are we Abraham's children? How are we chosen?

ABRAHAM'S ARGUMENT

Contrast Abraham's protest to God in Genesis 18:16–33 with the binding of Isaac in Genesis 22:1–19.

1. *"Abraham came forward and said, 'Will You sweep away the innocent along with the guilty? Far be it from You to do such a thing, to bring death upon the innocent as well as the guilty, so that innocent and*

guilty fare alike. Far be it from You! Shall not the Judge of all the earth deal justly?'" (Gen. 18:23,25)

On what basis does Abraham, and do we, have the right to challenge authority, be it human or divine?

Why doesn't Abraham challenge God regarding the sacrifice of his son Isaac? How might we resemble Abraham in this regard?

ARGUMENT AND PROTEST

For the protest of Moses, read Numbers 14; for Job, read the book of Job in its entirety.

1. *"Pardon, I pray, the iniquity of this people according to Your great kindness, as You have forgiven this people ever since Egypt."* (Num. 14:19)

   What strategy does Moses employ in appealing to change the mind of a higher power?

2. *"By God who has deprived me of justice . . . my lips will speak no wrong, nor my tongue utter deceit. Far be it from me to say you are right; until I die I will maintain my integrity."* (Job 27:2,4–5).

   What can we learn from Job's dramatic words?

3. "Every debate that is for the sake of heaven (*mahloket l'shem shamayim*) will make a lasting contribution. Every debate that is not for the sake of heaven will not make a lasting contribution." (Talmud, Avot 5:20)

   What debates are important to have in our personal and communal lives today?

4. "For three years there was a dispute between Beit Hillel and Beit Shammai. . . . Then a voice from heaven announced: both are the words of the living God." (Talmud, Eruvin 13b)

   Are there societal disputes today in which you perceive both sides to be right?

5. "[Beit Hillel prevailed] because [students of the school] were gentle and modest, and studied both their own opinions and the opinions of the other school, and always mentioned the words of the other school with great modesty and humility before their own." (Talmud, Eruvin 13b)

   How can we, personally and communally, make our debates more worthy?

6. "It says something about Judaism that both Hillel and Shammai, and many of their followers, remain revered figures . . . even when they embody opposite approaches to the law and life itself. It isn't simply the answer that is prized; it is the argument itself, the culture of disputation, the wrestling with the truth." (Rabbi Joseph Telushkin)

   How can we honor the culture of disputation in Judaism and in our country?

7. "There may be a time when we are powerless to prevent injustice, but there must never be a time when we fail to protest." (Elie Wiesel)

   How have we failed to protest in the face of injustice, and what can we do about it?

8. "Whoever is able to protest against the transgressions of his own family and does not do so is held responsible for the transgressions of his family. Whoever is able to protest against the transgressions of the people of his community and does not do so is held responsible for the transgressions of his community. Who-

ever is able to protest against the transgressions of the world and does not do so is responsible for the transgressions of the entire world." (Talmud, Shabbat 54b)

What transgressions of family, community, and world have weighed most heavily upon you? How can you protest them?

9. "There are some things in our society to which we should never be adjusted. We must never adjust ourselves to racial discrimination and racial segregation. We must never adjust ourselves to religious bigotry. We must never adjust ourselves to economic conditions that take necessities from the many to give luxuries to the few. We must never adjust ourselves to the madness of militarism and the self-defeating effects of physical violence." (Martin Luther King Jr.)

   In what ways have we as a society today adjusted ourselves to racial discrimination, religious bigotry, economic inequality, and violence, and what can we do to shake our complacency?

Chapter 2. Exploring Civil Disobedience

THE DEFIANCE OF THE MIDWIVES

For the prelude to the midwives' actions read Exodus 1:1–3, and then their actions in 1:15–21.

1. *"The midwives, fearing God, did not do as the king of Egypt had told them; they let the boys live."* (Exod. 1:17)

   What does the "fear of God" mean in our lives?

   What gives us the motivation and strength to practice civil disobedience?

   What injustices call for resistance today?

Read the story of Rahab's courage and resistance in Joshua 2:1–23, and the story of Esther in Esther 4:1–17 and 7:1–10.

1. *"I know that the Lord has given the country to you . . . for the Lord your God is the only God in heaven above and on earth below."* (Josh. 2: 9,11).

   What are the real reasons Rahab is willing to risk her life? When should we be like that?

2. *"Then I shall go to the king, though it is contrary to the law; and if I am to perish, I shall perish!"* (Esther 4:16)

   What made Esther overcome her initial reluctance to face the king? What personal fears obstruct us from taking a brave stand, and how can we overcome them?

3. *"Be strong and resolute, be not in fear, for the Lord your God marches with you."* (Deut. 31:6)

   How can faith alleviate our fears?

4. "Courage is never to let your actions be influenced by your fears." (Arthur Koestler)

   How can courage change the course of my life today?

5. "A person who negated a king's command because he was occupied with a mitzvah, even a minor one, behold, he is not liable." (Maimonides, Hilchot Melachim 3:9)

   Should this apply to conscientious objection to military service and acts of civil disobedience to unjust laws?

6. "Must the citizen ever for a moment, or in the least degree, resign his conscience to the legislator? Why has every man a conscience, then? I think that we should be men first, and subjects afterward.

It is not desirable to cultivate a respect for the law, so much as for the right." (Henry David Thoreau)

How does Thoreau's position have relevance today?

7. "When I look through my binoculars, I see children." (Colonel Eli Geva)

   Did Geva do the right thing by refusing to lead the assault on Beirut? What circumstances call for such action today?

8. "One may well ask: 'How can you advocate breaking some laws and obeying others?' The answer lies in the fact there are two types of laws: just and unjust. One has not only a legal but a moral responsibility to obey just laws. Conversely, one has a moral responsibility to disobey unjust laws." (Martin Luther King Jr.)

   On what basis should we decide what laws to obey and what to resist? What unjust laws, policies, or practices need change to in our society?

Chapter 3. Exploring Freedom

MOSES' ENCOUNTERS

Read the brief story of Moses' birth and youth in Exodus 2:1–22 as well as his encounter at the burning bush in Exodus 3:1–4:21, the story of his return to Egypt and encounters with Pharaoh in Exodus 4:24–13:16, and the Exodus itself in Exodus 13:17–18:27.

1. *"Some time after that, when Moses had grown up, he went out to his kinsfolk and witnessed their labors."* (Exod. 2:11)

   What does it mean to "go out" and witness today?

2. *"When the Lord saw that he had turned aside to look, God called to him out of the bush: "Moses! Moses!" He answered, "Here I am."* (Exod. 3:4)

   What calls today are in need of our response, "Here I am"?

3. *"But when Moses told this to the Israelites, they would not listen to Moses, their spirits crushed by cruel bondage."* (Exod. 6:9)

   What obstacles crush our spirit and prevent us from hearing the call to freedom?

FREEDOM

1. "The highest type of freedom in Judaism is *herut*. This implies spiritual freedom, not merely a cessation from work. That is why Passover is called *Zeman Herutenu*, the holiday of freedom. This is not merely the freedom from bondage of Egypt but . . . the Jewish people becoming a people. Pesach is a celebration of spiritual freedom, not mere physical freedom." (Nachum Ansel)

   How can we work toward greater "spiritual freedom" in our lives?

2. "God took us out from slavery (*avdut*) to freedom (*herut*), from despair to joy, from mourning to celebration, from darkness to radiance, from enslavement to redemption." (Passover Haggadah).

   How has the transformation described in the Haggadah happened in our current histories—personal, familial, and communal?

3. "In every generation each person should see themselves as if they went out from Egypt." (Passover Haggadah)

   How can we fulfill the charge of the Haggadah?

4. "The writing was God's writing, inscribed (*harut*) upon the tablets. Read 'freedom' (*herut*) rather than 'inscribed' upon the tablets." (Talmud, Avot 6:2 on Exodus 32:16)

   How do the commandments set us free?

5. "True freedom, in the rabbinic view, lies in servitude to God. The Israelites had been Pharaoh's slaves; in the wilderness they became God's servants—the Hebrew word (*avadim*) is the same. . . . He brought them . . . not at all a way of life free from regulation but rather a way of life to whose regulation they could

and did agree. The Israelites could be free only insofar as they accepted the discipline of freedom." (Michael Walzer)

In what ways do we practice the "discipline of freedom"?

6. "You can live in a dictatorship and be free—on one condition: that you fight the dictatorship. The man who thinks with his own mind, and keeps it uncorrupted, is free. But you can live in the most democratic country on earth, and if you're lazy, obtuse or servile within yourself, you're not free. Even without any violent coercion, you're a slave. You can't beg your freedom from someone. You have to seize it." (Ignazio Silone)

   In what ways are we as citizens free and not free?

Chapter 4. Exploring Equality

THE DAUGHTERS' CHALLENGE

Read the challenge of the five daughters in Numbers 27:1–11 and 36:1–12.

1. *"Let not our father's name be lost to his clan just because he had no son! Give us a holding among our father's kinsmen!"* (Num. 27:4)

   What is the unfinished agenda for women's equality today?

2. *"And the Lord said to Moses: The plea of Zelophehad's daughters is just."* (Num. 27:7)

   What is the unfinished agenda for equality for minorities and others today?

3. *"The plea of Zelophehad's daughters is just. . . . The plea of the Josephite tribe is just."* (Num. 27:7, 36:5)

   On what issues of inclusion and equality might we benefit from seeing both sides and effecting compromise?

Read the story of humanity's creation in Genesis 1 and 2.

1. *"And God created humanity in God's own image, in the divine image God created them; male and female God created them."* (Gen. 1:27)

   "Have we not all one Father? Did not one God create us?" (Mal. 2:10)

   "Are ye not as children of the Ethiopians unto me, O Children of Israel?" (Amos 9:7)

   "My house shall be called a house of prayer for all peoples." (Isa. 56:7)

   What, in your view, is the basis for inclusion and equality in society?

2. *"You shall have one law for stranger and citizen alike."* (Lev. 24:22)

   "There shall be one law for you and for the resident stranger; it shall be law for all time throughout the ages. You and the stranger shall be alike before the Lord; the same ritual and the same rule shall apply to you and to the stranger who resides among you." (Num. 15:15–16)

   What relevance does the Torah idea of having one law for both citizens and strangers have today (and who is the stranger)?

3. "Understand that 'one law for you' means that the law applies equally to all of you." (Talmud, Ketubot 33a)

   In what way is our political system discriminatory?

4. "Equality is the mother of justice, queen of all virtues." (Philo)

   Is there a place for affirmative action and remedial actions to correct inequality?

5. "It is a sacred duty to express most emphatically the complete religious equality of the female sex." (Breslau Reform Rabbinical Conference, 1845)

   What inequalities remain in religion, in government, and in the workplace?

6. "We must render visible the presence, experience, and deeds of women erased in traditional sources. To expand Torah, we must reconstruct Jewish history to include the history of women, and in doing so alter the shape of Jewish memory." (Judith Plaskow)

   How can we reconstruct the lost voices of women in the Bible and beyond?

7. "All people deserve dignity, integrity and equality. Therefore, we accord the same treatment both to homosexuals and heterosexuals that we now apply regardless of gender, age, disability, and birth religion. As we celebrate the love between heterosexuals, so too do we celebrate the love between gay and lesbian Jews. As we affirm that heterosexual marriages embody *kedushah* [holiness], so do we affirm that *kedushah* resides in committed relationships between gay and lesbian Jews." (Reconstructionist Movement)

   Why is this statement of marriage equality still controversial in the broader Jewish community, and where do you stand?

Chapter 5. Exploring Rebuke

SAMUEL'S WARNING

Read the Torah's admonition about kingship in Deuteronomy 17:14–20 and Samuel's rebuke of the people in 1 Samuel 8 and 12. Other prophetic rebukes, such as Elijah's, are recorded in 1 Kings—see especially chapters 13, 14, 18, 21. Isaiah (17) and Jeremiah (11) also rebuke.

1. *"All the elders of Israel assembled and came to Samuel at Ramah, and they said to him, "You have grown old, and your sons have not followed your ways."* (1 Sam. 8:4–5)

   How have our children, and/or our leaders, let us down (and vice versa)?

2. *"Therefore appoint a king for us, to govern us like all other nations."* (1 Sam. 8:5)

What changes need to take place in our families, communities, and country?

3. *"When he is seated on his royal throne, he shall have a copy of this Teaching written for him on a scroll by the priests. Let it remain with him and let him read in it all his life."* (Deut. 17:18–19)

What can we, and our leaders, do to be more accountable to the Torah . . . and to the Constitution of our country?

REBUKE

1. *"You shall surely rebuke your kinsman; incur no guilt because of him."* (Lev. 19:18)

What circumstances in my life call for warning or rebuke?

2. "But if the other will not rebuke him, he will hate him in his heart, and will cause him harm either then or at some other time." (*Sefer ha-Hinnukh*, 3:81, #239)

How has the failure to rebuke hurt myself or others?

3. "When one person wrongs another, the latter should not remain silent and despise him. Rather, he is commanded to make the matter known and ask him: Why did you do this to me? Why did you wrong me regarding this matter? If afterwards, [the person who committed the wrong] asks to forgive him, he must do so." (Maimonides, Hilchot De'ot 6:6)

When do we "let it go" and when do we speak up? Must we always forgive?

4. "He who rebukes another . . . should administer the rebuke in private, speak to the offender gently and tenderly, and point out that

he is only speaking for the wrongdoer's own good." (Maimonides, Hilchot De'ot 6:7)

What are the likely consequences of rebuking in the right way, and the wrong way?

5. "Whoever has the possibility of rebuking [sinners] and fails to do so is considered responsible for that sin, for he had the opportunity to rebuke them." (Maimonides, Hilchot De'ot 6:7)

   How do we become culpable when we fail to rebuke?

6. "And I declare to [Eli the high priest] that I sentence his house to endless punishment for the iniquity he knew about—how his sons committed sacrilege at will, and he did not rebuke them." (1 Sam. 3:13)

   How have I failed my children, and other family members, for not rebuking properly or at all?

7. "Love your critics and hate your flatterers." (Rabbi Yonah Gerondi, Sha'arei Teshuvah 13c)

   What is to be gained from following the advice of this medieval sage?

8. "Love unaccompanied by criticism is not love. . . . Peace unaccompanied by reproof is not peace." (Genesis Rabbah 54:3)

   How are love and criticism linked?

9. "Unconditional love is not uncritical love." (Rabbi Barry L. Schwartz)

   How does this statement apply to family and community?

10. "[Judaism is] a religion that will not worship power and the symbols of power—for that is what idols really were and are. . . . Judaism is a sustained critique of power. That is the conclusion I

have reached after a lifetime of studying our sacred texts." (Rabbi Jonathan Sacks)

How does Judaism express its "sustained critique" of power, and how do I?

11. "Had there been only a single verb I would have known that the law applies to a master reproving his disciple. How do we know that it applies even to a disciple reproving his master? From the phrase, *hokeach tokhiach*, implying, 'under all circumstances.'" (Talmud, Bava Metzia 31a)

Under what circumstances should we criticize our teachers?

12. "If two people were feuding, Aaron would walk up to one, sit down next to him and say, 'My child, don't you see how much your friend is tearing her heart out and rending her clothes?' The person would then say to himself: 'How can I lift up my head and look my friend in the face? I would be ashamed to see her because it is I who treated her foully.' Aaron would remain at his side until he had removed all rancor from his heart. Afterwards, Aaron would walk over to the other person, sit down next to her, and say: 'Don't you see how much your friend is eating his heart out and tearing his clothes?' And so this person, too, would think to herself: 'Woe unto me! How can I lift up my head and look my friend in the face? I would be ashamed to see him because it is I who treated him foully.' Aaron would sit with this person until she, too, had overcome the rancor in her heart. And finally when these two friends met, they would embrace and kiss each other. That is why it is said [that when Aaron died], 'And they wept for Aaron thirty days, the entire House of Israel' (Numbers 20:20)." (*Avot de-Rabbi Natan*, chapter 12)

How can we emulate Aaron the peacemaker?

Chapter 6. Exploring Righteousness

NATHAN'S CONFRONTATION WITH DAVID

Read the initial, and positive, encounter of Nathan with David as told in 2 Samuel 7:1–29, and continue with his epic confrontation with the king in 2 Samuel 11–12.

1. *"You acted in secret, but I will make this happen in the sight of all Israel and in broad daylight."* (2 Sam. 12:12)

   What are our secret sins?

2. *"David said to Nathan, 'I stand guilty before the Lord!'"* (2 Sam. 12:13)

   What are our sins of omission—instances where we did not do enough right (rather than doing something overtly wrong)?

3. *"And Nathan replied to David, "The Lord has remitted your sin; you shall not die. However, since you have spurned the enemies of the Lord by this deed, the child about to be born to you shall die."* (2 Sam. 12:13–14)

   For which of our sins will our repentance atone . . . and not atone?

ACCOUNTABILITY AND RIGHTEOUSNESS

1. "All is foreseen, yet freedom of choice is granted." (Talmud, Avot 3:19)

   How is this teaching manifest in our personal lives?

2. "Free will is bestowed on every human being. If one desires to turn to the good way and be righteous, he has the power to do so. If one wishes to turn toward the evil way and be wicked, he is at liberty to do so. . . . Every human being may become righteous like Moses our teacher, or wicked like Jeroboam; merciful or cruel, miserly or generous, and so with all other qualities." (Maimonides, *Mishneh Torah*, Laws of Repentance, 5:1–2)

   What choices have I made that make me a better person, and a worse person?

3. “Don’t remain passive when you see another about to act evilly, lest you share in the guilt.” (Rabbi Joseph Telushkin)

   In what ways has passivity led us astray?

4. “The irresistible is often only that which is not resisted.” (Justice Louis Brandeis)

   How does this adage apply to me?

5. “The difference between the wicked and the righteous is that the wicked are controlled by their hearts and the righteous have their hearts under their control.” (Genesis Rabbah 34:10)

   When have emotions overcome me to my detriment?

6. “At first the Evil Impulse is like a passer-by, then he is called a guest, and finally he becomes a master of the house.” (Talmud, Sukkah 52b)

   What examples from world and personal history come to mind?

7. “Who is a hero? He who subdues his Evil Impulse.” (Simeon be Zoma, Pirkei Avot, 4:1)

   When has self-control rendered you heroic?

8. “Whoever can stop the members of his household from committing a sin, but does not, is held responsible for the sins of his household. If he can stop the people of his city from sinning, but does not, he is held responsible for the sins of the people of his city.” (Talmud, Arakhin 16b)

   For what sins of family and community are we responsible due to lack of action?

9. “A rich man came to Jacob and sought his advice. Why must I give to the poor? Because they are responsible for your freedom, said Jacob. The man was astonished. How does giving to the poor bring about my freedom? You see, said Jacob, either the key to a

man's wallet is in his heart, or the key to a man's heart is in his wallet. So, until you express your charity, you are locked inside your greed." (Noah benShea, *Jacob the Baker*)

Do we do our share to help the poor? Is our key in our heart or in our wallet?

Chapter 7. Exploring Repentance

JUDAH'S TRANSFORMATION

Read Judah's journey from the betrayal of his brother in Genesis 37 to the incident with Tamar in Genesis 38 to the leadership role among his brothers in Genesis 43 to his encounter with Joseph in Genesis 44.

1. *"Then Judah said to his brothers, 'What do we gain by killing our brother and covering up his blood? Come, let us sell him to the Ishmaelites, but let us not do away with him ourselves. After all, he is our brother, our own flesh.'"* (Gen. 37:26–27)

   How do we defend yet betray our brothers (however defined)?

2. *"She is more in the right than I."* (Gen. 38:26)

   What confessions do we need to make to begin repentance?

3. *"For how can I go back to my father unless the boy is with me? Let me not be witness to the woe that would overtake my father!"* (Gen. 44:34)

   For what person or cause can we show greater empathy and be worthy of forgiveness?

REPENTANCE

Read the story of Cain and Abel in Genesis 4 and then passages in Deuteronomy 4 and 30 that highlight the return to God, along with selections from Jeremiah in chapters 3, 4, 7, and so on. The short book of Jonah (four chapters) should also be read, as it revolves around the repentance of the people of Nineveh.

1. *"Sin crouches at the door . . . yet you can be its master."* (Gen. 4:7)

   What are our temptations, and how might we overcome them?

2. *"God saw what they did, how they were turning back from their evil ways. And God renounced the punishment He had planned to bring upon them, and did not carry it out."* (Jon. 3:5–10)

   How might repentance change our lives?

3. "One hour of repentance and good deeds in this world is more beautiful than all the life in the world to come." (Talmud, Avot 4:17)

   What good may come to our family and community from our repentance?

4. "Repentance means that the sinner forsakes his sins, casts them out of his mind, and resolves in his heart to sin no more." (Maimonides, *Mishneh Torah*, Laws of Repentance, 2:2)

   What examples of true and complete repentance inspire you?

5. "Among the paths of repentance is for the penitent to: a) constantly call out before God, crying and entreating; b) perform charity according to his potential; c) separate himself far from the object of his sin; d) change his name, as if to say—I am a different person and not the same one who sinned; e) change his behavior in its entirety to the good and the path of righteousness; f) travel in exile from his home. Exile atones for sin because it causes a person to be submissive, humble and meek of spirit." (Maimonides, *Mishneh Torah*, Laws of Repentance, 2:4)

   What steps offered by Maimonides apply to my life?

6. "There are four steps to repentance: confession, remorse, asking forgiveness/repairing damage, and accepting responsibility to never repeat the sin." (Saadia Gaon, *Book of Beliefs* 5:5)

   Is my repentance complete?

7. "Rabbi Eliezer said, 'Repent one day before your death.' His disciples asked him, 'But does a person know what day he [or she] is going to die? He said, 'All the more reason, therefore, to repent today, lest one die tomorrow.'" (Talmud, Shabbat 153a)

   What repentance have I left undone, and what degree of urgency is there to complete it?

Chapter 8. Exploring Forgiveness

JOSEPH'S FORGIVENESS

Read about Joseph's forgiveness as told in Genesis 45 and 50.

1. *"Now, do not be distressed or reproach yourselves because you sold me hither; it was to save life that God sent me ahead of you."* (Gen. 45:5)

   To whom can we extend forgiveness, and why?

2. *"God has sent me ahead of you to ensure your survival on earth, and to save your lives in an extraordinary deliverance. So, it was not you who sent me here, but God."* (Gen. 45:7–8)

   What is the larger purpose I discern in my life?

3. *"But Joseph said to them, 'Have no fear! Am I a substitute for God? Besides, although you intended me harm, God intended it for good, so as to bring about the present result—the survival of many people. And so, fear not. I will sustain you and your children.' Thus he reassured them, speaking kindly to them."* (Gen. 50:19–21)

   For what mistakes we have committed do we need reassurance that we are forgiven?

Read about the pardon of the Israelites in Numbers 14. Likewise, review God's forgiveness of the people of Nineveh and Jonah's reaction to it as described in Jonah 3 and 4.

1. "To err is human; to forgive, divine." (Alexander Pope)

   How do our mistakes measure up to our forgiveness?

2. *"God saw what they did, how they were turning back from their evil ways. And God renounced the punishment He had planned to bring upon them, and did not carry it out."* (Jon. 3:5–10)

   Who has repented and is deserving of our forgiveness?

3. *"For a little while I forsook, but with vast love I will bring you back. In slight anger, for a moment, I hid my face from you. But with kindness everlasting I will take you back in love—said the Lord your redeemer."* (Isa. 54:7–8)

   What instances of neglect and anger are hindering our compassion and forgiveness?

4. *"[Moses said to God] 'Forgive, I pray, the iniquity of this people according to Your great kindness, as You have forgiven this people ever since Egypt.' And the Lord said, 'I forgive, as you have asked. Nevertheless . . . none of the men who . . . disobeyed Me shall see the land that I promised on oath to their fathers; none of those who spurn Me shall see it.'"* (Num. 14:19–23)

   How can we forgive another person but still hold that individual accountable?

5. "The Hebrew *salach* implies not the absolution of sin but the suspension of anger." (Jacob Milgrom)

   How might this understanding of *selicha* help us in our relationships?

6. "At first God intended to create the world by justice alone, but then God realized that the world could not endure and therefore gave precedence to mercy, allying it with justice." (Rashi)

   What can Rashi's comment teach us about how we are to act in the world?

7. "What does God pray? May it be My will that My compassion overcomes My anger, and that it may prevail over My justice when My children appeal to Me, that I may deal with them in mercy and in love." (Talmud, Berachot 7a)

   How is "God's prayer" an example for us?

8. "I wanted to be free, so I let it go." (Nelson Mandela)

   What do we need to let go of in order to be truly free?

9. "I set her down by the river, but you are still carrying her." (Zen parable)

   What are we still carrying that hinders our compassion?

10. "I will remember the courage of my friend in stone, and his unkindness in sand." (Persian parable)

    How does our attitude influence our capacity to forgive?

Chapter 9. Exploring Kindness

NAOMI, RUTH, AND BOAZ

Read Ruth's declaration and act of *hesed* in the first chapter of the book of Ruth, and then continue with the entirety of this short book to capture the spirit of compassion throughout. Read about Abraham's kindness toward the strangers in Genesis 18 and Rebecca's in Genesis 24.

1. *"Oh no, my daughters! My lot is far more bitter than yours, for the hand of the Lord has struck out against me."* (Ruth 1:13)

   What makes us embittered?

2. *"But Naomi said . . . May the Lord show hesed (kindness) to you, as you have shown hesed to the dead and to me."* (Ruth 1:8)

   How can we show *hesed* **to the living and to the dead?**

3. *"But Ruth replied, '. . . your people shall be my people, and your God my God.'"* (Ruth 1:16)

   How can we affirm our peoplehood and our faith and thereby show kindness?

KINDNESS

1. *"You shall each revere his mother and his father."* (Lev. 19:3)

   "You shall rise before the aged and show deference to the old." (Lev. 19:32)

   What more can we do to love and respect our parents and our elders?

2. *"You shall not pick your vineyard bare, or gather the fallen fruit of your vineyard; you shall leave them for the poor and the stranger."* (Lev. 19:10)

   How can we be more generous to the needy, personally and as a society?

3. *"Do not harden your heart and shut your hand against your needy kinsman."* (Deut. 15:7)

   How do we shut our eyes, our heart, and our hand to the needy around us?

4. "On three things the world stands: on Torah, on *Avodah* (prayer), and on *Gemilut Hasadim* (acts of kindness)." (Talmud, Avot 1:2)

   What acts of kindness are part of my life?

5. "Rabbi Simon said, 'When the Holy One, blessed be He, came to create Adam, the ministering angels formed themselves into groups and parties, some of them saying, *Let him be created,* whilst others urged, *Let him not be created.*' . . . Hesed said, '*Let*

him be created, because he will practice acts of hesed.'" (Genesis Rabbah 8:5)

What qualities or acts most define me?

6. "The quality of mercy . . . is twice blessed: it blesses him that gives and him that takes." (Shakespeare, *The Merchant of Venice*)

   How does practicing kindness bless others and ourselves?

7. *"Let not the wise man glory in his wisdom, not the mighty man in his might, nor the wealthy man in his wealth. But let him that glories, glory in this: that he understands and knows Me, that I am the Lord who does hesed, justice, and righteousness in the world. For in these things I delight, says the Lord."* (Jer. 9:12)

   What is our false worship, and what can we do to correct this?

8. "Compassion is the feeling of empathy which the pain of one being of itself awakens in another; and the higher and more human the beings are, the more keenly attuned are they to re-echo the note of suffering which, like a voice from heaven, penetrates the heart . . . the very nature of his heart must teach him that he is required above everything else to feel himself the brother of all beings, and to recognize the claim of all beings to his lobe and beneficence. Do not suppress this compassion, this sympathy, especially with the sufferings of your fellow. It is the warning voice of duty, which points out to you your brother in every sufferer." (Samson Raphael Hirsch, *Horeb* 17:125–126).

   How can we become more empathetic?

9. "This quintessential word lies at the heart of Jewish thought and feeling. All of Judaism's philosophy, ethics, ethos, leaning, education, hierarchy of values, are saturated with a sense of, and heightened sensitivity to, *rachmones*." (Leo Rosten, *The Joys of Yiddish*)

   Why is compassion considered to be central to our lives?

Chapter 10. Exploring Healing

NAAMAN'S HEALING

Read the story of Naaman in 2 Kings 5:1–17. Add the healing of the Shunamite woman's son in 2 Kings 4:1–37 and the precursor tale involving Elijah and the widow of Sidon's son in 1 Kings 17:20–24.

1. *"When Elisha, the man of God, heard that the king of Israel had rent his clothes, he sent a message to the king: 'Why have you rent your clothes? Let him come to me, and he will learn that there is a prophet in Israel.'"* (2 Kings 5:8)

   What makes us reluctant and afraid (like the king) to take on bold missions, and what can we learn from Elisha's response?

2. *"But his servants came forward and spoke to him. 'Sir,' they said, 'if the prophet told you to do something difficult, would you not do it? How much more when he has only said to you, Bathe and be clean.'"* (2 Kings 5:13)

   When do we make things more complicated than they need to be, and why?

3. *"'When I bow low in the temple of Rimmon, may the Lord pardon your servant in this.' And he said to him, 'Go in peace.'"* (2 Kings 5:18–19)

   What compromises do we make to get by? Are we as understanding as Elisha?

HEALING AND SAVING A LIFE

1. *"You shall keep My laws and My rules by the pursuit of which man shall live."* (Lev. 18:5)

   What is the foremost purpose of the commandments, in the view of tradition and in your view?

2. *"You shall not stand idly [stand by the blood] of your neighbor."* (Lev. 19:6)

   In what ways are we standing idly by?

3. "Whoever saves one life, it is as if he saved an entire world." (Talmud, Sanhendrin 4:5)

   When and how have you saved, or transformed, a life?

4. "The saving of life supersedes the Sabbath." (Talmud, Shabbat 132a)

   What tasks need to be the highest priority in your life, and why?

5. "We did everything to save lives despite Shabbat . . . we are here because the Torah orders us to save lives." (Mati Goldstein, commander of the ultra-Orthodox Jewish Zaka rescue organization, while working on the Sabbath during the 2010 Haiti earthquake mission)

   What life-saving or transformational work might await you?

6. "It is a religious precept to desecrate the Sabbath for any person afflicted with an illness that may prove dangerous; he who is zealous is praiseworthy while he who asks questions sheds blood." (Shulchan Arukh, Orach Chayyim 328:2)

   What more do we need to do to heal ourselves, or a loved one?

Chapter 11. Exploring Hope

JEREMIAH'S LAND PURCHASE AND PROPHECY

Read the account of Jeremiah's transaction and scroll writing in Jeremiah chapter 32. Then read about his prior incitements and public tribulation in chapters 25–26. Consider his message of consolation and hope in chapter 31.

1. *"Yet You, Lord God, said to me: 'Buy the land for money and call in witnesses'—when the city is at the mercy of the Chaldeans!"* (Jer. 32:25)

   What tangible acts can we do to demonstrate hope?

2. *"Thus said the Lord of Hosts, the God of Israel: 'Take these documents, this deed of purchase, the sealed text and the open one, and put them into an earthen jar, so that they may last a long time.'"* (Jer. 32:14)

   What would you write in an ethical will (a statement of your values to your children) that you would want to be remembered for a long time?

3. *"I will give them a single heart and a single nature to revere Me for all time, and it shall be well with them and their children after them."* (Jer. 32:39)

   In what ways does it behoove us to unify our families and our country so they will be well with us?

HOPE

1. "As long as there is life, there is hope." (Jerusalem Talmud, Berachot 9:1)

   What are your most cherished hopes?

2. *"As for me, I will hope always, and add to the many praises of You."* (Ps. 71:14)

   How can faith give you hope?

3. "I am a Jew because in every age when the cry of despair is heard, the Jew hopes." (Edmund Fleg)

   Why have the Jewish people been such exemplars of hope?

4. "We have not yet lost our hope, the hope of two thousand years, to be a free people in our own land." ("Hatikvah," "The Hope," national anthem of Israel, from the poem by Naphtali Imber)

   How is modern Israel a symbol of hope?

5. "Such a people, which discounts its present and has the eye fixed steadily on its future, which lives as it were on hope, is on that very account eternal, like hope." (Heinrich Graetz)

   What qualities engender hope?

6. "There is no hope unmingled with fear, and no fear unmingled with hope." (Baruch Spinoza)

   How are hope and fear connected in your life?

Chapter 12. Exploring Compassion

The tales of compassion, Jonah and Ruth, are both among the shortest books of the Bible, and can easily be read in their entireties. Review the compassion of Joseph in Genesis 43. See the chapter 9 section of this guide, on kindness, for related material.

JONAH'S LESSON

1. *"The people of Nineveh believed God. They proclaimed a fast, and great and small alike put on sackcloth. . . . God saw what they did, how they were turning back from their evil ways. And God renounced the punishment He had planned to bring upon them, and did not carry it out."* (Jon. 3:5,10)

   How can we be more forgiving and compassionate to those who have repented?

2. *"This displeased Jonah greatly, and he was grieved."* (Jon. 4:1)

   When and why have we been distrustful and resentful of repentance and forgiveness?

3. *"And should not I care about Nineveh, that great city, in which there are more than a hundred and twenty thousand persons who do not yet know their right hand from their left, and many beasts as well!"* (Jon. 4:11)

   What people and what causes deserve our greater concern?

COMPASSION

1. *"Love your neighbor as yourself."* (Lev. 19:18)

   Who might benefit from my greater compassion?

2. *"For I desire kindness, not sacrifice."* (Hosea 6:6)

   In what ways can I be a kinder, gentler person?

3. *"Have we not all one Father? Did not one God create us?"* (Mal. 2:10)

   How are people you struggle to relate to like yourself?

4. "Jews are compassionate children of compassionate parents, and one who shows no mercy for fellow creatures is assuredly not of the seed of Abraham, our father." (Talmud, Betzah 32a)

   What are my best expressions of compassion?

5. *"If your enemy is hungry, give him bread to eat."* (Prov. 25:21)

   How can I treat my adversaries more humanely?

6. "He who is merciful when he should be cruel will in the end be cruel when he should be merciful." (Midrash Samuel)

   When must I practice tough love or active opposition to those I care about?

7. "Do not suppress this compassion, this sympathy, especially with the sufferings of your fellowman. . . . See in it the admonition of God that you are to have no joy so long as a brother suf-

fers by your side." (Rabbi Samson Raphael Hirsch, *Horeb*, chap. 17, section 126)

What suffering in our community, country, and world must we address?

8. "This quintessential word lies at the heart of Jewish thought and feeling. All of Judaism's philosophy, ethics, ethos, learning, education, hierarchy of values, are saturated with a sense of, and heightened sensitivity to *rachmones*." (Leo Rosten, *The Joys of Yiddish*)

   What will it take to for others to call me a mensch?

Chapter 13. Exploring Joy

Read the story of Miriam in Exodus 2, and her moment of celebration in Exodus 15.

MIRIAM'S CELEBRATION

1. *"Then Miriam the prophetess, Aaron's sister, took a timbrel in her hand, and all the women went out after her in dance with timbrels."* (Exod. 15:20)

   What do you have to celebrate in your own life, and in the life of your community and people?

2. *"And Miriam chanted for them: 'Sing to the Lord, for He has triumphed gloriously.'"* (Exod. 15:21)

   What is the connection between your joy and your faith?

3. *"So Miriam was shut out of camp seven days; and the people did not march on until Miriam was readmitted."* (Num. 12:15)

   How can we return to the path of joy after we have suffered?

JOY

1. *"Weeping may tarry for the night, but joy comes in the morning."* (Ps. 30:6)

   What enables us to move on after a tragedy or crisis?

2. *"Eat your bread with joy; drink your wine with a merry heart."* (Eccles. 9:7)

   Why are we encouraged to make joy our "default" mode?

3. "Who lives in joy does his Creator's will." (Ba'al Shem Tov)

   How is joy a religious obligation?

4. "In the world to come we will be asked: What were the times when you could have rejoiced and did not?" (Jerusalem Talmud, Kiddushin 4:12; see also Talmud Ta'anit 11a, Ketubot 104a)

   What times of missed joy come to mind, and why did this happen?

5. "In this world, there is no perfect joy, unmixed with anxiety; no perfect pleasure, unmixed with envy." (Peskita Kahana 29:170a)

   When and how were your times of joy mixed with anxiety or sorrow?

Chapter 14. Exploring Faith

Read the story of Caleb in Numbers 13–14. Abraham's journey of faith can be gleaned from his saga in Genesis 12–22.

CALEB'S SPIRIT

1. *"Caleb hushed the people before Moses and said, 'Let us by all means go up, and we shall gain possession of it, for we shall surely overcome it.'"* (Num. 13:30)

   What situations have you faced that called for optimism in the face of pessimism?

2. *"If the Lord is pleased with us, He will bring us into that land, a land that flows with milk and honey, and give it to us; only you must not rebel against the Lord."* (Num. 14:8–9)

   What is the source of your optimism and faith?

3. *"But My servant Caleb, because he was imbued with a different spirit and remained loyal to Me—him will I bring into the land that he entered, and his offspring shall hold it as a possession."* (Num. 14:24)

   How can we evince the "different spirit" of Caleb in the face of our own challenges?

SPIRIT AND FAITH

1. *"So I promised you when you came out of Egypt, and My spirit is still in your midst. Fear not!"* (Hag. 2:5)

   How might God's spirit sustain us?

2. *"Not by might, nor by power, but by my spirit—said the Lord of Hosts."* (Zech. 4:6)

   How can faith trump might or power?

3. "Faith is clearer than sight." (Rabbi Menachem Mendel of Kotsk)

   How can faith enable us to discern things we might otherwise not see?

4. "Faith sees beyond fate." (Noah benShea)

   How is this true in your life, and in the life of the Jewish people?

5. "In Judaism faith is . . . the capacity of the soul to perceive the abiding . . . in the transitory, the invisible in the visible." (Rabbi Leo Baeck)

   What special insights have you derived from your spirituality or faith?

6. "With faith, there are no questions, and without faith there are no answers." (Chofetz Hayim)

   What questions still concern you; what answers have you arrived at?

Chapter 15. Exploring Prayer

Read the story of Hannah's prayer and subsequent birth of Samuel in 1 Samuel 1–2. Actual examples of personal prayer by individuals are scarce in the Bible. Yet Hannah's prayer (1 Samuel 2:1–10), like Jonah's prayer (Jonah 2:3–10) and David's prayer (2 Samuel 22) and the vast collection of Psalms they resemble, can be read for their intense spiritual feeling.

HANNAH'S PRAYER

1. *"In her wretchedness, she prayed to the Lord, weeping all the while."* (1 Sam. 1:10)

   What circumstances lead us to prayer?

2. *"Do not take your maidservant for a worthless woman; I have only been speaking all this time out of my great anguish and distress."* (1 Sam. 1:16)

   When have we misjudged another and overlooked this person's distress?

3. *"'Then go in peace,'" said Eli, 'and may the God of Israel grant you what you have asked of Him.' She answered, 'You are most kind to your handmaid.' So the woman left, and she ate, and was no longer downcast."* (1 Sam. 1:17–18)

   How can prayer and/or a kind word help us?

PRAYER

1. "What is the service [sacrifice] of the heart? It is prayer." (Talmud, Ta'anit 2a)

   How is prayer to be understood as a form of sacrifice?

2. "Prayer is the expression of man's longing and yearning for God in times of dire need and of overflowing joy." (Kauffman Kohler)

   Why pray both in times of need and in times of joy?

3. *"Out of the depths have I called You."* (Ps. 130:1)

   What should we expect when we pray?

4. *"The Lord is close to the brokenhearted; those crushed in spirit God delivers."* (Ps. 34:19) *"God heals their broken hearts, and binds up their wounds."* (Ps. 147:3)

   How can prayer heal a broken heart?

5. "The heart's cry to God is the highest form of prayer." "Tears smash through the gates and doors of heaven." (2 Zohar 245b)

   What is your definition of an answered prayer?

6. "Prayer invites God's presence to suffuse our spirit, God's will to prevail in our lives. Prayer may not bring water to parched fields, nor mend a broken bridge, nor rebuild a ruined city. But prayer can water an arid soul, mend a broken heart, and rebuild a weakened will." (Heschel, adapted, in *Mishkan T'filah*)

   What are the possibilities, and limitations, of prayer?

Chapter 16. Exploring Humility

Read Elijah's confrontation with the prophets of Ba'al in 1 Kings 18, his flight to the desert in chapter 19, and his problems with Ahab and Jezebel in chapter 21.

ELIJAH'S EXPERIENCE

1. *"He said to him, 'Why are you here, Elijah?' He replied, 'I am moved by zeal for the Lord, the God of Hosts, for the Israelites have forsaken Your covenant, torn down Your altars, and put Your prophets*

to the sword. I alone am left, and they are out to take my life.'" (1 Kings 19:9–10)

How does God's question and Elijah's answer resonate with you?

2. *"And after the fire—a soft murmuring sound. When Elijah heard it, he wrapped his mantle about his face and went out and stood at the entrance of the cave. Then a voice addressed him: 'Why are you here, Elijah?'"* (1 Kings 19:12–13)

   Why is God's question repeated before and after Elijah's experience at the cave?

3. *"The Lord said to him, 'Go back by the way you came . . . and anoint Elisha . . . to succeed you as prophet.'"* (1 Kings: 19:15–16)

   How have you been taught humility?

HUMILITY

1. "Through pride we are ever deceiving ourselves. But deep down below the surface of the average conscience a still, small voice says to us, something is out of tune." (Carl Jung)

   How are we deceiving ourselves, and what is out of tune?

2. "The human voice can never reach the distance that is covered by the still small voice of conscience." (Mahatma Gandhi)

   What is your conscience trying to tell you?

3. "This is a novum in history. The idea that a leader's highest virtue is humility must have seemed absurd, almost self-contradictory, in the ancient world . . . humility and majesty could not coexist. In Judaism, this entire configuration was overturned. Leaders were to serve, not to be served. Moses' highest accolade was to be called *eved Hashem*, God's servant." (Rabbi Jonathan Sacks)

   How can we maintain humility when we amass power and prestige?

4. "Humility is not thinking less of yourself; it is thinking of yourself less." (C. S. Lewis)

   In what ways can we incorporate Lewis's distinction?

5. "Those who have humility are open to things greater than themselves while those who lack it are not. That is why those who lack [humility] make you feel small while those who have it make you feel enlarged. Their humility inspires greatness in others." (Rabbi Jonathan Sacks)

   What are the blessings of humility?

6. *"To do justly, love mercy, and walk humbly with your God."* (Mic. 6:8)

   What constitutes a humble walk with God?

Chapter 17. Exploring Peace

Read Isaiah's vision in Isaiah 60:18–22 and 66:21–25. His famous passage on justice from chapter 58 (read on Yom Kippur) should also be read.

ISAIAH'S VISION OF PEACE

1. *"And they shall beat their swords into plowshares; and their spears into pruning hooks. Nation shall not take up sword against nation; they shall never again know war."* (Isa. 2:4)

   How can we realize peace as individuals, a family, and a nation?

2. *"The wolf shall dwell with the lamb."* (Isa. 11:6)

   With whom/what must we reconcile to make peace?

3. *"The cry "Violence!" shall no more be heard in your land."* (Isa. 60:18)

   Where is the cry of violence most pronounced,
   and where has it been most quieted?

1. *"Seek peace, and pursue it."* (Ps. 34:15)

   How can you be a seeker of peace?

2. "Be of the disciples of Aaron, one who loves peace and pursues it." (Talmud, Avot 1:12)

   What hero of peace do you wish to emulate?

3. "The blessing of the Holy One is peace." (Meg. 18a)

   How can God offer us peace?

4. "One who creates peace at home builds peace in all Israel." (Simeon ben Gamliel)

   What can we do in our own homes to further peace?

5. "Peace cannot be kept by force. It can only be achieved by understanding." (Albert Einstein)

   What challenges of tolerance and understanding stand before us?

5. *"Beat the swords into ploughshares."* (Isaiah). "Make musical instruments out of them." (Yehuda Amichai)

   What are the most inspirational examples of peace in our world today?

6. "Peace is the beauty of life. It is sunshine. It is the smile of a child, the love of a mother, the joy of a father, the togetherness of a family. It is the advancement of man, the victory of a just cause, the triumph of truth." (Menachem Begin)

   What are the foundations for a peaceful society?

Chapter 18. Exploring Wisdom

Read about the public reading of the Torah by Ezra in Nehemiah 8; Moses' declaration on standing in the covenant in Deuteronomy 29, and Josiah's discovery and recitation of the lost scroll in 2 Kings 22–23.

EZRA'S READING OF THE TORAH

1. *"On the first day of the seventh month, Ezra the priest brought the Teaching before the congregation, men and women and all who could listen with understanding."* (Neh. 8:2)

   What are we doing to bring Torah to ourselves and those around us?

2. *"They read from the scroll of the Teaching of God, translating it and giving the sense; so they understood the reading."* (Neh. 8:8)

   What does it mean to "translate" and to "give sense" to Torah for our generation?

3. *"'This day is holy to the Lord your God: you must not mourn or weep,' for all the people were weeping as they listened to the words of the Teaching."* (Neh. 8:9)

   What might sadden us when reading Torah, and why are we to celebrate instead?

WISDOM

1. *"It is a tree of life to them that hold fast to it."* (Prov. 3:18)

   How is the Torah a tree of life for us?

2. "Give me Yavneh and its sages." (Gittin 56b)

   What does this rallying cry mean to you today?

3. "From the time the Temple was destroyed, prophecy was taken away from the prophets and given to the sages . . . a sage is even greater than a prophet!" (Talmud, Bava Batra 12a)

   Should we aspire to be a sage rather than a prophet?

4. "The Bible is the portable homeland of the Jews." (Heinrich Heine)

   How does the Bible impact our lives?

5. "Torah is a Jew's sense of self, the beginning of it, and the foundation stone of it." (Chaim Potok)

   In what sense do you define yourself by the Torah?

6. "Genesis is the saga of a family. Exodus shows how that family became a people. [The Torah] tells who we are, where we came from, and what we are supposed to be." (Letty Pogrebin)

   What part of your identity is shaped by the Torah and by your faith?

7. "Torah is, effectively, our genetic code. Whether we embrace Torah and live it, or reframe it and live informed by its values, we always react to it—and that is a defining element of our experience on this planet." (David Lerman)

   How has reacting to the Torah and to religious experiences changed our lives?

Notes

The numerous citations in this book are brief in nature, educational in purpose, and covered under the commonly accepted "fair use" copyright provision. Nevertheless, Jewish tradition considers it praiseworthy to always identify and attribute sources. In fact the Talmud goes so far as to say, "for whosoever reports a thing in the name of him that said it brings deliverance into the world" (Hullin 104b and Avot 6:6). Wherever possible I have done so in this list of sources, with the most complete information I have. Book citations without a page number indicate that this information was not readily available at the time of this writing. Biblical citations are taken from the JPS TANAKH, with rare exceptions. Rabbinic citations are my own translation or that of varied sources. The lack of bibliographic information for any given source indicates that it was cited from the public domain or from a secondary source that did not identify its origin. Sources are indicated below by the page number in which they appear in this volume, in the order they are quoted on that page.

Preface

xv **"Others have considered history"**: Heschel, *The Prophets*, 171.

xvi **"The prophets' great contribution"**: This and the other Heschel quotes are taken from handwritten notes by Heschel I found in my research in the Heschel archives now located at Duke University.

xvi **"For the prophets"**: Lerner, *Jewish Renewal*, 131.

xviii **Scholars link the word *navi*:** Sarna, *JPS Torah Commentary: Genesis*, 142.

xviii **In fact, Heschel describes**: Heschel, *Moral Grandeur and Spiritual Audacity*, 400.

xix **"a very deep love"**: Heschel, December 10, 1972 (transcript). The interview is also reprinted in Heschel, *Moral Grandeur and Spiritual Audacity*, 395.

xxi **"the voice of cruelty"**: Lerner, *Jewish Renewal*, 90.

xxi **"No religious literature"**: Sacks, *Covenant & Conversation*, November 1, 2004.

xxi **In his study of biblical heroes**: Rabin, *Biblical Hero.*

xxii **The Talmud emphasizes:** Talmud, Avot 4:10; *Avot de-Rabbi Natan* 23a000.

xxiv **Heschel reminds us**: Heschel, *God in Search of Man*, 287.

xxiv **Bible scholar Nahum Sarna**: Sarna, *JPS Torah Commentary: Genesis*, 123.

xxiv **A celebrated passage**: Talmud, Sotah 14a.

xxiv **Much later, the Hasidic movement**: Ba'al Shem Tov in *Ketonet Pasim*, 75.

xxv **Elliot Wolfson**: Wolfson, "Walking as a Sacred Duty."

xxv **Henry David Thoreau's wonderful essay**: Thoreau, "Walking," in *Works of Henry David Thoreau*, 369–414.

xxv **In his book**: Weiner, *Geography of Genius*, 22.

xxvi **As scholar and theologian**: Brueggemann, *Prophetic Imagination*, 3.

xxvi **In an interview**: Heschel, December 10, 1972 (transcript); The interview is also reprinted in Heschel, *Moral Grandeur and Spiritual Audacity*, 395. See also Schwartz, "Abraham Joshua Heschel and *The Prophets*."

xxvi **The Reform movement**: Platforms of the Central Conference of American Rabbis: 1885, 1937, 1976, 1999.

xxviii **As Rabbi Walter Jacob explains**: Jacob, "Prophetic Judaism."

xxix **As Rabbi Sid Schwarz puts it**: Schwarz, *Judaism and Justice*, xxi.

xxix **In his famous "Letter"**: Martin Luther King Jr., "Letter from Birmingham City Jail," April 16, 1963, in King, *A Testament of Hope*, 289–302.

xxx **Perhaps the most stirring words**: Martin Luther King Jr. "Address to Synagogue Council of America," December 5, 1966 in Schneier, *Shared Dreams*, 185–86.

xxxi **Lerner laments**: Lerner, *Jewish Renewal*, 6.

xxxi **Celebrated Israeli author**: Amos and Fania Oz, *Jews and Words.*

xxxi **In his final interview**: Heschel, December 10, 1972 (transcript).

xxxi **Another Rabbinic source**: Tosefta, Sotah 13:2.

xxxii **Taking this a step further**: Held, *Heart of Torah*, 1:39.

xxxii **The Talmud itself**: Talmud, Shabbat 54b.

Introduction

xxxiv **"the first and most formative experience"**: Borowitz, *Renewing the Covenant*, 1–2.

xxxiv **"Prophecy, in its critical mode"**: Walzer, *In God's Shadow*, 13.

xxxvi **"In the Jewish Bible"**: Unterman, *Justice for All*, 15.

xxxvii **Walzer explains**: Walzer, *In God's Shadow*, 1, 3.

xxxix **"For the first time"**: Unterman, *Justice for All*, 24.

xl **"Sinai permanently exposes"**: Hartman, *A Heart of Many Rooms*, 259–66.

xli **"According to this version of the Ten Commandments"**: Tucker, "Parshat Yitro."

xliii **"their vitality lay in their movement"**: Chatwin, *The Songlines.*

xliv **Frederick Buechner**: Buechner, "Prophet."

xliv ***"stand in the breach"***: Muffs, "Who Will Stand in the Breach?"

xliv **"[The prophet] loves God"**: Held, *Heart of Torah,* 2:119.

xlvi **Heschel teaches us that this is God's first**: Heschel, *God in Search of Man,* 137, and *Man Is Not Alone,* 69.

xlvii **"the language of response"**: Rashi to Gen. 22:1.

l **"The [first concept] of holiness"**: Leibowitz, "Parashat Korah," in *Weekly Parasha,* 143.

l **"Following the introductory declaration"**: Unterman, *Justice for All,* 31–33.

li **Levenson cites a variety of biblical passages**: Levenson, *Love of God,* 4, and see also especially 7, 16, 19.

lii **"Greater is he**: Talmud, Bava Kamma 38a.

lii ***"Beloved is man"***: Talmud, Avot 3:14.

lviii **Jeremiah Unterman discerns seven distinct**: Unterman, *Justice for All,* 61.

lviii **An intriguing archeological footnote**: See the official website of the Kirbet Qeiyafa dig: http://qeiyafa.huji.ac.il/ostracon12_2.asp; and Unterman, *Justice for All,* 210n61.

lx **Lelyveld articulated and embodied the love**: Lelyveld, quoted in Schneier, *Shared Dreams,* 26.

lx **"Had the Israelites"**: Sacks, *Covenant & Conversation,* August 28, 2012.

lxi **Shalom Paul, puts it**: As quoted in Unterman, *Justice for All,* 99.

lxi **Shalom Speigel, echoes**: As quoted in Unterman, *Justice for All,* 99.

lxii **"that the way things are"**: Lerner, *Jewish Renewal,* 6.

1. Abraham's Argument

8 **Nobel Peace Prize-winner**: Wiesel, *A Jew Today,* 6.

9 **Torah teacher and psychotherapist**: Rosenblatt, *Wrestling with Angels,* 170.

10 **Indeed, "The Book of Job"**: Safire, *The First Dissident,* xiv, xix, 225.

11 **Two remarkable examples**: Levi Yitzhak of Berditchev (1740–1810), as cited in Schwartz, *Judaism's Great Debates,* 8–9, 97.

12 **the all-important Talmudic ethic**: Talmud, Shabbat 54b.

12 **When we protest, we follow**: Martin Luther King Jr. Many variations exist from his apparent first use of the phrase "We must never adjust ourselves" in a speech on September 23, 1959, to the Southern Christian Ministers Conference.

13 **"Every debate"**: Talmud, Avot 5:2, Eruvin 13b.

13 **As author Rabbi Joseph Telushkin**: Telushkin, *Hillel*, 84.

13 **The nineteenth-century German Jewish thinker**: Samson Raphael Hirsch (1808–1888), cited in Schwartz, *Judaism's Great Debates*, xii.

13 **The Hasidic leader:** Nachman of Bratzlav (1722–1810), cited in Schwartz, *Judaism's Great Debates*, xii.

14 **A contemporary teacher:** Or Rose, as cited in Schwartz, *Judaism's Great Debates*, 97.

14 **Elie Wiesel**: "Hope, Despair and Memory," Nobel Lecture, December 11, 1986.

2. Shiphrah's Defiance

20 **Moses Maimonides, rules that**: Maimonides, *Mishneh Torah*, Hilchot Melachim 3:9.

20 **Upon its founding**: Schwartz, "Tohar HaNeshek" (Purity of Arms). Citations from Ben-Gurion and Eli Geva are from this article.

21 **The following dialogue**: Bezmozgis, *The Betrayers*, 117–19.

22 **The nineteenth-century author**: Henry David Thoreau, "Resistance to Civil Government," 1849, in Thoreau, *Works*, 415–48.

22 **As a religious leader**: Martin Luther King Jr., "Letter from Birmingham City Jail," April 16, 1963, in King, *Testament of Hope*, 289–302.

3. Moses' Encounter

30 **Moses is willing to fulfill**: Talmud, Avot 2:5.

31 **Victorian poet**: Elizabeth Browning, *Aurora Leigh*.

31 **Philosopher Martin Buber:** Buber, *Ten Rungs*.

31 **Rabbi and mysticism master Lawrence Kushner:** Kushner, *Honey from the Rock*.

34 **As Elazar ben Yair, the leader of Masada**: Elazar ben Yair as quoted in Josephus, *Wars* 7.8.6–7.

34 **The Puritans saw themselves**: Thomas Paine, Benjamin Franklin, and Frederick Douglass, cited in Zola, "To Our Readers. . . ." See Hoberman, "God Loves the Hebrews," for a discussion of Jewish American and African American understandings of the Exodus, and the various books on the subject in his notes.

35 **The scholar Nahum Sarna**: Sarna, *JPS Torah Commentary: Exodus*, 118.

35 **As political philosopher**: Walzer, *Exodus and Revolution*.

36 **Rabbi Nachum Amsel**: Amsel, *Jewish Encyclopedia of Moral and Ethical Issues*, 35.

36 **As Heschel memorably expresses**: Heschel, as quoted in *Mishkan T'filah*, 45.

37 **By remembering and imagining**: Held, *Heart of Torah* 1:175.

37 **"So what is Moses saying?"**: From an interview with Sacks.

4. Tirzah's Challenge

45 **But as biblical scholar**: Unterman, *Justice for All*, 7.

46 **As biblical scholar Baruch Levine**: Levine, *JPS Torah Commentary: Leviticus*, 168.

46 **In the Talmud they are extolled**: Talmud, Bava Batra 199b.

47 **Ahead of his time**: Abraham Geiger, as cited in Plaut, *The Rise of Reform Judaism*, 253–55.

48 **Answering that call**: Plaskow, *Standing Again at Sinai.*

49 **In 1992, the small Reconstructionist**: Federation of Reconstructionist Congregations and Havurot statement, 1992.

49 **In 1996 the CCAR**: Central Conference of American Rabbis statements, 1996, 1998, 2000.

50 **In 1992 the all-important**: Committee on Jewish Laws and Standards, Rabbinical Assembly, 1992, 2006, 2012.

5. Samuel's Warning

61 **As Rabbi Jonathan Sacks**: Sacks, *Covenant & Conversation*, October 13, 2013.

61 **As biblical scholar Jeffrey Tigay notes**: Tigay, *JPS Torah Commentary: Deuteronomy*, 166.

63 **As Maimonides teaches**: Maimonides, Hilchot De'ot 6:6, Nachmanides to Lev. 19:17.

64 **Rabbi Jonathan Sacks explains**: Sacks, *Covenant & Conversation*, April 26, 2014.

64 **Maimonides extends the command**: Maimonides, Hilchot De'ot 6:7, Talmud, Avot 1:12.

64 **Another classic Rabbinic commentary**: *Avot de-Rabbi Natan* 12.

65 **Perhaps this is why**: Gerondi, *Sha'are Teshuvah*.

66 **The Rabbis ask Raba**: Talmud, Bava Metzi'a 31a.

66 **Rabbi Sharon Brous tells**: Brous, "The Prophets Shudder."

6. Nathan's Parable

76 **in the classic statement of Akiba**: Talmud, Avot 3:19.

76 **Maimonides best sums it up**: Maimonides, Laws of Repentance 5:1–2.

77 **As the Talmud well puts it**: Talmud, Sukkot 52b; Avot 4:1; B'rachot 28a.

79 **The contemporary storyteller**: benShea, *Jacob the Baker*.

7. Judah's Step Forward

89 **The noted biblical scholar**: Tigay, *JPS Torah Commentary: Deuteronomy*, 166.

89 **Another esteemed scholar**: Milgrom, *JPS Torah Commentary: Numbers*, 397.

90 **Among the numerous Talmudic teachings**: Talmud, Avot 4:17.

91 **"For transgressions against God"**: Talmud, Yoma 8:9.

91 **"Who is a hero?"**: Talmud, Avot 4:10.

92 **Maimonides adroitly notes**: Maimonides on Gen. 3:22.

92 **"four steps to repentance"**: Saadia Gaon (882–942), Book of Beliefs 5:5.

93 "**Among the paths of repentance"**: Maimonides, Laws of Repentance 2:2, 2:4.

93 **Rabbi and best-selling author**: Telushkin, *Jewish Literacy*.

8. Joseph's Cry

103 **In his autobiography**: Clinton, *My Life*.

105 **As biblical scholar**: Milgrom, *JPS Torah Commentary: Numbers*, 112.

106 **"At first God intended"**: Rashi to Genesis 1:1, 2:4.

106 **On June 17, 2015**: "How Do You Forgive a Murder?" *Time*, November 23, 2015.

107 **A remarkable passage**: Talmud, Berachot 7a.

107 **Rabbi Jonathan Sacks beautifully**: Sacks, *Covenant & Conversation*, December 17, 2014.

9. Ruth's Vow

113 **The ancient sage**: Midrash Ruth Rabbah 2:14–15.

113 **The contemporary scholar**: Eskenazi, *JPS Bible Commentary: Ruth*.

113 **In the words of the late Bible scholar:** Tikvah Frymer-Kensky, cited in Eskenazi, *JPS Bible Commentary: Ruth*.

115 **The Book of Ruth seems to**: Tamara Eskenazi, Alicia Ostriker, and Robert Hubbard Jr., all in *JPS Bible Commentary: Ruth*.

116 **"Boaz comforts"**: Pesikta de-Rav Kahana.

117 **The Talmud explains**: Talmud, Avot 1:2; Bezah 32b' Midrash B'reshith Rabbah 8:5.

117 **The talmudic sage Abba Saul**: *Mekhilta*, Shira 3.

118 **Rabbi Simlai**: Talmud, Sota 14a.

118 **When God appears to Abraham**: *Etz Hayim*, 99 to Gen. 18:1.

118 **"Hospitality to wayfarers":** Talmud, Shabbat 127a.
119 **As Rabbi Samson Raphael Hirsch**: Hirsch, *Horeb*, sect. 17.

10. Elisha's Invitation

128 **"We did everything to save lives"**: Amit Levy, "ZAKA Mission to Haiti 'Proudly Desecrating Shabbat,'" ynetnews.com, January 17, 2010.
128 **The Talmud famously teaches**: Talmud, Shabbat 132a; Shulchan Arukh, Orah Hayim 328:2; Talmud, Sanhedrin 4:5.
129 **They noted that the verse**: Talmud, Sotah 14a.

11. Jeremiah's Scroll

137 **Recall Heschel's definition**: Heschel, December 10, 1972 (transcript).
139 **An interesting passage**: *Mekhilta*, Bo, chap. 1.
140 **"The most common denominator":** Unterman, *Justice for All*, 153.
144 **"As long as there is life"**: Talmud (Jerusalem), Berachot 9:1.
144 **"Such a people"**: Graetz, *Gerschichte der Juden* 4 (1853), preface.
144 **"There is no hope unmingled with fear"**: Spinoza, *Ethics* (1677), III, 13.
145 **The French Jewish writer**: Fleg, *Why I Am a Jew*, 94.
145 **"We have not yet lost our hope"**: Naftali Herz Imber, "Tikvateinu" (1878).

12. Jonah's Lesson

151 **As Uriel Simon writes**: Simon, *The JPS Bible Commentary: Jonah*, 14.
152 **Furthermore, as Rabbi Steven Bob**: Bob, *Jonah and the Meaning of Our Lives*, 182, 226.
154 **"What does God pray?":** Talmud, Berachot 7a; Shabbat 133b; Betzah 32a/Sota 14a.
154 **Rabbinic midrash explains**: Midrash Samuel.
155 **The Talmud explicitly says**: Talmud, Sotah 14a.
155 **"Do not suppress this compassion":** Hirsch, *Horeb*, 17:126.
156 **Leo Rosten, author of the classic**: Rosten, *Joys of Yiddish*, 299.

13. Miriam's Celebration

165 **As the important feminist**: Eskenazi, *The Torah: A Women's Commentary*, 387.
166 **An ancient midrash**: Tanchuma Zav 13; Sifrei Numbers, 99.
166 **The pioneering feminist bible scholar**: Trible, "Miriam: Bible."
166 **As explained by scholar**: Meir, "Miriam: Midrash and Aggadah."
167 **The Talmud's description**: Talmud, Sukkah 4,5.

168 **They also taught in the Talmud**: Talmud, Avot 2:2,12.
168 **"Chasidim are moved"**: Baal Shem Tov (1698–1760) in Steinman, "Dancing Jews."
168 **Furthermore, the Baal Shem Tov taught**: Baal Shem Tov in *Keter Shem Tov*, Chabad.org.
168 **He quoted the Talmudic adage**: Talmud, Avot 2:12.
169 **"The Baal Shem Tov wiped away tears"**: Mendel, *Sefer Hasichot*, 5701, 132.
169 **They were mindful**: *Pesikta d'rav Kahana* 29:170a.

14. Caleb's Spirit

176 **Biblical scholar Jeremiah Unterman, however, directs**: Unterman, *Justice for All*, 5.
179 **"Ultimately, the question posed by the text"**: Held, *Heart of Torah*, 1:127.
179 **"Faith sees beyond fate"**: Quotes from Noah benShea, Leo Baeck, in benShea, *The Word*, 32.
180 **"Some see the world as it is":** Kennedy was paraphrasing at his brother's funeral his brother's use of the phrase that is originally derived from George Bernard Shaw in his play *Back to Methuselah.*

15. Hannah's Prayer

186 **The sincerity and humility**: Talmud, Berachot 4:1.
186 **Perhaps this is why**: Talmud, Megillah 14b.
187 **"the nightingale of the Psalms"**: Beecher, *Life Thoughts*, 11.
187 **Moses de Leon**: de Leon, *Zohar* 2:245b.
187 **"Prayer is the expression"**: Kohler, *Jewish Theology*, 271.
187 **The Talmud openly acknowledges**: Talmud, Ta'anit 2a.
188 **"The pious men"**: Talmud, Berachot 30b, 32b.
188 **As a Talmudic dictum teaches**: Talmud, Ta'anit 2a.
188 **"As a tree torn from the soil"**: Heschel, *Moral Grandeur and Spiritual Audacity*, 342, quoted in *Gates of Prayer*.
189 **"Prayer invites God's presence"**: Heschel, quoted in *Mishkan T'filah*, 47.

16. Elijah's Voice

195 **In some ways Elijah**: For the parallels between Moses and Elijah, see Verman, "Elijah."
197 **The midrash takes the humbling**: Midrash, Song of Songs, Rabbah 1:6.
198 **"The zealot takes the part of God"**: Sacks, *Covenant & Conversation*, July 11, 2015.

198 **Biblical scholar**: Kimelman, Kogan, Nelson, Brueggemann, and Held, all quoted in Held, *Heart of Torah*, 2:174–78.

200 **Noted critic Norman Podhoretz**: Podhoretz, *The Prophets*, 357.

201 **Pinchas, a grandson of Aaron**: Gelfand, "Pinchas, 5773."

201 **The *Mekhilta*, an ancient midrashic text**: *Mekhilta*, Bo, chap. 1.

202 **"This is a novum in history"**: Sacks, *Covenant & Conversation*, Behaalotcha, 5775.

203 **"humility is not thinking less of yourself"**: Often attributed to C. S. Lewis, but doubt has been cast on this; see http://www.cslewis.org/aboutus/faq/quotes-misattributed/.

17. Isaiah's Vision

214 **"One who creates peace"**: Talmud, Ketubot 16b–17a.

214 **"If your wife is short"**: Yevamot 65a.

214 **"Her food signifies"**: Maimonides, "Laws Concerning Marriage," *Mishneh Torah*, 12:1–2.

214 **"A woman must see"**: Jonah Gerondi, *Iggeret Teshuvah (Letter of Repentance)*.

215 **"A husband should speak"**: *Iggeret HaKodesh (The Holy Letter)*—attributed to Nachmanides.

215 **By virtue of a close reading**: Midrash, Simeon ben Gamliel; Leviticus Rabbah 9:9.

215 **The Talmud opines**: Talmud, Yevamot 65b.

215 **The Talmud echoes**: Talmud, Avot 1:12.

216 **In his poem**: Yehuda Amichai, quoted in *Mishkan T'filah*, 61.

217 **In November 1977**: Anwar el-Sadat, quoted in Schwartz, *Jewish Heroes, Jewish Values*, 85–87.

217 **Prime Minister Begin**: Menachem Begin, quoted in Schwartz, *Jewish Heroes, Jewish Values*, 85–87.

18. Ezra's Torah

223 **"A new verb is used"**: Halbertal, *People of the Book*, 15.

224 **As biblical scholar Michael Satlow**: Satlow, *How the Bible Became Holy*, 281.

225 **"Ezra was worthy"**: Talmud, Sanhedrin 21b.

228 **"The Jews every seventh day"**: Philo, *Life of Moses* 2:216.

229 **"Moses received the Torah"**: Talmud, Avot 1:1.

229 **"a man's table atones for him"**: Yochanan ben Zakkai, Talmud, Berakoth, 55a.

229 **"Give me Yavneh"**: Talmud, Gittin 56b.

229 **A celebrated passage**: Talmud, Peah1:1.

229 **"Turn [the Torah] again"**: Talmud, Avot 5:22.

230 **"Where two meet"**: Talmud, Avot 3:2.

230 **"If you have learned much Torah"**: Talmud, Avot 2:8.

230 **"From the time"**: Talmud, Bava Batra 1:8.

230 **"Every Jew"**: Maimonides, Laws of Talmud Torah 1:8.

231 **In modern times**: Heine, Potok, Pogrebin, Lerman, Finkelstein: quotes collected from various sermons.

Bibliography

Amsel, Nachum. *The Jewish Encyclopedia of Moral and Ethical Issues*. Northvale NJ: Jason Aronson, 1994.

Beecher, Henry Ward. *Life Thoughts*. Boston: Phillips, Sampson and Company, 1858.

benShea, Noah. *Jacob the Baker*. New York: Random House, 1990.

———. *The Word: A Spiritual Handbook*. New York: Villard, 1995.

Bezmozgis, David. *The Betrayers*. New York: Penguin, 2014.

Bob, Steven. *Jonah and the Meaning of Our Lives*. Philadelphia: JPS, 2016.

Borowitz, Eugene. *Renewing the Covenant*. Philadelphia: JPS, 1996.

Brous, Sharon. "The Prophets Shudder." Sermon, Yom Kippur 5773 (2013). www.ikar-la.org.

Brueggemann, Walter. *The Prophetic Imagination*. Minneapolis: Augsburg Fortress, 2001.

Buber, Martin. *The Prophetic Faith*. New York: Harper, 1949; new edition, Princeton NJ: Princeton University Press, 2016.

———. *Ten Rungs: Hasidic Sayings*. New York: Schocken, 1965.

Buechner, Frederick. "Prophet." *Quote of the Day* (blog), April 21, 2016. http://www.frederickbuechner.com/quote-of-the-day/2016/4/21/prophet.

Chatwin, Bruce. *The Songlines*. New York: Penguin, 1988.

Clinton, Bill. *My Life*. New York: Knopf, 2004.

Eskenazi, Tamara. *The JPS Bible Commentary: Ruth*. Philadelphia: JPS, 2011.

———, ed. *The Torah: A Women's Commentary*. New York: URJ Press, 2008.

Etz Hayim. New York: Rabbinical Assembly, 2001.

Fleg, Edmund. *Why I Am a Jew*. N.p., 1927.

Gates of Prayer. New York: CCAR, 1975.

Gelfand, Shoshana Boyd. "Pinchas, 5773." *Limmud on One Leg* (Torah commentary). http://limmud.org/publications/limmudononeleg/5773/pinchas/.

Halbertal, Moshe. *People of the Book: Canon, Meaning and Authority*. Cambridge MA: Harvard University Press, 1997.

Halbertal, Moshe, and Margalit, Avishai. *Idolatry*. Cambridge MA: Harvard University Press, 1992.
Hartman, David. *A Heart of Many Rooms*. Woodstock VT: Jewish Lights, 2001.
Held, Shai. *The Heart of Torah*. 2 vols. Philadelphia: JPS, 2017.
Heschel, Abraham Joshua. *God in Search of Man*. New York: Farrar, Straus and Cudahy, 1955.
———. *Man Is Not Alone*. Philadelphia: JPS, 1951.
———. *Moral Grandeur and Spiritual Audacity*. New York: Farrar, Straus and Giroux, 1996.
———. *The Prophets*. Philadelphia: JPS, 1962.
Hirsch, Samson Raphael. *Horeb*. New York: Soncino Press, 2002.
Hoberman, Michael. "God Loves the Hebrews: Exodus Typologies, Jewish Slaveholding, and Black Peoplehood in Antebellum America." *American Jewish Archives* 67, no. 2 (2015): 47–69.
Jacob, Walter. "Prophetic Judaism: The History of a Term." CCAR *Journal* (Spring 1979).
King, Martin Luther, Jr. *A Testament of Hope: The Essential Writings and Speeches of Martin Luther King, Jr.* San Francisco: Harper, 1986.
Kohler, Kaufman. *Jewish Theology*. New York: Macmillan, 1918.
Kushner, Lawrence. *Honey from the Rock*. Woodstock VT: Jewish Lights, 1990.
Laytner, Anson. *Arguing with God*. Northvale NJ: Jason Aronson, 1990.
Leibowitz, Yeshayahu. *Weekly Parasha*. New York: Chemed, 1990.
Lerner, Michael. *Jewish Renewal*. New York: Putnam, 1994.
Levenson, Jon. *The Love of God*. Princeton NJ: Princeton University Press, 2016.
Levine, Baruch. *The JPS Torah Commentary: Leviticus*. Philadelphia: JPS, 1989.
Meir, Tamar. "Miriam: Midrash and Aggadah." In *Jewish Women: A Comprehensive Historical Encyclopedia*. Jewish Women's Archive, March 20, 2009. https://jwa.org/encyclopedia/article/Miriam-midrash-and-aggadah.
Milgrom, Jeremy. *The JPS Torah Commentary: Numbers*. Philadelphia: JPS, 1990.
Mishkan T'filah: A Reform Siddur. New York: CCAR, 2007.
Muffs, Yohanan. "Who Will Stand in the Breach?" In *Love and Joy: Law, Language, and Religion in Ancient Israel*. New York and Cambridge MA: Jewish Theological Seminary and Harvard University Press, 1992.
Oz, Amos and Fania. *Jews and Words*. New Haven CT: Yale University Press, 2012.
Plaskow, Judith. *Standing Again at Sinai: Judaism from a Feminist Perspective*. San Francisco: Harper & Row, 1990.
Plaut, W. Gunther. *The Rise of Reform Judaism*. New York: World Union for Progressive Judaism, 1965; new edition, Philadelphia: JPS, 2015.

Podhoretz, Norman. *The Prophets*. New York: Free Press, 2002.
Rabin, Elliot. *The Biblical Hero*. Philadelphia: JPS, forthcoming.
Rosenblatt, Naomi. *Wrestling with Angels*. New York: Delacorte, 1995.
Rosten, Leo. *The Joys of Yiddish*. New York: Penguin, 1968.
Sacks, Jonathan. *Covenant & Conversation* (weekly Torah commentary). rabbisacks.org.
Safire, William. *The First Dissident*. New York: Random House, 1992.
Sarna, Nahum. *The JPS Torah Commentary: Genesis*. Philadelphia: JPS, 1989.
———. *The JPS Torah Commentary: Exodus*. Philadelphia: JPS, 1991.
Satlow, Michael. *How the Bible Became Holy*. New Haven CT: Yale University Press, 2014.
Schneier, Marc. *Shared Dreams: Martin Luther King, Jr. and the Jewish Community*. Woodstock VT: Jewish Lights, 2008.
Schwartz, Barry L. "Abraham Joshua Heschel and *The Prophets*: A Publishing Saga." CCAR *Journal* (Summer 2016).
———. *Jewish Heroes, Jewish Values*. Springfield NJ: Behrman House, 1996.
———. *Judaism's Great Debates*. Philadelphia: JPS, 2012.
———. "Tohar HaNeshek (Purity of Arms): Reclaiming a Jewish Ethic in War." CCAR *Journal* (Summer 1988).
Schwarz, Sid. *Judaism and Justice*. Woodstock VT: Jewish Lights, 2008.
Shapiro, Rami. *The Hebrew Prophets*. Nashville TN: SkyLight Paths, 2004.
Shire, Michael J. *The Jewish Prophets*. Woodstock VT: Jewish Lights, 2002.
Simon, Uriel. *The JPS Bible Commentary: Jonah*. Philadelphia: JPS, 1999.
Steinman, Eliezer. "The Dancing Jews." Chabad.org, n.d.
Telushkin, Joseph. *Hillel: If Not Now, When?* New York: Schocken, 2009.
———. *Jewish Literacy: The Most Important Things to Know about the Jewish Religion, Its People, and Its History*. New York: William Morrow, 2008. Reprinted at http://www.jewishvirtuallibrary.org/repentance.
Thoreau, Henry David. *Works of Henry David Thoreau*. New York: Avenel Books, 1981.
Tigay, Jeffrey. *The JPS Torah Commentary: Deuteronomy*. Philadelphia: JPS, 1996.
Trible, Phyllis. "Miriam: Bible." In *Jewish Women: A Comprehensive Historical Encyclopedia*. Jewish Women's Archive, March 20, 2009. https://jwa.org/encyclopedia/article/miriam-bible.
Tucker, Ethan. "Parashat Yitro." In *Ethan Tucker's Halakhic Essays*. Mechon Hadar, 5776 (2016). www.hadar.org.
Unterman, Jeremiah. *Justice for All: How the Bible Revolutionized Ethics*. Philadelphia: JPS, 2017.

Verman, Mark. "Elijah: The Peripatetic Prophet." *CCAR Journal* (Spring 2016): 85–98.

Walzer, Michael. *Exodus and Revolution.* New York: Basic Books, 1986.

———. *In God's Shadow: Politics in the Hebrew Bible.* New Haven CT: Yale, 2012.

Weiner, Eric. *The Geography of Genius.* New York: Simon and Schuster, 2016.

Wiesel, Elie. *A Jew Today.* New York: Vintage, 1979.

Wolfson, Elliot. "Walking as a Sacred Duty." In *Hasidism Reappraised*, edited by Ada Rapoport-Albert, 180–207. London: Littman Library of Jewish Civilization, 1997.

Wolpe, David. *David: The Divided Heart.* New Haven CT: Yale, 2014.

Zola, Gary. "To Our Readers . . ." *American Jewish Archives* 67, no. 2 (2015): v–x.